THE ROUGH GUIDE

MANDARIN

CHINESE

PHRASEBOOK

Compiled by

LEXUS

www.roughguides.com

Credits

Compiled by Lexus with Julian Ward and Xu Yinong
Lexus Series Editor: Sally Davies
Rough Guides Reference Director: Andrew Lockett
Rough Guides Series Editor: Mark Ellingham

First edition published in 1997.
Revised in 1999.
This updated edition published in 2006 by
Rough Guides Ltd,
80 Strand, London WC2R 0RL
345 Hudson St, 4th Floor, New York 10014, USA
Email: mail@roughguides.co.uk.

Distributed by the Penguin Group.

Penguin Books Ltd, 80 Strand, London WC2R 0RL
Penguin Putnam, Inc., 375 Hudson Street, NY 10014, USA
Penguin Group (Australia), 250 Camberwell Road, Camberwell,
Victoria 3124, Australia
Penguin Books Canada Ltd, 10 Alcorn Avenue, Toronto,
Ontario, Canada M4V 1E4
Penguin Group (New Zealand), Cnr Rosedale and Airborne Roads,
Albany, Auckland, New Zealand

Typeset in Bembo and Helvetica to an original design by Henry Iles.
Printed in Italy by L.E.G.O. S.p.A., Lavis (TN)

© Lexus Ltd 2006
288pp.

British Library Cataloguing in Publication Data
A catalogue for this book is available from the British Library.

ISBN 13: 978-1-84353-635-2
ISBN 10: 1-84353-635-8

5 7 9 8 6 4

The publishers and authors have done their best to ensure the
accuracy and currency of all information in The Rough Guide
Chinese Phrasebook however, they can accept no responsibility for
any loss or inconvenience sustained by any reader using the book.

Online information about Rough Guides can be found at our website
www.roughguides.com

CONTENTS

Introduction

The Rough Guide Mandarin Chinese dictionary phrasebook is a highly practical introduction to the contemporary language. Laid out in clear A-Z style, it uses key-word referencing to lead you straight to the words and phrases you want – so if you need to book a room, just look up 'room'. The Rough Guide gets straight to the point in every situation, in bars and shops, on trains and buses, and in hotels and banks.

The main part of the Rough Guide is a double dictionary: English-Chinese then Chinese-English. Before that, there's a section called **Basic Phrases** and to get you involved in two-way communication, the Rough Guide includes, in this new edition, a set of **Scenario** dialogues illustrating questions and responses in key situations such as renting a car and asking directions. You can hear these and then download them free from **www.roughguides. com/phrasebooks** for use on your computer or MP3 player.

Forming the heart of the guide, the **English-Chinese** section gives easy-to-use transliterations of the Chinese words wherever pronunciation might be a problem. Throughout this section, cross-references enable you to pinpoint key facts and phrases, while asterisked words indicate where further information can be found in a section at the end of the book called **How the Language Works**. This section sets out the fundamental rules of the language, with plenty of practical examples. You'll also find here other essentials like numbers, dates, telling the time and basic phrases. The **Chinese-English** section is in two parts: a dictionary, arranged phonetically, of all the words and phrases you're likely to hear (starting with a section of slang and colloquialisms); then a compilation, arranged by subject, of various signs, labels, instructions and other basic words you may come across in print or in public places.

Near the back of the book too the Rough Guide offers an extensive **Menu Reader**. Consisting of food and drink sections (each starting with a list of essential terms), it's indispensable whether you're eating out, stopping for a quick drink, or browsing through a local food market.

一路顺风
yílù shùnfēng!
have a good trip!

Basic
Phrases

Basic Phrases

yes
shìde
shur-dur
是的

no
bù
boo
不

OK
hǎo
how
好

hello
ní hǎo
nee how
你好

good morning
nǐ zǎo
nee dzow
你早

good evening
nǐ hǎo
ni how
你好

good night
wǎn'ān
wahn-ahn
晚安

goodbye/see you!
zàijiàn
dzai-jyen
再见

see you later
huítóujiàn
hway-toh-jyen
回头见

please
qǐng
ching
请

yes, please
hǎo, xièxie
how hsyeh-hsyeh
好谢谢

could you please-...?
qǐng nín-..., hǎo ma?
ching nin ... how mah
请您 ..., 好吗？

thank you
xièxie
hsyeh-hsyeh
谢谢

thank you very much
duōxiè
dwor-hsyeh
多谢

no, thank you
xièxie, wǒ bú yào
hsyeh-hsyeh wor boo yow
谢谢我不要

don't mention it
bú kèqi
boo kur-chee
不客气

how do you do?
nǐ hǎo
ni how
你好？

how are you?
nǐ hǎo ma?
mah
你好吗？

fine, thanks
hén hǎo, xièxie
hun how hsyeh-hsyeh
很好谢谢

nice to meet you
jiàndào nǐ hěn gāoxìng
jyen-dow nee hun gow-hsing
见到你很高兴

excuse me (to get past)
láojià
low-jyah
劳驾

(to get attention)
láojià, qǐng wèn-...
ching wun
劳驾请问

excuse me/sorry
duìbuqǐ
dway-boo-chee
对不起

sorry?/pardon me?
nǐ shuō shénme?
shwor shun-mur
你说什么？

I see/I understand
wǒ míngbai le
wor ming-bai lur
我明白了

I don't understand
wǒ bù dǒng
我不懂

do you speak English?
nín huì jiǎng Yīngyǔ ma?
hway jyang ying-yew mah
您会讲英语吗？

I don't speak-Chinese
wǒ búhuì jiǎng Hànyǔ
wor boo-hway hahn-yew
我不会讲汉语

could you speak more slowly?
qǐng shuō màn yìdiǎnr
ching shwor mahn yee-dyenr
请说慢一点儿

could you repeat that?
qǐng nǐ zài shuō yíbiàn, hǎo ma?
ching nee dzai shwor yee-byen how mah
请你再说一遍好吗？

9

Scenarios

1. Accommodation

is there an inexpensive hotel you can recommend?
▶ nǐ kěyǐ gěi wǒ tuījiàn yīge búguì de fàndiàn ma?
[nee kur-yee gay wor tway-jyen yee-gur boo-gway dur fahn-dyen mah]

                  duìbuqǐ, hǎoxiàng shì dōu mánle ◀
             [dway-boo-chee, how-hsiang shur doh mahn-lur]
             I'm sorry, they all seem to be fully booked

---

can you give me the name of a good middle-range hotel?
▶ nǐ kěyǐ gěi wǒ tuījiàn yīge zhōngjí fàndiàn ma?
[nee kur-yee gay wor tway-jyen yee-gur joong-jee fahn-dyen mah]

---

         wǒ lái kànkan, nǐ xiǎng zài shìzhōngxīn ma? ◀
       [wor lai kahn-kahn, nee hsyang dzai shur-joong-hsin mah]
       let me have a look, do you want to be in the centre?

---

if possible
▶ rúguǒ kěyǐ de huà
[roo-gwor kur-yee dur hwah]

---

     rúguǒ lí shìzhōngxīn shāo yuǎn yìdiǎnr, kěyǐ ma? ◀
   [roo-gwor lee shur-joong-hsin show-yew-ahn-yee-dyenr, kur-yee mah]
   do you mind being a little way out of town?

---

not too far out
▶ wǒ bù xiǎng tài yuǎn
[wor boo hsyang tai yew-ahn]

---

where is it on the map?
▶ nǐ kěyǐ zài dìtúshang gěi wǒ zhǐyīxià ma?
[nee kur-yee dzai dee-too shahng gay wor` jur-yee-hsyah mah]

---

can you write the name and address down?
▶ nǐ kěyǐ gěi wǒ bǎ míngzi hé dìzhǐ xiěxiàlái ma?
[nee kur-yee gay wor bah dee-jur hsyeh-hsyah-lai mah]

I'm looking for a room in a private house
▶ wǒ xiǎng zhù sīrén fáng
[wor hsyang joo sur-run fahng]

13

2. Banks

bank account	yínháng zhànghù	[yin-hahng jahng-hoo]
to change money	huàn qián	[hwahn-chyen]
cheque	zhīpiào	[jur-pyow]
to deposit	cúnqián	[tsun-chyen]
pin number	gèrén mìmǎ	[gur-run mee-mah]
pound	yīngbàng	[ying-bahng]
renminbi	rénmínbì	[run-min-bee]
to withdraw	qǔqián	[chew-chyen]

can you change this into renminbi?
▶ qǐng nín gěi wǒ huànchéng rénmínbì, kěyǐ ma?
[ching nin gay wor hwahn-chung run-min-bee, kur-yee mah]

nín yào shénme yàng de chāopiào? ◀
[nin yoh shun-mur yang dur chow-pyow]
how would you like the money?

small notes	big notes
▶ xiǎo chāopiào	▶ dà chāopiào
[hsyow chow-pyow]	[da chow-pyow]

do you have information in English about opening an account?
▶ nǐmen yǒu guānyú kāizhàng de yīngyǔ yìnshuāpǐn ma?
[nee-mun yoh gwahn-yew kai-jahng dur ying-yew yin-shwah-pin mah]

▶ yǒu, nín xiǎng kāi nǎzhǒng zhànghù?   **I'd like a current account** ◀
[yoh, nee hsyang kai nah-chung jahng-hoo]   huóqī cúnkuǎn ◀
yes what sort of account do you want?   [hwor-chee tsun-kwahn]

qǐng gěi wǒ kàn yīxià nínde hùzhào ◀
[ching gay wor kahn yee-hsyah neen-dur hoo-jow]
your passport, please

can I use this card to draw some cash?
▶ kěyǐ yòng zhège kǎ qǔ xiànjīn ma?
[kur-yee yoong jur-gur kah chew hsyan-jin mah]

nǐ děi dào chūnàyuán nàr qù ◀
[nee day dow choo-nah-yew-ahn nahr chew]
you have to go to the cashier's desk

I want to transfer this to my account at the Bank of China
▶ wǒ xiǎng bǎ qián zhuǎndào wǒ zài Zhōngguó yínháng de zhànghù
shàng qù
[wor hsyang bah chyen jwahn-dow wor dzai chung-gwor yin-hahng dur jahng-hoo-shahng chew]

hǎo, nínde diànhuà děi shōufèi ◀
[how, nin-dur dyen-hwah day shoh-fay]
OK, but we'll have to charge you for the phonecall

3. Booking a room

shower	línyù	[lin-yew]
telephone in the room	fángjiānlǐ de diànhuà	[fahng-jyen-lee dur dyen-hwah]
payphone in the lobby	dàtīnglǐ de tóubì diànhuà	[da-ting-lee dur toh-bee dyen-hwah]

do you have any rooms?
▶ yǒu fángjiān ma?
[yoh fahng-jyen mah]

jǐge rén? ◀
[jee-gur run]
for how many people?

for one / for two
▶ yīge rén / liǎngge rén
[yee-gur run / lyang-gur run]

yǒu fángjiān ◀
[yoh fahng-jyen]
yes, we have rooms free

▶ zhù jǐge wǎnshang?
[joo jee-gur wahn-shahng]
for how many nights?

just for one night
yīge wǎnshang
[yee-gur wahn-shahng]

how much is it?
▶ duōshǎo qián?
[dwor-show chyen]

dài xǐzǎojiān de jiǔbǎi yuán renminbi, búdài xǐzǎojiān de qībǎi yuán ◀
[dai hshee-dzow-jyen dur jyoh-bai yew-ahn run-min-bee, boo dai hshee-dzow-jyen dur chee-bai yew-ahn]
900 yuan with bathroom and 700 yuan without bathroom

does that include breakfast?
▶ bāokuò zǎocān ma?
[bow-kwor dzow-tsahn mah]

can I see a room with bathroom?
▶ wǒ kěyǐ kàn yīxià dài xǐzǎojiān de fángjiān ma?
[wor kur-yee kahn yee-hsyah dai hshee-dzow-jyen dur fahng-jyen mah]

ok, I'll take it
▶ hǎo, wǒ yàole
[how wor yow-lur]

when do I have to check out?
▶ wǒ shénme shíhou jiézhang líkāi?
[wor shun-mur shur-hoh jyeh-jahng lee-kai]

is there anywhere I can leave luggage?
▶ yǒu cún xínglǐ de dìfāng ma?
[yow tsun hsing-lee dur dee-fahng mah]

4. Car hire

automatic	zìdòng huàndǎng	[dzur-doong hwahn-dahng]
full tank	yóuxiāng mǎnde	[yoh-hsyang mahn-dur]
manual	shǒudòng huàndǎng	[show-doong hwahn-dahng]
rented car	zūde chē	[dzoo-dur chur]

I'd like to rent a car
▶ wǒ xiǎng zū chē
[wor hsyang dzoo chur]

duō cháng shí jiān? ◀
[dwor chahng shur-jyen]
for how long?

two days | I'll take the ...
▶ liǎng tiān | ▶ wǒ yào ...
[lyang-tyen] | [wor yow]

is that with unlimited mileage?
▶ kāi duō cháng lù yǒu xiànzhì ma?
[kai dwor-chahng loo yoh hsyen-jur mah]

méiyou xiànzhì ◀
[may-yoh hsyen-jur]
it is

wǒ kàn yìxià nǐde jiàshǐ zhí zhǎo, hǎo ma? ◀
[wor kahn yee-hsyah nee-dur jyah-shur jur-jow, how mah]
can I see your driving licence please?

hái yào nǐde hùzhào ◀
[hai yow nee-dur hoo-jow]
and your passport

is insurance included?
▶ bāokuò bǎoxiǎn ma?
[bow-kwor bow-hsyen mah]

bāokuò, búguò nín děi xiān fù yìqiān yuán ◀
[bow-kwor, boo-gwor nin day hsyen foo yee-chyen yew-ahn]
yes, but you have to pay the first 1000 yuan

qǐng nín fù yìqiān yuán yājīn, hǎo ma? ◀
[ching nin foo yee-chyen yew-ahn yah-jin, how mah]
can you leave a deposit of 1000 yuan?

and if this office is closed, where do I leave the keys?
▶ rúguǒ nǐmen zhèr guānménle, wǒ bǎ yàoshi fàng zài nǎr?
[roo-gwor nee-mun jer gwahn-mun-lur, wor bah yow-shur fahng dzai nahr]

fàng zài nàge hézi lǐ ◀
[fahng dzai nah-gur hur-dzur lee]
you drop them in that box

download these scenarios as MP3s from:

5. Communications

ADSL modem	tiáozhì jiětiáoqì	[tyow-jur jyeh-tyow-chee]
dial-up modem	diànhuá tiáozhì jiětiáoqì	[dyen-hwah tyow-jur jyeh-tyow-chee]
dot	diàn	[dyen]
Internet	hùliánwǎng	[hoo-lyen-wahng]
mobile (phone)	shǒujī	[show-jee]
password	mìmǎ	[mee-mah]
telephone socket	diànhua chāzuò	[dyen-hwah chah-dzwor]
adaptor	zhuǎnhuàn	[jwahn-hwahn]
wireless hotspot	wúxiàn rèdiǎn	[woo-hsyen rur-dyen]

is there an Internet café around here?
▶ zhèr fùjìn yǒu wǎngbā ma?
[jur foo-jin yoh wahng-bah mah]

can I send email from here?
▶ wǒ kěyǐ zài zhèr fā diànzǐ yóujiàn ma?
[wor kur-yee dzai zher fah dyen-dzur yoh-jyen mah]

where's the at sign on the keyboard?
▶ jiànpán shàngde "at sign" zài nǎr?
[jyen-pan shahng-dur "at sign" dzai nahr]

can you switch this to a UK keyboard?
▶ wǒ kěyǐ yòng yìngshì jiànpán ma?
[wor kur-yee yoong ying-shur jyen-pan mah]

can you help me log on?
▶ nǐ kěyǐ bāng wǒ jìnrù míngdàn ma?
[nee kur-yee bahng wor jin-roo ming-dan mah]

can you put me through to ...?
▶ qǐng nín gěi wǒ jiē ...?
[ching nin gay wor jyeh ...]

I'm not getting a connection, can you help?
▶ wǒ bù néng jìnrù, bāng ge máng, hǎo ma?
[wor boo nung jin-roo, bahng-gur mahng, how mah]

where can I get a top-up card for my mobile?
▶ nǎr mài shǒujī chōngzhí kǎ?
[nahr mai show-jee choong-jur kah]

zero	**five**
líng	wǔ
[ling]	[woo]
one	**six**
yī	liù
[yee]	[lyoh]
two	**seven**
èr	qī
[ur]	[chee]
three	**eight**
sān	bā
[san]	[bah]
four	**nine**
sì	jiǔ
[sur]	[jyoh]

6. Directions

hi, I'm looking for Nán Jiē
▶ wǒ zhǎo Nán Jiē
[wor jow Nan Jyeh]

duìbuqǐ, méi tīngshuōguo zhè tiáo jiē ◀
[dway-boo-chee, may ting-shwor-gwor juh tyow jyeh]
sorry, never heard of it

hi, can you tell me where Nán Jiē is?
▶ qǐng wèn, Nán Jiē zài nǎr?
[ching wun, Nan Jyeh dzai nar]

wǒ duì zhège dìfang yě bù shúxi ◀
[wor dway juh-gur dee-fahng yur boo shoo-hshee]
I'm a stranger here too

hi, Nán Jiē, do you know where it is?

qǐng wèn, nǐ zhīdao Nán Jiē zài nǎr ma?
[ching wun, nee jur-dow Nan Jyeh dzai nar mah]

where?
zài nǎr?
[dzai nar]

which direction?
nǎge fāngxiàng?
[nah-gur fahng-hsyang]

▶ dàole dì'èrge hónglǜdēng, wǎng zuǒ guǎi
[dow-luh dee-er-gur hoong-lyew-dung, wahng dzwor gwai]
left at the second traffic lights

▶ guòle lùkǒu
[gwor-luh loo-koh]
around the corner

▶ zhīhòu, zǒu yòubiān dìyī tiáo lù
[jur-hoh, dzoh yoh-byen dee-yee tyow loo]
then it's the first street on the right

duìmiàn [dway-myen] **opposite**	jìn [jin] **near**	yìzhí wǎng qián zǒu [yee-jur wahng chyen dzoh] **straight ahead**	zài nàr [dzai nar] **over there**
guǎi [gwai] **turn (off)**	qiánmiàn [chyen-myen] **in front of**		zài...zhīhòu [dzai...jur-hoh] **just after**
guòle [gwor-luh] **past the**	wǎng huí [wahng hway] **back**	yòubiān [yoh-byen] **on the right**	zuǒbiān [dzwor-byen] **on the left**
jiē [jyeh] **street**	xià yīge [hsyah yee-gur] **next**	yuǎn [yew-ahn] **further**	

18

7. Emergencies

accident	shìgù	[shur-goo]
ambulance	jiùhùchē	[jyoh-hoo-chur]
consul	lǐngshì	[ling-shur]
embassy	dàshǐguǎn	[da-shur-gwahn]
fire brigade	xiāofángduì	[hsyow-fahng-dway]
police	jǐngcháju	[jing-chah-joo]

help!
▶ jiùmìng!
[jyoh-ming]

can you help me?
▶ bāngge máng, hǎo ma?
[bahng-gur mahng, how mah]

please come with me! it's really very urgent
▶ qǐng gēn wǒ lái! yòu jǐnjí qíngkuàng
[ching gun wor lai! yoh jin-jee ching-kwahng]

I've lost (my keys)
▶ wǒ diūle (yàoshi)
[wor dyoh-lur (yow-shur)]

(my car) is not working
▶ (wǒde chē) bù gōngzuòle
[(wor-dur chur) boo goong-dzwor-lur]

(my purse) has been stolen
▶ (wǒde qiánbāo) bèi tōule
[(wor-dur chyen-bow) bay tow-lur]

I've been mugged
▶ wǒ bèi rén qiǎngle
[wor bay run chyang-lur]

nínde míngzi? ◀
[nin-dur ming-dzur]
what's your name?

wǒ kànkan nínde húzhào, hǎo ma? ◀
[wor kahn-kahn nin-dur hoo-jow, how mah]
I need to see your passport

I'm sorry, all my papers have been stolen
▶ duìbuqǐ, wǒ suǒyǒu de wénjiàn bèi tōule
[dway-boo-chee, wor swor-yoh dur wun-jyen bay toh-lur]

www.roughguides.com/phrasebooks   **19**

8. Friends

hi, how're you doing?
▶ nǐ hǎo ma?
[nee how mah]

wǒ hěn hǎo, nǐ ne? ◀
[wor hun how, nee nuh]
ok, and you?

yeah, fine   not bad
▶ hěn hǎo   ▶ búcuò
[hun how]   [boo-tswor]

d'you know Mark?
▶ nǐ rènshi Mǎkè ma?
[nee run-shur Mah-kuh mah]

and this is Hannah
▶ zhè shì Hànnà
[juh shur Han-nah]

wǒmen yǐjing rènshile ◀
[wor-mun yee-jing run-shur-luh]
yeah, we know each other

where do you know each other from?
▶ nǐmen shì zènme rènshide?
[nee-mun shur dzen-mur run-shur-dur]

▶ wǒmen shì zài Lúkè jiā rènshide
[wor-mun shur dzai loo-kur jyah run-shur-dur]
we met at Luke's place

that was some party, eh?
▶ nàge yànhuì bàng jíle, duì budui
[nah-gur yen-hway bang jee-luh, dway boo-dway]

shì zuìhǎo de ◀
[shur dzway-how dur]
the best

are you guys coming for a beer?
▶ zánmen hējiǔ qù ba?
[dzahn-mun huh-jyoh chew bah]

hǎo, zǒu ba ◀
[how, dzoh bah]
cool, let's go

wǒ búqù, wǒ yào qù jiàn Luólā ◀
[wor boo-chew, wor yow chew jyen Lwor-lah]
no, I'm meeting Lola

ok, that's cool too
▶ hǎo ba
[how bah]

see you at Luke's place tonight
▶ wǎnshang zài Lúkè jiā jiànmiàn
[wahn-shahng dzai Loo-kur jyah jyen-myen]

huítóu jiàn ◀
[hway-toh jyen]
see you

9. Health

I'm not feeling very well
▶ wǒ juéde bù shūfu
[wor jew-eh-dur boo shoo-foo]

can you get a doctor?
▶ qǐng gěi wǒ zhǎo ge yīshēng
[ching gay wor jow-gur yee-shung]

▶ nǎr bù shūfu?
[nahr boo shoo-foo]
where does it hurt?

it hurts here
zhèr téng ◀
[jur tung]

▶ zǒngshi téng ma?
[dzoong-shur tung mah]
is the pain constant?

it's not a constant pain
bù zǒngshi téng ◀
[boo dzoong-shur tung]

can I make an appointment?
▶ wǒ kěyǐ yùyuē yīshēng ma?
[wor kur-yee yew-yew-eh yee-shung mah]

can you give me something for ...?
▶ gěi wǒ diǎnr...yào, hǎo ma?
[gay wor dyanr...yow, how mah]

yes, I have insurance
▶ wǒ yǒu bǎoxiǎn
[wor yoh bow-hsyen]

antibiotics	kàngjūnsù	[kahng-joon-soo]
antiseptic ointment	kàngjūn yóugāo	[kahng-joon yoh-gow]
cystitis	pángguāngyán	[pahng-gwahng-yen]
dentist	yáyī	[yah-yee]
diarrhoea	lādùzi	[lah-doo-dzur]
doctor	yīshēng	[yee-shung]
hospital	yīyuàn	[yee-yew-ahn]
ill	shēngbìngle	[shung-bing-lur]
medicine	yào	[yow]
painkillers	zhǐténgyào	[jur-tung-yow]
pharmacy	yàofáng	[yow-fahng]
to prescribe	kāi yàofāng	[kai yow-fahng]
thrush	ékǒuchuāng	[ur-koh-chwahng]

10. Language difficulties

a few words	jǐge zì	[jee-gur dzur]
interpreter	kǒutóu fānyì	[koh-tow fahn-yee]
to translate	fānyì	[fahn-yee]

nǐde xìnyòngkǎ bèi jùle ◀
[nee-dur hsin-yoong-kah bay-jew-lur]
your credit card has been refused

what, I don't understand; do you speak English?
▶ shénme? wǒ bù dǒng; nǐ huì shuō yīngyǔ ma?
[shun-mur wor boo doong; nee hway shwor ying-yew mah]

xìnyòngkǎ wúxiàole ◀
[hsin-yoong-kah woo-hsyow-lur]
this isn't valid

could you say that again?   **slowly**
▶ qǐng zài shuō yīxià, hǎo ma?   màn diǎnr ◀
[ching dzai shwor yee-hsyah, how mah]   [mahn dyenr]

I understand very little Chinese
▶ wǒ zhǐ huì yīdiǎnr zhōngwén
[wor jur hway yee-dyenr choong-wun]

I speak Chinese very badly
▶ wǒ zhōngwén shuōde bù hǎo
[wor choong-wun shwor-dur boo how]

nǐ bù néng yòng zhège kǎ fùqián ◀
[nee boo nung yoong jur-gur kah foo chyen]
you can't use this card to pay

▶ dǒngle ma?   **sorry, no**
[doong-lur mah]   duìbuqǐ, wǒ hái shì bù míngbai ◀
do you understand?   [dway-boo-chee, wor hai shur boo ming-bai]

is there someone who speaks English?
▶ zhèr yǒu rén huì yīngwén ma?
[jur yoh run hway ying-wun mah]

oh, now I understand   **is that ok now?**
▶ hǎo, wǒ míngbaile   ▶ xíngle ma?
[how wor ming-bai-lur]   [hsing-lur mah]

11. Meeting people

hello
▶ nǐ hǎo
[nee how]

nǐ hǎo, wǒ jiào Shèn, xìng Wáng ◀
[nee how, wor jyow Shun, hsing Wahng]
hello, my name's Wang Shen

Graham, from England, Thirsk
▶ wǒ shì yīngguórén, wǒ jiào Graham, shì Thirsk rén
[wor shur ying-gwor-run, wor jyow Graham, shur Thirsk run]

Thirsk wǒ bù zhīdào, zài nǎr? ◀
[Thirsk wor boo jur-dow, dzai nar]
don't know that, where is it?

not far from York, in the North; and you?
▶ zài Yīnggélán běibù, lí York bù yuǎn; nǐ ne?
[dzai Ying-guh-lan bay-boo, lee York boo yewahn; nee nur]

wǒ shì Lúndūn rén; nǐ shì yígè rén lái de ma? ◀
[wor shur Lun-dun run; nee shur yee-gur run lai duh mah]
I'm from London; here by yourself?

no, I'm with my wife and two kids
▶ búshì, wǒ gēn wǒ àiren hé liǎngge háizi yìqǐ láide
[boo-shur, wor gun wor ai-run huh lyang-gur hai-dzur yee-chee lai-dur]

what do you do?
▶ nǐ zuò shénme gōngzuò?
[nee dzwor shun-mur goong-dzwor]

▶ wǒ shì gǎo diànnǎode
[wor shur gow dyen-nao-dur]
I'm in computers

me too
▶ wǒ yě shì
[wor yeh shur]

here's my wife now
▶ zhè shì wǒ àiren
[jur shur wor ai-run]

hěn gāoxìng rènshí nín ◀
[hun gow-hsing run-shur nin]
nice to meet you

12. Post offices

airmail	hángkōng	[hahng-kung]
post card	míngxìnpiàn	[ming-hsin-pyen]
post office	yóujú	[yoh-jew]
stamp	yóupiào	[yoh-pyow]

---

what time does the post office close?
▶ yóujú jǐdiǎn guānmén?
[yoh-jew jee-dyen gwahn-mun]

▶ gōngzuòrì wǔdiǎn
[gung-dzow-rur woo-dyen]
five o'clock weekdays

---

is the post office open on Saturdays?
▶ yóujú xīngqīliù kāimén ma?
[yoh-jew hsing-chee-lyow kai-mun mah]

zhídào zhōngwǔ ◀
[jur dow joong-woo]
until midday

I'd like to send this registered to England
▶ wǒ yào wǎng yīngguó jì guàhàoxìn
[wor yow wahng ying-gwor jee gwah-how-hsin]

méi wèntí, guàhàoxìn shí yuán ◀
[may wun-tee, gwah-how-hsin shur yew-ahn]
certainly, that will cost 10 yuan

---

and also two stamps for England, please
▶ hái yào liǎng zhāng dào yīngguó de yóupiào
[hai yow lyang-jahng dow ying-gwor dur yoh-pyow]

---

do you have some airmail stickers?
▶ yǒu hángkōng yóujiàn biāoqiān ma?
[yoh hahng-kung yoh-jyen byow-chyen mah]

---

do you have any mail for me?
▶ yǒu wǒde xìn ma?
[yoh wor-dur hsin mah]

国际	guójì	international
信	xìn	letters
国内	guónèi	domestic
包裹	bāoguǒ	parcels
待领邮件	dàilǐng yóujiàn	poste restante

13. Restaurants

bill	zhàngdān	[jahng-dan]	menu	càidān	[tsai-dan]
table	zhuōzi	[jwor-dzur]			

can we have a non-smoking table?
▶ wǒmen yào bù chōuyānde zhuōzi, kěyì ma?
[wor-mun yow boo choh-yen-dur jwor-dzur, kur-yee mah]

there are two of us
▶ wǒmen liǎngge rén
[wor-mun lyang-gur run]

there are four of us
▶ yīgòng sìgerén
[yee-gung sur-gur run]

what's this?
▶ zhè shì shénme?
[jur shur shun-mur]

yī zhǒng yú ◀
[yee joong yew]
it's a type of fish

shì běndì tèchǎn ◀
[shur bun-dee tur-chahn]
it's a local speciality

qǐng jìnlái kànkan ◀
[ching jin-lai kahn-kahn]
come inside and I'll show you

we would like two of these, one of these, and one of those
▶ zhège liǎngge, zhège yīge, nàge yige
[jur-gur lyang-gur, jur-gur yee-gur, nah-gur yee-gur]

▶ hē diǎnr shénme?
[hur dyenr shun-mur]
and to drink?

red wine
▶ hóng pútaójiǔ
[hung poo-tow-jyoh]

white wine
▶ bái pútaójiǔ
[bai poo-tow-jyoh]

a beer and two orange juices
▶ yībēi píjiǔ, liǎng bēi júzizhī
[yee-bay pee-jyoh, lyang bay jew-dzur-jur]

some more bread please
▶ qǐng zài lái xiē miànbāo
[ching dzai lai hsyeh myen-bow]

▶ chīde hǎo ma?
[chur-dur how mah]
how was your meal?

excellent!, very nice!
▶ hěn hǎo! búcuò!
[hun how boo-tswor]

▶ hái yào shénme ma?
[hai yow shun-mur mah]
anything else?

just the bill thanks
▶ wǒmen fù zhàngdān, hǎo ma?
[wor-mun foo jahng-dan, how mah]

14. Shopping

mǎi diǎnr shénme? ◀
[mai dyenr shun-mur]
can I help you?

can I just have a look around?
▶ wǒ kànkan, kěyǐ ma?
[wor kahn-kahn, kur-yee mah]

yes, I'm looking for ...
▶ wǒ xiǎng mǎi...
[wor hsyang mai]

how much is this?
▶ duōshǎo qián?
[dwor-show chyen]

sānshí èr yuán ◀
[san-shur ur yew-ahn]
thirty-two yuan

OK, I think I'll have to leave it; it's a little too expensive for me
▶ wǒ búyào, yǒu diǎnr tài guì
[wor boo-yow, yoh dyenr tai gway]

zhège zěnme yàng? ◀
[jur-gur dzun-mur yang]
how about this?

can I pay by credit card?
▶ shōu xìnyòngkǎ ma?
[shoh hsin-yoong-kah mah]

it's too big
▶ tài dàle
[tai dah-lur]

it's too small
▶ tài xiǎole
[tai hsyow-lur]

it's for my son – he's about this high
▶ gěi wǒ érzi mǎide – tā zhème gāo
[gay wor ur-dzur mai-dur, tah jur-mur gow]

▶ hái yào biéde ma?
[hai yow byeh-dur mah]
will there be anything else?

that's all thanks
▶ búyàole, xièxie
[boo-yow-lur, hsyeh-hsyeh]

make it twenty yuan and I'll take it
▶ wǒ zhǐ xiǎng fù èrshí yuán, kěyǐ ma?
[wor jur hsyang foo ur-shur yew-ahn, kur-yee mah]

fine, I'll take it
▶ xíng
[hsing]

dà jiǎnjià	[dah-jyen-jyah]	sale
fùkuǎntái	[foo kwahn-tai]	cash desk
guānmén	[gwahn-mun]	closed
huàn	[hwahn]	to exchange
kāimén	[kai-mun]	open

download these scenarios as MP3s from:

15. Sightseeing

art gallery	měishùguǎn	[may-shoo-gwahn]
bus tour	zuò dà bāshì lǚyóu	[dzwor dah bah-shur lyew-yoh]
city centre	shì zhōngxīn	[shur joong-hsin]
closed	guānmén	[gwahn-mun]
guide	dǎoyóu	[dow-yoh]
museum	bówùguǎn	[bor-woo-gwahn]
open	kāimén	[kai-mun]

I'm interested in seeing the old town
▶ wǒ duì cānguān lǎochéng yǒu xìngqù
[wor dway tsan-gwahn low-chung yoh hsing-chew]

are there guided tours?
▶ yǒu dǎoyóu tuán ma?
[yoh dow-yoh twahn mah]
duìbuqǐ, dōu dìngmǎnle ◀
[dway-boo-chee, doh ding-mahn-lur]
I'm sorry, it's fully booked

how much would you charge to drive us around for four hours?
▶ wǒmen zuò nǐde chē sìge xiǎoshí, duōshǎo qián?
[wor-mun, dzwor nee-dur chur sur-gur hsyow-shur dwor-show chyen]

can we book tickets for the concert here?
▶ wǒmen kěyǐ zài zhèr dìng yīnyuèhuì de piào ma?
[wor-mun kur-yee dzai jur ding yin-yew-eh-hway dur pyow mah]

▶ kěyǐ, qǐngwèn, nǐnde míngzi?
[kur-yee, ching-wun, nin-dur ming-dzur]
yes, in what name?
shénme xìnyòngkǎ? ◀
[shun-mur hsin-yoong-kah]
which credit card?

where do we get the tickets?
▶ zài nǎr qǔ piào?
[dzai nahr chew pyow]
jiù zài rùkǒu (qǔ piào) ◀
[jyoh dzai roo-koh (chew pyow)]
just pick them up at the entrance

is it open on Sundays?
▶ xīngqītiān kāimén ma?
[hsing-chee tyen kai-mun mah]

how much is it to get in?
▶ ménpiào duōshǎo qián?
[mun-pyow dwor-show chyen]

are there reductions for groups of 6?
▶ liùgèrén yīqǐ yǒu méiyou yōuhuì?
[lyoh-gur-run yee-chee yoh may-yoh yoh-hway]

that was really impressive!
▶ zhēn shì hǎojíle!
[jun shur how-jee-lur]

16. Trains

to change trains	huàn huǒchē	[hwahn hwor-chur]
platform	zhàntái	[jahn-tai]
return	wǎngfǎnpiào	[wahng-fahn-pyow]
single	dānchéngpiào	[dahn-chung-pyow]
station	huǒchēzhàn	[hwor-chur-jahn]
stop	tíngchē	[ting-chur]
ticket	huǒchēpiào	[hwor-chur-pyow]

how much is ...?
▶ ... duōshǎo qián?
[dwor-show chyen]

a single, second class to ...
▶ yìzhāng dānchéngpiào, èrděng chēxiāng, dào ...
[yee-jahng, dhan-chur-pyow, ur-dung chur-hsyang, dow]

two returns, second class to ...
▶ liǎngzhāng wǎngfǎnpiào, èrděng chēxiāng, dào ...
[lyang-jahng, wahng-fahn-pyow, ur-dung chur-hsyang, dow]

for today	**for tomorrow**	**for next Tuesday**
▶ jīntiānde	▶ míngtiānde	▶ xià xīngqīèrde
[jin-tyen-dur]	[ming-tyen-dur]	[hsyah hsing-chee-ur-dur]

tèkuài jiàshōu ◀
[tur-kway jyah-shoh]
there's a supplement for the express

nǐ yào dìng zuòwèi ma? ◀
[nee yow ding dzwor-way mah]
do you want to make a seat reservation?

nǐ děi zài Shànghǎi huànchē ◀
[nee day dzai Shahng-hai hwahn-chur]
you have to change at Shanghai

is this seat free?
▶ zhège zuò yǒurén zuò ma?
[jur-gur dzwor yow-run dzwor mah]

excuse me, which station are we at?
▶ qǐngwèn, zhèshì shénme zhàn?
[ching-wun, jur shur shun-mur jahn]

is this where I change for Suzhou?
▶ shì zài zhèr huàn dào Sūzhōu de huǒchē ma?
[shur dzai jur hwahn dow Soo-joh dur hwor-chur mah]

English

→

Chinese

A

a, an*

about: about 20-èr shí zuǒyòu [dzwor-yoh]
二十左右

it's about 5 o'clock wǔdiǎn (zhōng) zuǒyòu
五点钟左右

a film about China guānyú Zhōngguó de diànyǐng
[gwahn-yew – dur dyen-ying]
关于中国的电影

above* (zài)-... shàng [(dzai)-... shahng]
在 ... 上

abroad guówài [gwor-wai]
国外

absorbent cotton yàomián [yow-myen]
药棉

accept jiēshòu [jyeh-shoh]
接受

accident shìgù [shur-goo]
事故

there's been an accident chūle ge shìgù
[choo-lur gur]
出了个事故

accurate zhǔnquè [jun-chew-eh]
准确

ache téng [tung]
疼

my back aches wǒ hòubèi téng [wor hoh-bay]
我后背疼

acrobatics zájì [dzah-jee]
杂技

across: across the road zài mǎlù duìmiànr [dzai mah-loo dway-myenr]
在马路对面儿

acupuncture zhēnjiǔ [jun-jyoh]
针灸

adapter duōyòng chātóu [dwor-yoong chah-toh]
多用插头

address dìzhǐ [dee-jur]
地址

what's your address? nín zhù nǎr? [joo]
您住哪儿？

address book tōngxùnlù [toong-hsyewn-loo]
通讯录

admission charge: how much is the admission charge? rùchǎng fèi shì duōshao qián? [roo-chahng fay shur dwor-show chyen]
入场费是多少钱？

adult dàrén [dah-run]
大人

advance: in advance tíqián [tee-chyen]
提前

aeroplane fēijī [fay-jee]

飞机

after yǐhòu [yee-hoh]

以后

after you nǐ xiān qù ba [nee hsyen chew bah]

你先去吧

after lunch wǔfàn hòu [woo-fahn]

午饭后

afternoon xiàwǔ [hsyah-woo]

下午

in the afternoon xiàwǔ

下午

this afternoon jīntiān xiàwǔ [jin-tyen]

今天下午

aftershave xūhòushuǐ [hsyew-hoh-shway]

须后水

afterwards yǐhòu [yee-hoh]

以后

again zài [dzai]

再

age niánjì [nyen-jee]

年纪

ago: a week ago yíge xīngqī yǐqián [yee-gur hsing-chee yee-chyen]

一个星期以前

an hour ago yíge xiǎoshí yǐqián [hsyow-shur]

一个小时以前

agree: I agree wǒ tóngyì [wor toong-yee]

我同意

AIDS àizībìng [ai-dzur-bing]

爱滋病

air kōngqì [koong-chee]

空气

by air zuò fēijī [dzwor fay-jee]

坐飞机

air-conditioning kōngtiáo [koong-tyow]

空调

airmail: by airmail hángkōng(xìn) [hahng-koong(-hsin)]

航空信

airmail envelope hángkōng xìnfēng [hsin-fung]

航空信封

airplane fēijī [fay-jee]

飞机

airport fēijīchǎng [–chahng]

飞机场

to the airport, please qǐng dài wǒ dào fēijīchǎng [ching dai wor dow]

请带我到飞机场

airport bus jīchǎng bānchē [jee-chahng bahn-chur]

机场班车

alarm clock nàozhōng [now-joong]

闹钟

alcohol (drink) jiǔ [jyoh]

酒

all: all of it quánbù [chew-ahn-

boo]
全部

that's all, thanks gòule, xièxie
[goh-lur hsyeh-hsyeh]
够了谢谢

allergic: I'm allergic to-... wǒ
duì-... guòmǐn [wor dway-...
gwor-min]
我对 ... 过敏

allowed: is it allowed? zhè
yúnxǔ-ma? [jur yun-hsyew-
mah]
这允许吗？

all right hǎo [how]
好

I'm all right wǒ méi shìr [wor
may shur]
我没事儿

are you all right? nǐ méi shìr
ba? [nee may-shur bah]
你没事儿吧？

(greeting) ní hǎo ma? [nee how]
你好吗？

almost chàbuduō [chah-boo-
dwor]
差不多

alone yíge rén [yee-gur run]
一个人

already yǐjing
已经

also yě [yur]
也

although suīrán [sway-rahn]
虽然

altogether yígòng

[yee-goong]
一共

always zǒng [dzoong]
总

am*: I am shì [shur]
是

a.m.: at seven a.m. shàngwǔ
qī diǎn [chee dyen]
上午七点

amazing (surprising) méi
xiǎngdào [may hsyang-dow]
没想到

(very good) liǎobùqǐ [lyow-boo-
chee]
了不起

ambulance jiùhùchē [jyoh-hoo-
chur]
救护车

call an ambulance! (kuài) jiào
jiùhùchē! [(kwai) jyow
jyoh-hoo-chur]
（快）叫救护车

America Měiguó [may-gwor]
美国

American (adj) Měiguó
美国

I'm American wǒ shì Měiguó
rén [wor shur – run]
我是美国人

among zài-... zhī zhōng [dzai-...
jur joong]
在 ... 之中

amp: a 13-amp fuse shísān
ānpéi de bǎoxiǎnsī [shur-sahn
ahn-pay dur bow-hsyen-sur]
十三安培的保险丝

and hé [hur]
和

angry shēngqì [shung-chee]
生气

animal dòngwù [doong-woo]
动物

ankle jiǎobózi [jyow-bor-dzur]
脚脖子

annoying: how annoying! zhēn
tǎoyàn! [jun tow-yahn]
真讨厌

another (different) lìng yíge
[yee-gur]
另一个
(one more) yòu yíge [yoh]
又一个

can we have another room?
wǒ xiǎng huàn lìngwài yíge
fángjiān [wor hsyang hwahn ling-
wai]
我想换另外一个房间

another beer, please qǐng zài
lái yì bēi píjiǔ [ching dzai lai yee]
请再来一杯啤酒

antibiotics kàngjūnsù [kahng-
jyewn-soo]
抗菌素

**antique: is it a genuine
antique?** shì zhēn gǔdǒng
ma? [shur jurn goo-doong mah]
是真古董吗？

antique shop wénwù
shāngdiàn [wun-woo shahng-
dyen]
文物商店

antiseptic fángfǔjì [fahng-foo-
jee]
防腐剂

any: do you have any-...? nǐ
yǒu ... ma? [nee yoh ... mah]
你有 ... 吗？

sorry, I don't have any
duìbuqǐ, wǒ méiyǒu [dway-
boo-chur wor may-yoh]
对不起我没有

anybody shéi [shay]
谁

does anybody speak English?
shéi huì shuō Yīngyǔ? [hway
shwor ying-yoo]
谁会说英语？

there wasn't anybody there
zàinàr shénme rén dōu
méiyou [zai-nar shun-mur run doh
may-yoh]
在那儿什么人都没有

anything shénme [shun-mur]
什么

dialogues

anything else? hái yào
shénme? [hai yow]
nothing else, thanks bú
yào, xièxie [hsyeh-hsyeh]

**would you like anything
to drink?** nǐ yào hé diǎnr
shénme? [hur dyenr]
I don't want anything,

thanks wǒ shénme dōu bú yào, xièxie [wor – doh]

apart from chúle-... yǐwài [choo-lur]
除了 ... 以外

apartment dānyuán [dahn-yew-ahn]
单元

aperitif kāiwèijiǔ [kai-way-jyoh]
开胃酒

appendicitis lánwěiyán [lahn-way-yen]
阑尾炎

appetizer lěngpánr [lung-pahnr]
冷盘儿

apple píngguǒ [ping-gwor]
苹果

appointment yuēhuì [yew-eh-hway]
约会

dialogue

good morning, how can I help you? nín zǎo, wǒ néng bāng shénme máng ma? [dzow wor nung bahng shun-mur mahng mah]
I'd like to make an appointment wǒ xiǎng dìng ge yùehùi [hsyang ding gur]
what time would you like?

nín xiǎng yuē shénme shíjian[yew-eh]
three o'clock sān diǎn (zhōng) [dyen (joong)]
I'm afraid that's not possible, is four o'clock all right? duìbùqǐ sān diǎn bù xíng, sì diǎn (zhōng) xíng ma? [dway-boo-chee – hsing – mah]
yes, that will be fine xíng, kěyǐ [kur-yee]
the name was? nín guì xìng? [gway]

apricot xìngzi [hsing-dzur]
杏子

April sìyuè [sur-yew-eh]
四月

are*: we are wǒmen shì [wor-mun shur]
我们是
you are (sing) nǐ shì
你是
(pl) nǐmen shì [nee-mun]
你们是
they are tāmen shì [tah-mun]
他们是

area (measurement) miànjì [myen-jee]
面积
(region) dìqū [dee-chew]
地区

arm gēbo [gur-bor]
胳膊

army jūnduì [chewn-dway]
军队

arrange: will you arrange it for us? nǐ néng tì wǒmen ānpái yí xià ma? [nung tee wor-mun ahn-pai yee hsyah mah]
你能替我们安排一下吗？

arrive dào [dow]
到

when do we arrive? wǒmen shénme shíhou dàodá? [wor-mun shun-mur shur-hoh dow-dah]
我们什么时候到达？

has my fax arrived yet? wǒ gěi nǐ fā de chuánzhēn dàole ma? [wor gay nee fah dur chwahn-jun dow-lur mah]
我给你发的传真到了吗？

we arrived today wǒmen jīntiān gāng dào [jin-tyen gahng]
我们今天刚到

art yìshù [yee-shoo]
艺术

art gallery měishùguǎn [may-shoo-gwahn]
美术馆

as: as big as... gēn ... yíyàng dà [gun ... yee-yang dah]
跟 ... 一样大

as soon as possible jǐnkuài [jin-kwai]
尽快

ashtray yānhuī gāng [yahn-hway gahng]
烟灰缸

ask (someone to do something) qǐng [ching]
请

(a question) wèn [wun]
问

could you ask him to-...? nǐ néng bù néng qǐng tā ...? [nung – tah]
你能不能请他 ... ？

asleep: she's asleep tā shuìzháole [tah shway-jow-lur]
他睡着了

aspirin āsīpǐlín [ah-sur-pee-lin]
阿斯匹林

asthma qìchuǎn [chee-chwahn]
气喘

at*: at my hotel zài wǒ zhú de fàndiàn [dzai wor joo dur]
在我住的饭店

at the railway station zài huǒchē zhàn
在火车站

at six o'clock liùdiǎn zhōng [lyoh-dyen joong]
六点钟

at Li Zhen's zài Lǐ Zhēn jiā [jyah]
在李真家

ATM zìdòng qǔkuǎnjī [dzur-doong chew-kwahn-jee]
自动取款机

attendant (on train) chéngwùyuán [chung-woo-yew-ahn]

乘务员

August bāyuè [bah-yew-eh]

八月

aunt (father's sister, unmarried)

gūgu

姑姑

(father's sister, married) gūmǔ

姑母

(mother's sister, unmarried) yímǔ

姨母

(mother's sister, married) yímā

[yee-mah]

姨妈

Australia Àodàlìyà [or-dah-lee-yah]

澳大利亚

Australian (adj) Àodàlìyà

澳大利亚

I'm Australian wǒ shì

Àodàlìyà rén [wor shur – run]

我是澳大利亚人

automatic (adj) zìdòng [dzur-doong]

自动

autumn qiūtiān [chyoh-tyen]

秋天

in the autumn qiūtiān

秋天

average (ordinary) yíbàn [yee-bahn]

一般

on average píngjūn [ping-jyewn]

平均

awake: is he awake? tā xǐngle

ma? [tah hsing-lur mah]

他醒了吗？

away: is it far away? yuǎn ma?

[yew-ahn]

远吗？

awful zāogāole [dzow-gow-lur]

糟糕了

B

baby yīng'ér [ying-er]

婴儿

baby food yīng'ér shíwù [shur-woo]

婴儿食物

baby's bottle nǎipíng

奶瓶

baby-sitter línshí kān

xiǎoháir de [lin-shur kahn hsyow-hair dur]

临时看小孩儿的

back hòu [hoh]

后

(of body) hòubèi [bay]

后背

at the back zài hòumian [dzai hoh-myen]

在后面

can I have my money back?

qǐng bǎ qián huán gěi wǒ ba

[ching bah chyen hwahn gay wor bah]

请把钱还给我吧

to come back huílai [hway–]
回来
to go back huíqu [–chew]
回去
backache bèitòng [bay-toong]
背痛
bad huài [hwai]
坏
a bad headache tóu téng de lìhai [toh tung dur lur-hai]
头疼得利害
bag dàizi [dai-dzur]
袋子
(handbag) shǒutíbāo [shoh-tee-bow]
手提包
(suitcase) shǒutíxiāng [shoh-tee-hsyang]
手提箱
baggage xíngli [hsing-lee]
行李
baggage check (US) xíngli jìcúnchù [jee-tsun-choo]
行李寄存处
baggage claim xíngli tíqǔchù [tee-chew-choo]
行李提取处
bakery miànbāodiàn [myen-bow-dyen]
面包店
balcony yángtái
阳台
a room with a balcony dài yángtái de fángjiān [dur fahng-jyen]
带阳台的房间
ball qiú [chyoh]
球
ballet bāléiwǔ [bah-lay-woo]
芭蕾舞
ballpoint pen yuánzhūbǐ [yew-ahn-joo-bee]
圆珠笔
bamboo zhúzi [joo-dzur]
竹子
bamboo shoots zhúsǔn [joo-sun]
竹笋
banana xiāngjiāo [hsyang-jyow]
香蕉
band (musical) yuèduì [yew-eh-dway]
乐队
bandage bēngdài [bung-dai]
绷带
Bandaid® xiàngpí gāo [hsyang-pee gow]
橡皮膏
bank (money) yínháng [yin-hahng]
银行
bank account zhànghù [jahng-hoo]
帐户
banquet yànhuì [yen-hway]
宴会
bar jiǔbājiān [jyoh-bah-jyen]
酒吧间

a bar of chocolate yí kuàir qiǎokèlì [yee kwair chyow-kur-lee]
一块儿巧克力

barber's lǐfàdiàn [lee-fah-dyen]
理发店

dialogue

> **how much is this?** zhèi ge duōshao qián? [jay gur dwor-show chyen]
>
> **30 yuan** sān shí kuài qián [kwai chyen]
>
> **that's too expensive, how about 20?** tài guì le, èr shí kuài, zénme yàng? [gway lur – dzun-mur]
>
> **I'll let you have it for 25** èr shí wǔ kuài ba [bah]
>
> **can you reduce it a bit more?** zài jiǎn yí diǎnr ba [dzai jyen yee dyenr]
>
> **OK, it's a deal** hǎo ba [how]

basket kuāng [kwahng]
筐

bath xǐzǎo [hshee-dzow]
洗澡

can I have a bath? wǒ néng xǐ ge zǎo ma? [wor nung hshee gur dzow mah]
我能洗个澡吗？

bathroom yùshì [yew-shur]
浴室

with a private bathroom dài xǐzǎojiān de fángjiān [dai hshee-dzow-jyen dur fahng-jyen]
带洗澡间的房间

bath towel yùjīn [yew-jin]
浴巾

bathtub zǎopén [dzow-pun]
澡盆

battery diànchí [dyen-chur]
电池

bay hǎiwān [hai-wahn]
海湾

be* shì [shur]
是

beach hǎitān [hai-tahn]
海滩

on the beach zài hǎitānshang [dzai –shahng]
在海滩上

bean curd dòufu [doh-foo]
豆腐

beans dòu [doh]
豆

French beans sìjìdòu [sur-jee-doh]
四季豆

broad beans cándòu [tsahn-doh]
蚕豆

string beans jiāngdòu [jyang-doh]
豇豆

soya beans huángdòu [hwahng-doh]
黄豆

bean sprouts dòu yár
豆芽儿

beard húzi [hoo-dzur]
胡子

beautiful (object) měilì
[may-lee]
美丽

(woman) piàoliang
[pyow-lyang]
漂亮

(view, city, building) měi
美

(day, weather) hǎo [how]
好

because yīnwéi [yin-way]
因为

because of-... yóuyú ... [yoh-yew]
由于

bed chuáng [chwahng]
床

I'm going to bed now wǒ
yào shuì le [wor yow shway
lur]
我要睡了

bedroom wòshì [wor-shur]
卧室

beef niúròu [nyoh-roh]
牛肉

beer píjiǔ [pee-jyoh]
啤酒

two beers, please qǐng lái
liǎng bēi píjiǔ [ching]
请来两杯啤酒

before: before-... ... yǐqián

[yee-chyen]
... 以前

begin kāishǐ [kai-shur]
开始

when does it begin? shénme
shíhou kāishǐ? [shun-mur shur-
hoh]
什么时候开始？

beginner chūxuézhě [choo-yew-
eh-jur]
初学者

behind zài-... hòumian [dzai-...
hoh-myen]
在 ... 后面

behind me zài wǒ hòumian
[wor]
在我后面

believe xiāngxìn [hsyang-hsin]
相信

below* zài-... xiàmian [dzai-...
hsyah-myen]
在 ... 下面

(less than) zài-... yǐxià [yee-
hsyah]
在 ... 以下

belt yāodài [yow-dai]
腰带

bend (in road) lùwánr [loo-
wahnr]
路弯儿

berth (on train) wòpù [wor-poo]
卧铺

beside: beside the-... zài-...
pángbiān [dzai-... pahng-byen]
在 ... 旁边

best zuìhǎo [dzway-how]
最好

better: even better gèng hǎo [gung how]
更好

a bit better hǎo yì diǎnr [dyenr]
好一点儿

are you feeling better? hǎo diǎnr le ma? [lur mah]
好点儿了吗？

between zài-... zhī jiān [dzai-... jur-jyen]
在 … 之间

bicycle zìxíngchē [dzur-hsing-chur]
自行车

big dà [dah]
大

too big tài dà le [lur]
太大了

it's not big enough búgòu dà [boo-goh]
不够大

bill zhàngdānr [jahng-dahnr]
帐单儿

(US: money) chāopiào [chow-pyow]
钞票

could I have the bill, please? qǐng bāng wǒ jiézhàng, hǎo ma? [ching bahng wor jyeh-jahng how mah]
请帮我结帐好吗？

bin lājī xiāng [lah-jee hsyang]
垃圾箱

bird niǎo [nyow]
鸟

birthday shēngrì [shung-rur]
生日

happy birthday! zhù nǐ shēngrì kuàilè! [joo – kwai-lur]
祝你生日快乐

biscuit bǐnggān [bing-gahn]
饼干

bit: a little bit yìdiǎnr [yee-dyenr]
一点儿

a big bit yídàkuàir [yee-dah-kwair]
一大块儿

a bit expensive yǒu diǎn guì
有点贵

bite (by insect) yǎo [yow]
咬

bitten by a dog ràng gǒu gěi yǎoshāng le [rahng goh gay yow-shahng]
让狗给咬伤了

bitter (taste etc) kǔ
苦

black hēi [hay]
黑

blanket tǎnzi [tahn-dzur]
毯子

blind xiā [hsyah]
瞎

blocked dǔzhùle [doo-joo-lur]
堵住了

blond (adj) jīnhuángsè [jin-hwahng-sur]

金黄色

blood xiě [hsyeh]

血

high blood pressure gāo xuèyā [gow hsyew-eh-yah]

高血压

blouse nǚchènshān [nyew-chun-shahn]

女衬衫

blow-dry: I'd like a cut and blow-dry wǒ xiǎng lǐfà hé chuīfēng [wor hsyang lee-fah hur chway-fung]

我想理发和吹风

blue lánsè [lahn-sur]

蓝色

blue eyes lán yǎnjing [lahn yahn-jing]

蓝眼睛

boarding pass dēngjì kǎ [dung-jee kah]

登记卡

boat chuán [chwahn]

船

(for passengers) kèchuán [kur-chwahn]

客船

body shēntǐ [shun-tee]

身体

boiled egg zhǔ jīdàn [joo jee-dahn]

煮鸡蛋

boiled rice mǐfàn [mee-fahn]

米饭

boiled water kāishuǐ [kai-shway]

开水

bone gǔ [goo]

骨

book (noun) shū [shoo]

书

(verb) dìng [ding]

订

can I book a seat? wǒ néng dìng ge zuòwei ma? [wor nung – gur dzwor-way mah]

我能订个座位吗？

dialogue

I'd like to book a table for two/three wǒ xiǎng dìng liǎng/sān ge rén yì zhuō de wèizi [wor hsyang – gur run yee jwor dur way-dszur]

what time would you like it booked for? nín yào jǐdiǎn zhōng? [yow jee-dyen joong]

half past seven qī diǎn bàn

that's fine xíng [hsing]

and your name? nín guì xìng? [gway]

bookshop, bookstore shūdiàn [shoo-dyen]

书店

boot (footwear) xuēzi [hsyew-

42

eh-dzur]

靴子

(of car) xínglixiāng [hsing-lee-hsyang]

行李箱

border (of country) biānjiè [byen-jyeh]

边界

border region biānjìng

边境

bored: I'm bored fán sǐ le [fahn sur-lur]

烦死了

boring méi jìnr [may]

没劲儿

born: I was born in Manchester wǒ shì zài Mànchéng shēng de-[wor shur dzai – shung dur]

我是在曼城生的

I was born in 1960 wǒ shì yí jiǔ liù líng nián-shēng de

我是一九六零年生的

borrow jiè [jyeh]

借

may I borrow-...? wǒ kěyǐ jiè yíxia-... ma? [wor kur-yee jyeh yee-hsyah-... mah]

我可以借一下 ... 吗？

both liǎngge dōu [lyang-gur doh]

两个都

bother: sorry to bother you duìbuqǐ dǎjiǎo nín le [dway-boo-chee dah-jyow nin lur]

对不起打搅您了

bottle píngzi [ping-dzur]

瓶子

a bottle of beer yì píng píjiǔ

一瓶啤酒

bottle-opener kāi píng qì [chee]

开瓶器

bottom dǐr [deer]

底儿

(of person) pìgu

屁股

at the bottom of the road lù de jìntóu [loo dur jin-toh]

路的尽头

box hézi [hur-dzur]

盒子

a box of chocolates yí hé qiǎokèlì [hur chyow-kur-lee]

一盒巧克力

box office shòupiào chù [shoh-pyow]

售票处

boy nánhái [nahn-hai]

男孩

boyfriend nán péngyou [nahn pung-yoh]

男朋友

bra xiōngzhào [hsyoong-jow]

胸罩

bracelet shǒuzhuó [shoh-jwor]

手镯

brandy báilándì [bai-lahn-dee]

白兰地

bread (baked) miànbāo [myen-bow]

面包

(steamed) mántou [mahn-toh]

馒头

white bread bái miànbāo

白面包

brown bread hēi miànbāo
[hay]

黑面包

wholemeal bread quánmài
miànbāo [chew-ahn-mai]

全麦面包

break (verb) dǎpò [dah-por]

打破

I've broken the-... wǒ
dǎpòle ... [wor dah-por-lur]

我打破了 ...

I think I've broken my ...
wǒde ... kěnéng huàile [wor-
dur ... kur-nung hwai-lur]

我的 ... 可能坏了

breakdown gùzhàng [goo-
jahng]

故障

breakfast zǎofàn [dzow-fahn]

早饭

break-in: I've had a break-in
(in room) wǒde fángjiān ràng
rén gěi qiàole mén le [wor-dur
fahng-jyen rahng run gay chyow-lur
mun lur]

我的房间让人给撬了门了

breast xiōng [hsyoong]

胸

breeze wēifēng [way-fung]

微风

bridge (over river) qiáo

[chyow]

桥

brief duǎn [dwahn]

短

briefcase gōngwénbāo [goong-
wun-bow]

公文包

bright (light etc) mínglliàng
[ming-lyang]

明亮

brilliant (idea, person) gāomíng
[gow-ming]

高明

bring dàilái

带来

I'll bring it back later wǒ guò
xiē shíhou dàihuílái [wor gwor
hsyeh shur-hoh dai-hway-lai]

我过些时候带回来

Britain Yīngguó [ying-gwor]

英国

British (adj) Yīngguó

英国

I'm British wǒ shì Yīngguó
rén [wor shur – run]

我是英国人

brochure shuōmíng shū [shwor-
ming]

说明书

broken (object) pòle [por-lur]

破了

(leg etc) duànle [dwahn-lur]

断了

(not working) huàile [hwai-lur]

坏了

brooch xiōngzhēn [hsyoong-jun]

胸针

brother xiōngdì

[hsyoong-dee]

兄弟

(older) gēge [gur-gur]

哥哥

(younger) dìdi

弟弟

brother-in-law (elder sister's
husband) jiěfū [jyeh-foo]

姐夫

(younger sister's husband) mèifu
[may-foo]

妹夫

(wife's elder brother) nèixiōng
[nay-hsyoong]

内兄

(wife's younger brother) nèidì [nay-
dee]

内弟

(husband's elder brother) dàbó
[dah bor]

大伯

(husband's younger brother)
xiǎoshū [hsyow-shoo]

小叔

brown zōngsè [dzoong-sur]

棕色

brush shuāzi [shwah-dzur]

刷

bucket tǒng [toong]

桶

Buddha Fó [for]

佛

Buddhism Fójiào [for-jyow]

佛教

Buddhist (adj) Fójiàotú

佛教徒

buffet car cānchē
[tsahn-chur]

餐车

building fángzi [fahng-dzur]

房子

(multi-storey) dàlóu [dah-loh]

大楼

bunk: bottom bunk xià pù
[hsyah]

下铺

middle bunk zhōng pù [joong]

中铺

top bunk shàng pù [shahng]

上铺

bureau de change wài huì
duìhuàn bù
[hway dway-hwahn]

外汇兑换部

burglary dàoqiè [dow-chyeh]

盗窃

Burma Miǎndiàn [myen-dyen]

缅甸

burn (noun) shāoshāng [show-
shahng]

烧伤

(verb) ránshāo [rahn-show]

燃烧

burnt: this is burnt (food)
shāojiāole [show-jyow-lur]

烧焦了

bus (public transport) gōnggòng

qìchē [goong-goong chee-chur]

公共汽车

(limited stop) shìqūchē [shur-chew-chur]

市区车

(in suburbs) jiāoqūchē [jyow-chew-chur]

郊区车

(long-distance) chángtú qìchē [chahng-too chee-chur]

长途汽车

what number bus is it to-...?
dào ... qù zuò jǐ lù chē? [dow ... chew dzwor jee lu chur]

到 ... 去坐几路车？

when is the next bus to-...?
dào ... qù de xià (yì) bān chē shì jídiǎn? [dow ... chew dur hsyah (yee) bahn chur shur jee-dyen]

到 ... 去的下一班车是几点？

what time is the last bus?
mòbānchē shì jǐ diǎn? [mor-bahn-chur shur jee dyen]

末班车是几点？

dialogue

does this bus go to-...?
zhèi liàng chē qù ... ma? [jay lyang chur chew ... mah]

no, you need a number-...
bú qù, nǐ yào zùo ... hào chē [chew nee yow zwor ... how chur]

business shēngyi [shung-yee]

生意

(firm, company) gōngsī [goong-sur]

公司

bus station gōnggòng qìchē zǒngzhàn [goong-goong chee-chur dzoong-jahn]

公共汽车总站

bus stop gōnggòng qìchē zhàn [jahn]

公共汽车站

busy (road etc) rènào [rur-now]

热闹

(person) hěn máng [hun mahng]

很忙

I'm busy tomorrow wǒ míngtian hěn máng [wor ming-tyen hun mahng]

我明天很忙

but kěshi [kur-shur]

可是

butcher's ròu diàn [roh dyen]

肉店

butter huángyóu [hwahng-yoh]

黄油

button niǔkòu [nyoh-koh]

纽扣

buy mǎi

买

where can I buy-...? zài nǎr néng mǎidào-...? [dzai nar nung mai-dow]

在哪儿能买到 ... ？

by: by bus zuò gònggōng

qìchē [dzwor]

坐公共汽车

written by-... shì ... xiě de
[shur ... sheh dur]

是 ... 写的

by the window zài chuānghu
pángbiān [dzai]

在窗户旁边

by the sea zài hǎibiān

在海边

by Thursday xīngqī sì zhī
qián [jur chyen]

星期四之前

bye zàijiàn [dzai-jyen]

再见

C

cabbage báicài [bai-tsai]

白菜

cabin (on ship) chuáncāng
[chwahn-tsahng]

船舱

cake dàngāo [dahn-gow]

蛋糕

cake shop gāodiǎndiàn [gow-
dyen-dyen]

糕点店

call (verb: to phone) dǎ diànhuà
[dah dyen-hwah]

打电话

what's it called? zhèige jiào
shénme? [jay-gur jyow shun-mur]

这个叫什么？

he/she is called-... (given name)
tā jiào ... [tah jyow]

他叫 ...

(surname) tā xìng ... [hsing]

他姓 ...

please call the doctor qǐng bǎ
yīshēng jiào lái [ching bah yee-
shung jyow]

请把医生叫来

**please give me a call at 7.30
a.m. tomorrow** qǐng
míngtiān zǎoshàng qī diǎn
bàn gěi wǒ dǎ diànhuà
[ching ming-tyen dzow-shahng
chee dyen bahn gay wor dah dyen-
hwah]

请明天早上七点半给
我打电话

please ask him to call me
qǐng tā dǎ diànhuà gěi wǒ [tah
dah – gay]

请他打电话给我

call back: I'll call back later
(phone back) wǒ guò yì huìr
zài dǎ lái [gwor yee hwayr dzai
dah]

我过一回儿再打来

**call round: I'll call round
tomorrow** wǒ míngtiān lái
zhǎo nǐ [jow]

我明天来找你

camcorder shèxiàngjī [shur-
hsyang-jee]

摄相机

camera zhàoxiàngjī [jow-

hsyang-jee]
照相机

can (noun) guàntou [gwahn-toh]
罐头

a can of beer yí guànr píjiǔ
一罐儿啤酒

can: can you-...? nǐ néng-...
ma? [nung-... mah]
你能 ... 吗？

can I have-...? qǐng gěi wǒ
...? [ching gay wor]
请给我 ... ？

I can't-... wǒ bù néng-...
我不能 ...

Canada Jiānádà [jyah-nah-dah]
加拿大

Canadian (adj) Jiānádà
加拿大

I'm Canadian wǒ shì
Jiānádàrén [wor shur –run]
我是加拿大人

canal yùnhé [yewn-hur]
运河

cancel (reservation etc) tuì [tway]
退

candies tángguǒ [tahng-gwor]
糖果

candle làzhú [lah-joo]
蜡烛

can-opener kāiguàn dāojù
[kai-gwahn dow-joo]
开罐刀具

Cantonese (adj) Guǎngdōng
[gwahng-doong]
广东

(language) Guǎngdōnghuà
[–hwah]
广东话

(person) Guǎngdōng rén [run]
广东人

cap (hat) màozi [mow-dzur]
帽子

(of bottle) pínggài [ping-gai]
瓶盖

car xiǎo qìchē [hsyow
chee-chur]
小汽车

by car zuò xiǎo qìchē
[dzwor]
坐小汽车

card kǎpiàn [kah-pyen]
卡片

here's my (business) card
zhèi shì wǒde míngpiàn [jay
shur wor-dur ming-pyen]
这是我的名片

Christmas card shèngdàn kǎ
[shung-dahn kah]
圣诞卡

birthday card shēngrì kǎ
[shung-rur kah]
生日卡

cardphone cíkǎ diànhuà [tsur-
kah dyen-hwah]
磁卡电话

careful: be careful! xiǎoxīn!
[hsyow-hsin]
小心

car ferry lúndù [lun-doo]
轮渡

car park tíngchēchǎng [ting-
chur-chahng]

停车场

carpet dìtǎn [dee-tahn]

地毯

car rental qìchē chūzū [chee-
chur choo-dzoo]

汽车出租

carriage (of train) chēxiāng
[chur-hsyang]

车厢

carrot húluóbo [hoo-lwor-bor]

胡萝卜

carry ná [nah]

拿

cash (noun) xiànqián [hsyen-
chyen]

现钱

will you cash this for me? nǐ
néng tì wǒ huàn chéng xiàn
qián ma? [nung tee wor hwahn
chung – mah]

你能替我换成现钱吗？

cash desk jiāokuǎnchù [jyow-
kwahn-choo]

交款处

cash dispenser zìdòng
qúkuǎnjī [dzur-doong chew-
kwahn-jee]

自动取款机

cassette cídài [tsur-dai]

磁带

cassette recorder lùyīnjī [loo-
yin-jee]

录音机

castle chéngbǎo [chung-bow]

城堡

casualty department jíjiùshì
[jee-jyoh-shur]

急救室

cat māo [mow]

猫

catch (verb) zhuā [jwah]

抓

**where do we catch the bus
to-...?** qù-... zài nǎr shàng
chē? [chew-... dzai – chur]

去 ... 在哪儿上车？

cathedral dà jiàotáng [dah
jyow-tahng]

大教堂

Catholic (adj) tiānzhǔjiào [tyen-
joo-jyow]

天主教

cauliflower càihuā [tsai-hwah]

菜花

cave shāndòng [shahn-doong]

山洞

(dwelling) yáodòng
[yow-doong]

窑洞

cemetery mùdì

墓地

centigrade shèshì [shur-shur]

摄氏

centimetre límǐ [lee-mee]

厘米

central zhōngyāng
[joong-yang]

中央

central heating nuǎnqì [nwahn-chee]

暖气

centre zhōngxīn [joong-hsin]

中心

how do we get to the city centre? qù shì zhōngxīn zénme zǒu? [chew shur joong-hsin dzun-mur dzoh]

去市中心怎么走？

certainly dāngrán [dahn-grahn]

当然

certainly not dāngrán bù

当然不

chair yǐzi [yee-dzur]

椅子

Chairman Mao Máo zhǔxí [mow jyew-hshee]

毛主席

change (noun: money) língqián [ling-chyen]

零钱

(verb: money) duìhuàn [dway-hwahn]

兑换

can I change this for-...? nín néng bāng wǒ duìhuàn chéng ... ma? [nung bahng wor dway-hwahn chung ... mah]

您能帮我兑换成 ... 吗？

I don't have any change wǒ yìdiǎnr língqián yě méi yǒu [wor yee-dyenr ling-chyen yur may yoh]

我一点儿零钱也没有

can you give me change for a hundred-yuan note? yí bǎi kuài nín zhǎodekāi ma? [kwai nin jow-dur-kai mah]

一百块您找得开吗？

dialogue

do we have to change (trains)? zhōngtú yào huàn chē ma? [joong-too yow hwahn chur mah]

yes, change at Hangzhou yào zài Hángzhōu huàn chē [yow dzai]

no, it's a direct train bú yòng huàn chē, zhè shì zhídáchē [yoong – jur shur jur-dah-chur]

changed: to get changed huàn yīfu [hwahn yee-foo]

换衣服

character (in Chinese writing) zì [dzur]

字

charge (noun) shōufèi [shoh-fay]

收费

cheap piányi [pyen-yee]

便宜

do you have anything cheaper? yǒu piányi diǎnr de ma? [yoh pyen-yee dyenr dur mah]

有便宜点儿的吗？

check: could you check
the-bill, please? qǐng ba
zhàngdān jiǎnchá yíxià, hāo
ma? [ching bah jahng-dahn jyen-
chah yee-syah how mah]

请把帐单检查一下好
吗？

check (US: bill) zhàngdānr
[jahng-dahnr]

帐单儿

check in dēngjì [dung-jee]

登记

where do we have to check
in? wǒmen yào zài nár
dēngjì? [wor-men yow dzai nar]

我们要在哪儿登记？

cheerio! zàijiàn! [dzai-jyen]

再见

cheers! (toast) gānbēi! [gahn-
bay]

干杯

cheese nǎilào [nai-low]

奶酪

chemist's yàofáng [yow-
fahng]

药房

cherry yīngtao [ying-tow]

樱桃

chess guójì xiàngqí [gwor-jee
hsyang-chee]

国际象棋

to play chess xià qí [hsyah
chee]

下棋

Chinese chess xiàngqí

[hsyang-chee]

象棋

chest (body) xiōng [hsyoong]

胸

chicken (meat) jīròu [jee-roh]

鸡肉

child háizi [hai-dzur]

孩子

child minder bǎomǔ [bow-moo]

保姆

chin xiàba [hsyah-bah]

下巴

china cíqì [tsur-chee]

瓷器

China Zhōngguó [joong-gwor]

中国

China tea Zhōngguo chá
[chah]

中国茶

Chinese (adj) Zhōngguó [joong-
gwor]

中国

(person) Zhōngguó rén [run]

中国人

(spoken language) Hànyǔ [hahn-
yew]

汉语

(written language) Zhōngwén
[joong-wun]

中文

the Chinese Zhōngguó
rénmín [run-min]

中国人民

Chinese leaf báicài [bai-tsai]

白菜

Chinese-style Zhōngshì [joong-shur]

中式

chips zhá tǔdòu tiáo [jah too-doh tyow]

炸土豆条

(US) (zhá) tǔdòupiànr [too-doh-pyenr]

（炸）土豆片儿

chocolate qiǎokèlì [chyow-kur-lee]

巧克力

milk chocolate nǎiyóu qiǎokèlì [nai-yoh]

奶油巧克力

plain chocolate chún qiǎokèlì

纯巧克力

a hot chocolate yì bēi rè qiǎokèlì (yǐnliào) [bay rur – (yin-lyow)]

一杯热巧克力（饮料）

choose xuǎn [hsyew-ahn]

选

chopsticks kuàizi [kwai-dzur]

筷子

Christmas Shèngdàn jié [shung-dahn jyeh]

圣诞节

Christmas Eve Shèngdànqiányè [–chyen-yur]

圣诞前夜

Merry Christmas! Shèngdàn kuàilè! [kwai-lur]

圣诞快乐

church jiàotáng [jyow-tahng]

教堂

cigar xuějiā [hsyew-eh-jyah]

雪茄

cigarette xiāngyān [hsyang-yen]

香烟

cinema diànyǐng yuàn [dyen-ying yew-ahn]

电影院

circle yuánquān [ywahn-kwahn]

圆圈

(in theatre) lóutīng [loh-ting]

楼厅

city chéngshì [chung-shur]

城市

city centre shì zhōngxīn [shur joong-hsin]

市中心

clean (adj) gānjìng [gahn-jing]

干净

can you clean these for me? nǐ néng tì wǒ xǐyixǐ, ma? [nung tee wor hshee-yee-hshee mah]

你能替我洗一洗吗？

clear (water) qīngchè [ching-chur]

清澈

(speech, writing) qīngxī [ching-hshee]

清晰

(obvious) míngxiǎn [–hsyen]

明显

clever cōngming [tsoong-ming]

聪明

cliff xuányá [hsyew-ahn-yah]
悬崖

climbing páshān [pah-shahn]
爬山

clinic zhěnsuǒ [jun-swor]
诊所

cloakroom yīmàojiān [yee-mow-jyen]
衣帽间

clock zhōng [joong]
钟

close (verb) guān [gwahn]
关

dialogue

what time do you close?
nǐmen shénme shíhou
guān mén? [nee-mun shun-mur shur-hoh – mun]

we close at 8 p.m. on
weekdays and 6 p.m. on
Saturdays zhōurì xiàwǔ bā
diǎn, xīngqī liù xiàwǔ liù
diǎn [joh-rur]

do you close for lunch? chī
wǔfàn de shíhou guān mén
ma? [chur woo-fahn dur shur-hoh – mah]

yes, between 1 and
3.30 p.m. shì de, cóng yī
diǎn dào sān diǎn bàn yě
guān mén [shur dur tsoong – dow – yur]

closed guānménle [gwahn-mun-lur]
关门了

cloth (fabric) bùliào [bool-yow]
布料
(for cleaning etc) mābù [mah-boo]
抹布

clothes yīfu [yee-foo]
衣服

clothes line shàiyīshéng [shai-yee-shung]
晒衣绳

clothes peg yīfu jiāzi [yee-foo jyah-dzur]
衣服夹子

cloudy duōyún [dwor-yewn]
多云

coach (bus) chángtú qìchē [chahng-too chee-chur]
长途汽车
(tourist bus) lǚyóu chē [lyew-yoh chur]
旅游车
(on train) kèchē [kur-chur]
客车

coach station chángtú qìchēzhàn [chang-too chee-chur-jahn]
长途汽车站

coach trip zuò chángtú qìchē lǚxíng [dzwor chahng-too chee-chur lyew-hsing]
坐长途汽车旅行

coast hǎibīn
海滨

coat (long coat) dàyī [dah-yee]
大衣

coathanger yījià [yee-jyah]
衣架

cockroach zhāngláng [jahng-lahng]
蟑螂

code (for phoning) diànhuà qūhào [dyen-hwah chew-how]
电话区号

what's the (dialling) code for Beijing? Běijīng de diànhuà qūhào shì duōshao? [dur – shur dwor-show]
北京的电话区号是多少？

coffee kāfēi [kah-fay]
咖啡

two coffees, please qǐng lái liǎng bēi kāfēi [ching]
请来两杯咖啡

coin yìngbì [ying-bee]
硬币

Coke® Kěkǒukělè [kur-koh-kur-lur]
可口可乐

cold lěng [lung]
冷

I'm cold wǒ juéde hěn lěng [wor jyew-eh-dur hun lung]
我觉得很冷

I have a cold wǒ gǎnmào le [gahn-mow lur]
我感冒了

collapse: he's collapsed tā kuǎle [tah kwah-lur]
他垮了

collar yīlǐng
衣领

collect qǔ-... [chew]
取

I've come to collect-... wǒ lái qǔ-... [wor]
我来取

collect call duìfāng fùkuǎn [dway-fahng foo-kwahn]
对方付款

college xuéyuàn [hsyew-eh-yew-ahn]
学院

colour yánsè [yahn-sur]
颜色

do you have this in other colours? yǒu biéde yánsè de ma? [yoh byeh-dur – dur mah]
有别的颜色吗？

colour film cǎisè jiāojuǎnr [tsai-sur jyow-jyew-ahnr]
彩色胶卷儿

comb shūzi [shoo-dzur]
梳子

come lái
来

dialogue

where do you come from? nǐ shì cóng nǎr láide? [shur tsoong nar lai-dur]
I come from Edinburgh

wǒ shì cóng Àidīngbǎo lái de [wor]

come back huílai [hway-lai]
回来
I'll come back tomorrow wǒ míngtiān huílai [ming-tyen]
我明天回来
come in qǐng jìn [ching jin]
请进
comfortable shūfu [shoo-foo]
舒服
communism gòngchánzhǔyì [goong-chahn-joo-yee]
共产主义
Communist Party Gòngchándǎng [–dahng]
共产党
Communist Party member gòngchándǎngyuán [–dahng-yew-ahn]
共产党员
compact disc jīguāng chàngpiàn [jee-gwahng chahng-pyen]
激光唱片
company (business) gōngsī [goong-sur]
公司
compass zhǐnánzhēn [jur-nahn-jun]
指南针
complain mányuàn [mahn-yew-ahn]
埋怨

complaint bàoyuàn [bow-yew-ahn]
抱怨
I have a complaint to make wǒ xiǎng tí yí ge yìjiàn [wor hsyang tee yee gur yee-jyen]
我想提一个意见
completely wánwánquánquán [wahn-wahn-chahn-chahn]
完完全全
computer diànnǎo [dyen-now]
电脑
concert yīnyuèhuì [yin-yew-eh-hway]
音乐会
concussion nǎozhèndàng [now-jun-dahng]
脑震荡
conditioner (for hair) hùfàsù [hoo-fah-soo]
护发素
condom bìyùntào [bee-yewn-tow]
避孕套
conference huìyì [hway-yee]
会议
congratulations! gōngxǐ! gōngxǐ! [goong-hshee]
恭喜恭喜
connecting flight xiánjiē de bānjī [hsyen-jyeh dur bahn-jee]
衔接的班机
connection (in travelling) liányùn [lyen-yewn]
联运

(rail) zhōngzhuǎn [joong-jwahn]
中转

constipation biànbì [byen-bee]
便秘

consulate lǐngshìguǎn [ling-shur-gwahn]
领事馆

contact (verb) liánxi [lyen-hshee]
联系

contact lenses yǐnxíng yǎnjìng [yin-hsing yahn-jing]
隐型眼镜

contraceptive bìyùn yòngpǐn [bee-yewn yoong-pin]
避孕用品

convenient fāngbiàn [fahng-byen]
方便

that's not convenient bù fāngbiàn
不方便

cooker lúzào [loo-dzow]
炉灶

cookie xiǎo bǐnggān [hsyow bing-gahn]
小饼干

cool liángkuai [lyang-kwai]
凉快

corner: on the corner jiējiǎor [jyeh-jyowr]
街角儿

in the corner qiángjiǎor [chyang-jyowr]
墙角儿

correct (right) duì [dway]
对

corridor zǒuláng [dzoh-lahng]
走廊

cosmetics huàzhuāngpǐn [hwah-jwahng-pin]
化妆品

cost (noun) jiàqián [jyah-chyen]
价钱

how much does it cost? duōshao qián? [dwor-show chyen]
多少钱？

cotton miánhuā [myen-hwah]
棉花

cotton wool yàomián [yow-myen]
药棉

couchette wòpù [wor-poo]
卧铺

cough késou [kur-soh]
咳嗽

cough medicine zhǐké yào [jur-kur yow]
止咳药

could: could you-...? nín kěyi-... ma? [kur-yee-... mah]
您可以 ... 吗？

I couldn't-... wǒ bù néng ... [wor boo nung]
我不能

country (nation) guójiā [gwor-jyah]
国家

(countryside) xiāngcūn 〖hsyang-tsun〗

乡村

couple (two people) fūfù 〖foo-foo〗

夫妇

a couple of-... liǎngge-... 〖lyang-gur〗

两个 ...

courier xìnshǐ 〖hsin-shur〗

信使

course: of course dāngrán 〖dahn-grahn〗

当然

of course not dāngrán bù

当然不

cousin (son of mother's brother: older than speaker) biǎogē 〖byow-gur〗

表哥

(younger than speaker) biǎodì

表弟

(son of father's brother: older than speaker) tángxiōng 〖tahng-hsyoong〗

堂兄

(younger than speaker) tángdì

堂弟

(daughter of mother's brother: older than speaker) biǎojiě 〖byow-jyeh〗

表姐

(younger than speaker) biǎomèi 〖byow-may〗

表妹

(daughter of father's brother: older

than speaker) tángjiě 〖tahng-jyeh〗

堂姐

(younger than speaker) tángmèi 〖tahng-may〗

堂妹

cow nǎiniú 〖nain-yoh〗

奶牛

crab pángxiè 〖pahng-hsyeh〗

螃蟹

craft shop gōngyìpǐn shāngdiàn 〖goong-yee-pin shahng-dyen〗

工艺品商店

crash (noun: vehicle) zhuàng chē 〖jwahng chur〗

撞车

crazy fēng 〖fung〗

疯

credit card xìnyòng kǎ 〖hsin-yoong kah〗

信用卡

do you take credit cards? shōu xìnyòng kǎ ma? 〖show – mah〗

收信用卡吗？

dialogue

can I pay by credit card? wǒ kéyǐ yòng xìnyòng kǎ jiāo kuǎn ma? 〖wor kur-yee yoong hsin-yoong kah jyow kwahn mah〗

which card do you want to use? nín yóng de shì

shénme kǎ? [dur shur shun-mur kah]

Mastercard/Visa

yes, sir kěyǐ [kur-yee]

what's the number? duōshao hàomǎ? [dwor-show how-mah]

and the expiry date? jǐ shí guòqī? [jee shur gwor-chee]

crisps (zhá) tǔdòupiànr [(jah) too-doh-pyenr]
（炸）土豆片儿

crockery cānjù [tsahn-jyew]
餐具

crossing (by sea) guòdù [gwor-doo]
过渡

crossroads shízì lùkǒu [shur-dzur loo-koh]
十字路口

crowd rénqún [run-chewn]
人群

crowded yōngjǐ [yoong-jee]
拥挤

crown (on tooth) yáguàn [yah-gwahn]
牙冠

cruise zuò chuán lǚxíng [dzwor chwahn lyew-sing]
坐船旅行

crutches guǎizhàng [gwai-jahng]
拐杖

cry (verb) kū
哭

Cultural Revolution wénhuà dà gémìng [wun-hwah dah gur-ming]
文化大革命

cup bēizi [bay-dzur]
杯子

a cup of tea/coffee, please yì bēi chá/kāfēi [bay]
一杯茶／咖啡

cupboard guìzi [gway-dzur]
柜子

cure (verb) zhìyù [jur-yew]
治愈

curly juǎnqūde [jwahn-chew-dur]
卷曲的

current (electric) diànliú [dyen-lyoh]
电流
(in water) shuǐliú [shway-lyoh]
水流

curry gālì [gah-lee]
咖喱

curtains chuānglián [chwahng-lyen]
窗帘

cushion diànzi [dyen-dzur]
垫子

custom fēngsú [fung-soo]
风俗

Customs hǎiguān [hai-gwahn]
海关

cut (noun) dāoshāng [dow-shahng]
刀伤

I've cut myself wǒ bǎ zìjǐ gēshāng le [wor bah dzur-jee gurshahng lur]

我把自己割伤了

cutlery dāochā cānjù [dow-chah
tsahn-jew]

刀叉餐具

cycling qí zìxíngchē [chee dzur-
hsing-chur]

骑自行车

cyclist qí zìxíngchē de rén
[dur run]

骑自行车的人

D

dad bàba [bah-bah]

爸爸

daily měi tiān [may tyen]

每天

damage (verb) sǔnhuài [syewn-
hwai]

损坏

damaged sǔnhuài le

损坏了

I'm sorry, I've damaged this
duìbùqǐ, wó bǎ zhèi ge nòng
huài le [dway-boo-chee wor bah
jay gur noong hwai lur]

对不起我把这个弄坏了

damn! zāole! [dzow-lur]

糟了

damp (adj) cháoshī [chow-shur]

潮湿

dance (noun) wǔdǎo [woo-dow]

舞蹈

(verb) tiàowǔ [tyow-woo]

跳舞

would you like to dance? nǐ
xiǎng tiàowǔ ma? [hsyang
– mah]

你想跳舞吗？

dangerous wēixiǎn [way-hsyen]

危险

Danish (adj) Dānmài [dahn-mai]

丹麦

dark (adj) àn [ahn]

暗

(colour) shēnsè [shunsur]

深色

it's getting dark tiān hēile
[tyen hay-lur]

天黑了

date*: **what's the date today?**
jīntiān jǐ hào? [jin-tyen jee how]

今天几号？

**let's make a date for next
Monday** zánmen xiàge
xīngqīyī jiànmiàn [zahn-mun
hsyah-gur – jyen-myen]

咱们下个星期一见面

daughter nǚ'ér [nyew-er]

女儿

daughter-in-law érxífur [er-
hshee-foor]

儿媳妇儿

dawn límíng

黎明

at dawn tiān gāng liàng [tyen
gahng lyang]

天刚亮

day tiān tyen]
天

the day after dìèr tiān
第二天

the day after tomorrow
hòutiān [hoh-tyen]
后天

the day before qián yì tiān
[chyen]
前一天

the day before yesterday
qiántiān [chyen-tyen]
前天

every day měitiān [may-tyen]
每天

all day zhěngtiān [jung-tyen]
整天

in two days' time liǎng tiān
nèi [nay]
两天内

have a nice day zhù nǐ wánr
de gāoxìng [joo nee wahnr dur
gow-hsing]
祝你玩儿得高兴

day trip yírìyóu [yee-rur-yoh]
一日游

dead sǐle [sur-lur]
死了

deaf ěr lóng [loong]
耳聋

deal (business) mǎimài
买卖

it's a deal! yì yán wéi dìng!
[yee yahn way]
一言为定

death sǐwáng [sur-wahng]
死亡

December shí'èr yuè [shur-er
yew-eh]
十二月

decide juédìng [jyew-eh-ding]
决定

we haven't decided yet
wǒmen hái méi juédìng [wor-
mun hai may]
我门还没决定

decision juédìng
决定

deck (on ship) jiábǎn [jyah-
bahn]
甲板

deep shēn [shun]
深

definitely yídìng
一定

definitely not yídìng bù
一定不

degree (qualification) xuéwèi
[hsyew-eh-way]
学位

delay (noun) wǎndiǎn [wahn-
dyen]
晚点

deliberately gùyì [goo-yee]
故意

delicious hǎochī [how-chur]
好吃

deliver sòng [soong]
送

delivery (of mail) sòngxìn

[soong-hsin]
送信

Denmark Dānmài [dahn-mai]
丹麦

dentist yáyī [yah-yee]
牙医

dialogue

> it's this one here zhèr zhèi
> kē [jer jay kur]
> this one? zhèi kē ma? [mah]
> no, that one bù, shì nèi kē
> [shur nay]
> here? zhèr?
> yes duì [dway]

dentures jiǎyá [jee-ah-yah]
假牙

deodorant chúchòujì [choo-
choh-jee]
除臭剂

department (administrative) bù
部

(academic) xì [hshee]
系

department store bǎihuò
dàlóu [bai-hwor dah-loh]
百货大楼

departure lounge hòujīshì
[hoh-jee-shur]
候机室

depend: it depends on-... nà
yào kàn-... [nah yow kahn]
那要看 ...

deposit yājīn [yah-jin]
押金

dessert tiánpǐn [tyen-pin]
甜品

destination mùdìdì
目的地

develop (film) chōngxǐ [choong-
hshee]
冲洗

dialogue

> could you develop these
> films? qǐng nín bāng wǒ
> chōngxǐ yíxià zhèi xiē
> jiāojuǎnr, hǎo ma? [ching nin
> bahng wor choong-hshee yee-
> hsyah jay hsyeh jyow-jyew-ahnr
> how mah]
> yes, certainly kěyǐ [kur-yee]
> when will they be ready?
> shénme shíhou néng
> chōng hǎo? [shun-mur shur-
> hoh nung choong how]
> tomorrow afternoon
> míngtian xiàwǔ [ming-tyen
> hsyah-woo]
> how much is the four-hour
> service? sì xiǎoshí fúwù
> duōshao qián? [sur hsyow-
> shur foo-woo dwor-show]

diabetic (noun) tángniàobìng
rén [tahng-nyow-bing run]
糖尿病人

glish → Chinese

dial (verb) bōhào [bor-how]
拨号

dialling code diànhuà qūhào
[dyen-hwah chew-how]
电话区号

diamond zuànshí [dzwahn-shur]
钻石

diaper niàobù [nyow-boo]
尿布

diarrhoea lā dùzi [lah doo-dzur]
拉肚子

**do you have something for
diarrhoea?** nǐ yǒu zhì lā dùzi
de yào ma? [nee yoh jur lah doo-
dzur dur yow mah]
你有治拉肚子的药吗？

diary rìjì [rur-jee]
日记

dictionary cídiǎn [tsur-dyen]
词典

didn't* see not

die sǐ [sur]
死

diet jìkǒu [jee-koh]
忌口

I'm on a diet wǒ zài jìkǒu [wor
dzai]
我在忌口

I have to follow a special diet
wǒ děi chī guīdìng de
yǐnshí [day chur gway-ding dur
yin-shur]
我得吃规定的饮食

difference bùtóng [boo-toong]
不同

what's the difference? yǒu
shénme bùtóng? [yoh shun-
mur]
有什么不同？

different bùtóng
不同

difficult kùnnan [kun-nahn]
困难

difficulty kùnnan
困难

dining room cāntīng [tsahn-ting]
餐厅

dinner (evening meal) wǎnfàn
[wahn-fahn]
晚饭

to have dinner chī wǎnfàn
吃晚饭

direct (adj) zhíjiē [jur-jyeh]
直接

(flight) zhífēi [jur-fay]
直飞

is there a direct train? yǒu
zhídá huǒchē ma? [yoh jur-dah
hwor-chur mah]
有直达火车吗？

direction fāngxiàng [fahng-
hsyang]
方向

which direction is it? zài něige
fāngxiàng? [dzai nay-gur]
在哪个方向？

is it in this direction? shì
zhèige fāngxiàng ma? [shur
jay-gur – mah]
是这个方向吗？

director zhǔrèn [joo-run]
主任

dirt wūgòu [woo-goh]
污垢

dirty zāng [dzahng]
脏

disabled cánfèi [tsahn-fay]
残废

is there access for the disabled? yǒu cánjírén de tōngdào ma? [you tsahn-jee–run dur toong-dow mah]
有残疾人的通道吗？

disaster zāinàn [dzai-nahn]
灾难

disco dísīkē [dee-sur-kur]
迪斯科

discount jiǎnjià [jyen-jyah]
减价

is there a discount? néng jiǎnjià ma? [nung – mah]
能减价吗？

disease jíbìng
疾病

disgusting ěxīn [ur-hsin]
恶心

dish (meal) cài [tsai]
菜

(bowl) diézi [dyeh-dzur]
碟子

disk (for computer) ruǎnpán [rwahn-pahn]
软盘

disposable nappies/diapers (yícìxìng) niàobù [(yee-tsur-hsing) nyow-boo]
（一次性）尿布

distance jùlí
距离

in the distance zài yuǎnchù [dzai yew-ahn-choo]
在远处

district dìqū [dee-chew]
地区

disturb dárǎo [dah-row]
打扰

divorced líhūn [lee-hun]
离婚

dizzy: I feel dizzy wǒ tóuyūn [wor toh-yewn]
我头晕

do (verb) zuò [dzwor]
作

what shall we do? nǐ xiǎng zuò shénme? [hsyang – shun-mur]
你想作什么？

how do you do it? gāi zěnme zuò? [dzun-mur]
该怎么做？

will you do it for me? máfan nǐ bāng wǒ zuò yíxià, hǎo ma? [mah-fahn nee bahng wor dzwor yee-hsyah how mah]
麻烦你帮我做一下好吗？

dialogues

how do you do? nín hǎo?
[how]

nice to meet you jiàn dào
nín zhēn gāoxìng [jyen dow
nin jun gow-hsing]

what do you do? (work) nǐ
shì zuò shénme gōngzuò
de? [shur – goong-dzwor dur]

I'm a teacher, and you? wǒ
shì jiàoshī, nǐ ne? [wor –
nur]

I'm a student wǒ shì
xuésheng

**what are you doing this
evening?** nǐ jīnwǎn zuò
shénme? [jin-wahn]

**we're going out for a drink,
do you want to join us?**
wǒmen chū qù hē jiǔ, nǐ
xiǎng gēn wǒmen yí kuàir
qù ma? [wor-mun choo chew
hur jyoh nee hsyang gun – kwair
chew mah]

do you want more rice? nǐ
hái yào fàn, ma? [yow fahn]

I do, but she doesn't wǒ
yào, tā bú yào [wor yow tah]

doctor yīshēng [yee-shung]
医生

please call a doctor qǐng nǐ
jiào ge yīshēng [ching nee jyow
gur]
请你叫个医生

dialogue

where does it hurt? nǎr
téng? [tung]

right here jiù zài zhèr [jyoh
dzai jer]

does that hurt now?
xiànzài hái téng ma?
[hsyahn-dzai – mah]

yes hái téng

**take this prescription to
the chemist** ná zhèi gè
yàofāng dào yàodiàn qù
pèi yào [nah jay gur yow-fahng
dow yow-dyen chew pay yow]

document wénjiàn [wun-jyen]
文件

dog gǒu [goh]
狗

domestic flight guónèi
hángbān [gwor-nay
hahng-bahn]
国内行班

don't!* búyào! [boo-yow]
不要

don't do that! bié zhème zuò
[byeh jur-mur zwor]
别这么做

see **not**

door mén [mun]
门

doorman bǎménrde [bah-munr-dur]
把门儿的

double shuāng [shwahng]
双

double bed shuāngrén chuáng [–run chwahng]
双人床

double room shuāngrén fáng(jiān) [fahng(jyen)]
双人房（间）

down xià [hsyah]
下

down here jiù zài zhèr [jyoh dzai jer]
就在这儿

put it down over there gē zài nàr
搁在那儿

it's down there on the right jiù zài yòubian [yoh-byen]
就在右边

it's further down the road zài wǎng qián [wahng chyen]
再往前

downstairs lóuxià [loh-hsyah]
楼下

dozen yì dá [dah]
一打

half a dozen bàn dá [bahn]
半打

dragon lóng [loong]
龙

draught beer shēng píjiǔ [shung pee-jyoh]
生啤酒

draughty: it's draughty zhèr tōngfēng [jer toong-fung]
这儿通风

drawer chōuti [choh-tee]
抽屉

drawing huìhuà [hway-hwah]
绘画

dreadful zāotòule [dzow-toh-lur]
糟透了

dress (noun) liányīqún [lyen-yee-chewn]
连衣裙

dressed: to get dressed chuān yīfu [chwahn]
穿衣服

dressing gown chényī [chun-yee]
晨衣

drink (noun: alcoholic) jiǔ [jyoh]
酒

(non-alcoholic) yǐnliào [yin-lyow]
饮料

(verb) hē [hur]
喝

a cold drink yì bēi léngyǐn [yee bay lung-yin]
一杯冷饮

can I get you a drink? hēdiǎnr shénme ma? [dyenr shun-mur mah]
喝点儿什么吗？

what would you like (to

drink)? nǐ xiǎng hē diǎnr shénme? 〖hsyang〗

你想喝点儿什么？

no thanks, I don't drink xièxie, wǒ bú huì hē jiǔ 〖hsyeh-hsyeh wor boo hway hur jyoh〗

谢谢我不会喝酒

I'll just have a drink of water wǒ hē diǎnr shuǐ ba 〖shway bah〗

我喝点儿水吧

drinking water yǐnyòngshuǐ 〖yin-yoong-shway〗

饮用水

is this drinking water? zhè shuǐ kěyǐ hē ma? 〖jur shway kur-yee hur ma〗

这水可以喝吗？

drive (verb) kāichē 〖kai-chur〗

开车

we drove here wǒmen kāichē lái de 〖wor-mun kai-chur lai dur〗

我们开车来的

I'll drive you home wǒ kāichē sòng nǐ huíjiā 〖wor kai-chur soong nee hway-jyah〗

我开车送你回家

driver sījī 〖sur-jee〗

司机

driving licence jiàshǐ zhízhào 〖jyah-shur jur-jow〗

驾驶执照

drop: just a drop, please (of drink) zhēn de yì diǎnr,

xièxie 〖jun dur yee dyen hsyeh-hsyeh〗

真的一点儿谢谢

drugs (narcotics) dúpǐn 〖doo-pin〗

毒品

drunk (adj) hēzuìle 〖hur-dzway-lur〗

喝醉了

dry (adj) gān 〖gahn〗

干

dry-cleaner gānxǐdiàn 〖gahn-hshee-dyen〗

干洗店

duck (meat) yā 〖yah〗

鸭

due: he was due to arrive yesterday tā yīnggāi shì zuótiān dào 〖tah ying-gai dzwor-tyen dow〗

他应该昨天到

when is the train due? huǒchē jǐ diǎn dào? 〖hwor-chur jee shur〗

火车几点到？

dull (pain) yǐnyǐn zuòtòng 〖dzwor-toong〗

隐隐作痛

(weather) yīntiān 〖yin-tyen〗

阴天

during zài-... de shíhou 〖dzai-... dur shur-hoh〗

在 ... 的时候

dust huīchén 〖hway-chun〗

灰尘

dustbin lājīxiāng [lah-jee-hsyang]
垃圾箱

Dutch (adj) Hélán [hur-lahn]
荷兰

duty-free (goods) miǎnshuì
[myen-shway]
免税

duty-free shop miǎnshuì
shāngdiàn [shahng-dyen]
免税商店

dynasty cháodài [chow-dai]
朝代

E

each (every) měi [may]
每

how much are they each? yí
ge yào duōshao qián? [yee gur
yow dwor-show chyen]
一个要多少钱？

ear ěrduo [er-dwor]
耳朵

earache: I have earache wó
ěrduo téng [wor – tung]
我耳朵疼

early zǎo [dzow]
早

early in the morning yì zǎo
一早

I called by earlier wǒ zǎo xiē
shíhou láiguo [wor – hsyeh shur-
hoh lai-gwor]
我早些时候来过

earrings ěrhuán [er-hwahn]
耳环

east dōng [doong]
东

in the east dōngbiān [doong-
byen]
东边

East China Sea Dōng Hǎi
东海

easy róngyì [roong-yee]
容易

eat chī [chur]
吃

we've already eaten, thanks
xièxie, wǒmen yǐjing chīle
[hsyeh-hsyeh wor-mun –chur-lur]
谢谢我们已经吃了

economy class jīngjìcāng
[–tsahng]
经济舱

egg jīdàn [jee-dahn]
鸡蛋

either: either-... or-...
huòzhe-... huòzhe-... [hwor-
jur]
或者 ... 或者 ...

either of them něi liǎngge dōu
kěyǐ [nay lyang-gur doh kur-yee]
那两个都可以

elastic band xiàngpíjīnr
[hsyahng–]
橡皮筋儿

elbow gēbozhǒur [gur-bor-
johr]
胳膊肘儿

electric diàn [dyen]
电

electric fire diàn lúzi [loo-dzur]
电炉子

electrician diàngōng [dyen-goong]
电工

electricity diàn [dyen]
电

elevator diàntī [dyen-tee]
电梯

else: something else biéde dōngxi [byeh-dur doong-hshee]
别的东西

somewhere else biéde dìfāng [dee-fahng]
别的地方

dialogue

would you like anything else? hái yào biéde ma?
[yow – mah]

no, nothing else, thanks bú yào le, xièxie [lur hsyeh-hsyeh]

email diànzi yóujiàn [dyen-dzur yoh-jyen]
电子邮件

embassy dàshíguǎn [dah-shur-gwahn]
大使馆

embroidery cìxiù [tsur-hsyoh]
刺绣

emergency jǐnjí qíngkuàng [ching-kwahng]
紧急情况

this is an emergency!
jiùmìng! [jyoh-ming]
救命

emergency exit ānquánmén [ahn-choo-en-mun]
安全门

emperor huángdì [hwahng-dee]
皇帝

empress huánghòu
皇后

empty kōng [koong]
空

end (noun) mòduān [mor-dwahn]
末端

at the end of the street zhèi tiáo jiē de jìntóu [jay tyow jyeh dur jin-toh]
这条街的尽头

when does it end? shénme shíhou jiéshù? [shun-mur shur-hoh jyeh-shoo]
什么时候结束？

engaged (toilet) yǒurén [yoh-run]
有人
(phone) zhànxiàn [jahn-hsyen]
占线
(to be married) dìnghūnle [ding-hun-lur]
定婚了

England Yīngguó [ying-gwor]
英国

English (adj) Yīngguó [ying-gwor]
英国

(language) Yīngyǔ [ying-yew]
英语

I'm English wǒ shì Yīngguó rén [wor shur – run]
我是英国人

do you speak English? ni huìbuhuì shuō Yīngyǔ? [hway-boo-hway shwor]
你会不会说英语？

enjoy: to enjoy oneself wánr de hěn kāixīn [wahnr dur hun kai-hsin]
玩儿得很开心

dialogue

how did you like the film? nǐ juéde diànyǐng zěnme yàng? [jyew-eh-dur dyen-ying dzun-mur yang]
I enjoyed it very much, did you enjoy it? wǒ juéde hěn hǎo, nǐ ne? [wor – hun how nee nur]

enjoyable lìng rén yúkuàide [run yew-kwai-dur]
令人愉快的

enormous dàjíle [dah-jee-lur]
大极了

enough: that's enough gòule [goh-lur]
够了

there's not enough bú gòu
不够

it's not big enough bú gòu dà
不够大

entrance (noun) rùkǒuchù [roo-koh-choo]
入口处

envelope xìnfēng [hsin-fung]
信封

equipment shèbèi [shur-bay]
设备

(for climbing, sport etc) qìxiè [chee-hsyeh]
器械

especially tèbié [tur-byeh]
特别

essential zhòngyào [joong-yow]
重要

it is essential that-... ... shì juéduì bìyào de [shur jyew-eh-dway bee-yow dur]
... 是决对必要的

Europe Ōuzhōu [oh-joh]
欧洲

European (adj) Ōuzhōu
欧洲

even shènzhi [shun-jur]
甚至

even if-... jìshǐ-... yě [jee-shur-... yur]
即使 ... 也

evening wǎnshang [wahn-shahng]

晚上

this evening jīntiān wǎnshang [jin-tyen]

今天晚上

in the evening wǎnshang

晚上

evening meal wǎnfàn [wahn-fahn]

晚饭

eventually zuìhòu [dzway-hoh]

最后

ever céngjīng [tsung-jing]

曾经

dialogue

have you ever been to the Great Wall? nǐ qùguo Chángchéng ma? [chew-gwor-- mah]

yes, I was there two years ago qùguo, liǎng nián qián qùguo [chew-gwor lyang nyen chyen chew-gwor]

every měige [may-gur]

每个

every day měitiān [may-tyen]

每天

everyone měige rén [may-gur run]

每个人

everything měijiàn shìr [may-jyen shur]

每件事儿

(objects) suǒyǒu de dōngxi [swor-yoh dur doong-hshee]

所有的东西

everywhere měige dìfang [may-gur dee-fahng]

每个地方

exactly! duìjíle! [dway-jee-lur]

对极了

exam kǎoshì [kow-shur]

考试

example lìzi [lee-dzur]

例子

for example lìrú [lee-roo]

例如

excellent hǎojíle [how-jee-lur]

好极了

except chúle-... yǐwài [choo-lur]

除了 ... 以外

excess baggage chāozhòng xíngli [chow-joong hsing-lee]

超重行李

exchange rate duìhuàn lǜ [dway-hwahn lew]

兑换率

exciting (day) cìji [tsur-jee]

刺激

excuse me (to get past) láojià [low-jyah]

劳驾

(to get attention) láojià, qǐng wèn-... [ching wun]

劳驾请问

(to say sorry) duìbuqǐ [dway-boo-chee]

对不起

exhausted (tired) lèisǐle [lay-sur-lur]

累死了

exhibition (of paintings etc) zhǎnlǎn [jan-lan]

展览

(trade fair etc) jiāoyì huì [jyow-yee hway]

交易会

exit chūkǒu [choo-koh]

出口

where's the nearest exit? zuì jìn de chūkǒu zài nǎr? [dzway jin dur choo-koh dzai]

最近的出口在哪儿？

expensive guì [gway]

贵

experienced yǒu jīngyàn [yoh jing-yen]

有经验

explain jiěshì [jyeh-shur]

解释

can you explain that? nǐ néng jiěshì yíxià ma? [nung – yee-syah mah]

你能解释一下吗？

express (mail) kuàidì [kwai-dee]

快递

(train) kuàichē [kwai-chur]

快车

extension (telephone) fēnjī [fun-jee]

分机

extension 221, please qǐng guà èr èr yāo [ching gwah er er yow]

请挂二二一

extra: can we have an extra one? qǐng zài lái yíge? [dzai lai yee-gur]

请再来一个？

do you charge extra for that? hái yào qián ma? [hai yow chyen mah]

还要钱吗？

extremely fēicháng [fay-chahng]

非常

eye yǎnjing [yahn-jing]

眼睛

will you keep an eye on my suitcase for me? máfan nín bāng wǒ kān yíxià tíbāo, hǎo ma? [mah-fahn nin bahng wor kahn yee-hsyah tee-bow how mah]

麻烦您帮我看一下提包好吗？

eyeglasses yǎnjìng [yahn-jing]

眼镜

F

face liǎn [lyen]

脸

factory gōngchǎng [goongchahng]

工厂

Fahrenheit huáshì [hwah-shur]

华氏

faint (verb) yūn [yewn]

晕

she's fainted tā yūndǎole [tah yewn-dow-lur]

她晕倒了

I feel faint wǒ juéde yǒu diǎn (tóu) yūn [wor jyew-eh-dur yoh dyen (toh)]

我觉得有点（头）晕

fair (adj) gōngpíng [goong-ping]

公平

fake màopái [mow-pai]

冒牌

fall (verb: person) shuāidǎo [shwai-dow]

摔倒

she's had a fall tā shuāile yì jiāo [tah shwai-lur yee jyow]

她摔了一交

fall (US) qiūtiān [chyoh-tyen]

秋天

in the fall qiūtiān

秋天

false jiǎ [jyah]

假

family jiātíng [jyah-ting]

家庭

famous yǒumíng [yoh-ming]

有名

fan (electrical) fēngshàn [fung-

shahn]

风扇

(hand-held) shànzi [shahn-dzur]

扇子

(sports) qiúmí [chyoh-mee]

球迷

fantastic (wonderful) tàihǎole [tai-how-lur]

太好了

far yuǎn [yew-ahn]

远

dialogue

is it far from here? lí zhèr yuǎn ma? [jer – mah]
no, not very far bú tài yuǎn
well, how far? duō yuǎn ne? [dwor – nur]
it's about 20 kilometres èr shí gōnglǐ zuǒyòu [goong-lee dzwor-yoh]

fare chēfèi [chur-fay]

车费

Far East Yuǎndōng [yew-ahn-doong]

远东

farm nóngchǎng [noong-chahng]

农场

fashionable shímáo [shur-mow]

时髦

fast kuài [kwai]

快

fat (person) pàng [pahng]
胖
(on meat) féiròu [fay-roh]
肥肉

father fùqīn [foo-chin]
父亲

father-in-law yuèfù [yew-eh-foo]
岳父

faucet shuǐlóngtóu [shway-loong-toh]
水龙头

fault cuò [tswor]
错

sorry, it was my fault duìbuqǐ shì wǒde cuò [dway-boo-chee shur wor-dur tswor]
对不起是我的错

it's not my fault bú shì wǒde cuò
不是我的错

faulty yǒu máobìng [yoh mow-bing]
有毛病

favourite zuì xǐhuan de [dzway hshee-hwahn dur]
最喜欢的

fax (noun) chuánzhēn [chwahn-jun]
传真

to send a fax fā chuánzhēn [fah]
发传真

February èryuè [er-yew-eh]
二月

feel gǎnjué [gahn-jyew-eh]
感觉

I feel hot wǒ juéde hěn rè [wor jyew-eh-dur hun rur]
我觉得很热

I feel unwell wǒ juéde bú tài shūfu [–dur – shoo-foo]
我觉得不太舒服

I feel like going for a walk wǒ xiǎng qù zǒuzǒu [hsyahng chew dzoh-dzoh]
我想去走走

how are you feeling? nǐ juéde zěnme yàng le? [nee jyew-eh-dur dzun-mur – lur]
你觉得怎么样了？

I'm feeling better wǒ hǎo diǎnr le [how dyenr]
我好点儿了

fence zhàlan [jah-lahn]
栅栏

ferry bǎidù
摆渡

festival jiérì [jyeh-ree]
节日

fetch qǔ [chew]
取

I'll fetch him wǒ qù jiào tā lái [wor – jyow tah]
我去叫他来

will you come and fetch me later? děng huìr nǐ lái jiē wǒ, hǎo ma? [dung hwayr – jyeh]
等会儿你来接我好吗？

feverish fāshāo [fah-show]

发烧

few: a few yì xiē [yee-hsyeh]

一些

a few days jǐ tiān [tyen]

几天

fiancé wèihūnfū [way-hun-foo]

未婚夫

fiancée wèihūnqī [way-hun-chee]

未婚妻

field tiándì [tyen-dee]

田地

(paddy) dàotián [dow-tyen]

稻田

fill in tián [tyen]

填

do I have to fill this in? wǒ yào tián zhèi zhāng biǎo ma? [wor yow tyen jay jahng byow mah]

我要填这张表吗？

filling (in cake, sandwich) xiànr [hsyenr]

馅儿

(in tooth) bǔ yá [byew yah]

补牙

film (movie) diànyǐng [dyen-ying]

电影

(for camera) jiāojuǎnr [jyow-jew-ahnr]

胶卷儿

dialogue

do you have this kind of film? nǐ yǒu zhèi zhǒng jiāojuǎnr ma? [yoh jay-joong jyow-jyew-ahnr mah]

yes, how many exposures? yǒu, nǐ yào duōshao zhāng de? [yow dwor-show jahng dur]

36 sān shí liù zhāng (de)

filthy zāng [dzahng]

脏

find (verb) zhǎodào [jow-dow]

找到

I can't find it wǒ zhǎobúdào [wor jow-boo-dow]

我找不到

I've found it zhǎodàole [jow-dow-lur]

找到了

find out zhǎochū [jow-choo]

找出

could you find out for me? nǐ néng tì wǒ diàochá yíxià ma? [nung tee wor dyow-chah yee-hsyah mah]

你能替我调查一下吗？

fine (weather) qínglǎng [ching-lang]

晴朗

(punishment) fákuán [fah-kwahn]

罚款

dialogues

how are you? nǐ hǎo ma?
[how mah]
I'm fine, thanks hěn hǎo,
xièxie [hun how hsyeh-hsyeh]

is that OK? zhèyàng xíng
ma? [jur-yang hsing mah]
that's fine, thanks xíng,
xièxie

finger shóuzhǐ [shoh-jur]
手指
finish (verb) zuò wán [dzwor
wahn]
作完
I haven't finished yet wǒ hái
méi nòng wán [wor hai may
noong wahn]
我还没弄完
when does it finish? shénme
shíhou néng wán? [shun-mur
shur-hoh nung]
什么时候能完？
fire huǒ [hwor]
火
(blaze) huǒzāi [hwor-dzai]
火灾
fire! zháohuǒle! [jow-hwor-lur]
着火了
can we light a fire here? zhèr
néng diǎn huǒ ma? [jer nung
dyen hwor mah]
这儿能点火吗？

fire alarm huǒjǐng [hwor-
jing]
火警
fire brigade xiāofángduì
[hsyow-fahng-dway]
消防队
fire escape tàipíngtī
太平梯
fire extinguisher mièhuǒqì
[myeh-hwor-chee]
灭火器
first dìyī
第一
I was first wǒ dìyī [wor]
我第一
first of all shǒuxiān [shoh-
hsyen]
首先
at first qǐchū [chee-choo]
起初
the first time dìyí cì [tsur]
第一次
first on the left zuǒbian dì
yīge [zwor-byen – gur]
左边第一个
first aid jíjiù [jee-jyoh]
急救
first-aid kit jíjiùxiāng
[–hsyahng]
急救箱
first class (travel etc) yīděng
[yee-dung]
一等
first floor èr lóu [er loh]
二楼

(US) yī lóu
一楼

first name míngzi [ming-dzur]
名子

fish (noun) yú [yew]
鱼

fit: it doesn't fit me zhè duì
wǒ bù héshì [jur dway wor boo
hur-shur]
这对我不合适

fitting room shì yī shì [shur yee
shur]
试衣室

fix: can you fix this? (repair) nǐ
néng bǎ zhèige xiū hǎo ma?
[nung bah jay-gur hsyoh how mah]
你能把这个修好吗？

fizzy yǒuqìde [yoh-chee-dur]
有气的

flag qí [chee]
旗

flannel (xǐliǎn) máojīn [(hshee-
lyen) mow-jin]
洗脸毛巾

flash (for camera)
shǎnguāngdēng [shahn-gwahng-
dung]
闪光灯

flat (noun: apartment) dānyuán
[dahn-yew-ahn]
单元

(adj) píngtǎn [ping-tahn]
平坦

I've got a flat tyre wǒde
chētāi biěle [wor-dur chur-tai

byeh-lur]
我的车胎瘪了

flavour wèidao [way-dow]
味道

flea tiàozǎo [tyow-dzow]
跳蚤

flight hángbān [hahng-bahn]
航班

flight number hángbān hào
[how]
航班号

flood hóngshuǐ [hoong-shway]
洪水

floor (of room: wooden) dìbǎn
地板

(storey) lóu [loh]
楼

(in hotel etc) céng [tsung]
层

on the floor zài dìshang [dzai
dee-shahng]
在地上

florist huādiàn [hwah-dyen]
花店

flower huā [hwah]
花

flu liúgǎn [lyoh-gahn]
流感

**fluent: he speaks fluent
Chinese** tā Hànyǔ jiǎngde
hěn liúlì [tah hahn-yew jyang-dur
hun lyoh-lee]
他汉语讲得很流利

fly (noun) cāngying [tsahng-ying]
苍蝇

(verb) fēi [fay]

飞

can we fly there? dào nàr yǒu fēijī ma? [dow nar yoh fay-jee mah]

到那儿有飞机吗？

fog wù

雾

foggy: it's foggy yǒu wù [yoh]

有雾

folk dancing mínjiān wǔdǎo [min-jyen woo-dow]

民间舞蹈

folk music mínjiān yīnyuè [yin-yew-eh]

民间音乐

food shíwù [shur-woo]

食物

(in shops) shípǐn [shur-pin]

食品

food poisoning shíwù zhòngdú [joong-doo]

食物中毒

food shop, food store shípǐn diàn [shur-pin dyen]

食品店

foot (measurement) yīngchǐ [ying-chur]

英尺

(of person) jiǎo [jyow]

脚

to go on foot bùxíng [boo-hsing]

步行

football (game) zúqiúsài [dzoo-chyoh-sai]

足球赛

(ball) zúqiú [dzoo-chyoh]

足球

for*: do you have something for-...? (illness) nǐ yǒu zhì... de yào ma? [yoh –jur yow mah]

你有治 ... 的药吗？

dialogues

who are the dumplings for? zhèi xiē jiǎozi shì shéi (jiào) de? [jay hsyeh jyow-dzur shur shay (jyow) dur]

that's for me shì wǒ de [shur wor]

and this one? zhèi gè ne? [jay gur nur]

that's for her shì tā de [shur tah]

where do I get the bus for Beijing? qù Běijīng zài nár zuò chē? [chew – dzai nar dzwor chur]

the bus for Beijing leaves from Donglu Street qù Běijīng de chē zài Dōnglù kāi [chew – dur chur dzai]

how long have you been here? nǐ lái zhèr duō cháng shíjiān le? [jer dwor chahng shur-jyen lur]

I've been here for two days, how about you? wǒ láile liǎng tiān le, nǐ ne? [wor lai-lur lyang tyen lur nee nur]

I've been here for a week wǒ láile yíge xīngqī le [yee-gur hsing-chee lur]

Forbidden City Gùgōng [goo-goong]
故宫

foreign wàiguó [wai-gwor]
外国

foreigner wàiguó rén [run]
外国人

forest sēnlín [sun-lin]
森林

forget wàng [wahng]
忘

I forget, I've forgotten wǒ wàngle [wor –lur]
我忘了

fork (for eating) chā [chah]
叉

(in road) chàlù [chah-loo]
岔路

form (document) biǎo [byow]
表

formal (dress) zhèngshì [jung-shur]
正式

fortnight liǎngge xīngqī [lyang-gur hsing-chee]
两个星期

fortunately xìngkuī [hsing-kway]
幸亏

forward: could you forward my mail? nín néng bāng wó zhuǎn yíxià xìn ma? [nung bahng wor jwahn yee-hsyah hsin mah]
您能帮我转一下信吗？

forwarding address zhuǎnxìn dìzhǐ [jwahn-hsin dee-jur]
转信地址

fountain pēnquán [pun-chew-ahn]
喷泉

foyer xiūxītīng [hsyoh-see-ting]
休息厅

fracture (noun) gǔzhé [gyew-jur]
骨折

France Fǎguó [fah-gwor]
法国

free zìyóu [dzur-yoh]
自由

(no charge) miǎn fèi [myen fay]
免费

is it free (of charge)? miǎn fèi de ma? [dur mah]
免费的吗？

French (adj) Fǎguó [fah-gwor]
法国

(language) Fǎyǔ [fah-yew]
法语

French fries zhá tǔdòu tiáo [jah too-doh tyow]
炸土豆条

frequent jīngcháng [jing-chahng]

经常

how frequent is the bus to the Forbidden City? dào Gùgōng qù de gōnggòng qìchē duōcháng shíjian kāi yì bān? [dow goo-goong chew dur goong-goong chee-chur dwor-chahng shur-jyen kai yee bahn]

到故宫去的公共汽车多长时间开一班？

fresh (weather, breeze) qīngxīn [ching-hsin]

清新

(fruit etc) xiān [hsyen]

鲜

fresh orange juice xiān júzhī [jyew-jur]

鲜桔汁

Friday xīngqī wǔ [hsing-chee-woo]

星期五

fridge bīngxiāng [–hsyahng]

冰箱

fried (shallow-fried) jiānde [jyen-dur]

煎的

(deep-fried) zháde [jah-dur]

炸

(stir-fried) chǎode [chow-dur]

炒

fried egg jiān jīdàn [jyen jee-dahn]

煎鸡蛋

fried noodles chǎomiàn [chow-myen]

炒面

fried rice chǎofàn [chow-fahn]

炒饭

friend péngyou [pung-yoh]

朋友

friendly yǒuhǎo [yoh-how]

友好

friendship yǒuyì [yoh-yee]

友谊

friendship store yǒuyì shāngdiàn [yoh-yee shahng-dyen]

友谊商店

from* cóng [tsoong]

从

how far is it from here? lí zhèr duō yuǎn? [jer dwor ywahn]

离这儿多远？

when does the next train from Suzhou arrive? cóng Sūzhōu lái de xià yì bān huǒchē jǐdiǎn dàodá? [tsoong soo-joh lai dur hsyah yee bahn hwor-chur jee-dyen dow-dah]

从苏州来的下一班火车几点到达？

from Monday to Friday cóng xīngqī yī dào xīngqī wǔ [tsoong hsing-chee-yee dow hsing-chee]

从星期一到星期五

from next Thursday cóng xià xīngqī sì qǐ [hsyah – sur chee]

从下星期四起

dialogue

> **where are you from?** nǐ shì nár de rén? ⟦shur nar-duh run⟧
> 你是哪儿的人？
> **I'm from Slough** wǒ shì Slough láide rén ⟦wor shur – lai-dur⟧

front qiánmian ⟦chyen-myen⟧
前面
  in front, at the front zài qiánbianr ⟦dzai chyen-byenr⟧
  在前边儿
  in front of the hotel zài fàndiàn qiánmian ⟦dzai fahn-dyen chyen-myen⟧
  在饭店前面

frozen bīngdòngde ⟦bing-doong-dur⟧
冰冻的

fruit shuǐguǒ ⟦shway-gwor⟧
水果

fruit juice guǒzhī ⟦gwor-jur⟧
果汁

full mǎn ⟦mahn⟧
满
  it's full of-... lǐmian dōu shì ... ⟦lee-myen doh shur⟧
  里面都是 …
  I'm full wǒ bǎole ⟦wor bow-lur⟧
  我饱了

full board shí zhù quán bāo ⟦shur joo choo-en bow⟧
食住全包

fun: it was fun hěn hǎo wánr ⟦hun how wahnr⟧
很好玩儿

funeral zànglǐ ⟦dzahng-lee⟧
葬礼

funny (strange) qíguài ⟦chee-gwai⟧
奇怪
  (amusing) yǒu yìsi ⟦yoh yee-sur⟧
  有意思
  (comical) huájī ⟦hwah-jee⟧
  滑稽

furniture jiājù ⟦jyah-jew⟧
家具

further: it's further down the road zài wǎng qián zǒu ⟦dzai wahng chyen soh⟧
再往前走

dialogue

> **how much further is it to the Forbidden City?** dào Gùgōng hái yǒu duōshao lù? ⟦dow – yoh dwor-show⟧
> **about 5 kilometres** dàyuē wǔ gōnglǐ (lù) ⟦dah-yew-eh woo goong-lee⟧

future jiānglái ⟦jyang-lai⟧
将来
  in future jiānglái
  将来

G

game (cards etc) yóuxì [yoh-hshee]

游戏

(match) bǐsài

比赛

(meat) yěwèi [yur-way]

野味

garage (for fuel) jiāyóu zhàn [jyah-yoh jahn]

加油站

(for repairs) qìchē xiūlíchǎng [chee-chur hsyoh-lee-chahng]

汽车修理厂

(for parking) chēkù [chur-koo]

车库

garden huāyuán [hwah-yew-ahn]

花园

garlic dàsuàn [dah-swahn]

大蒜

gas méiqì [may-chee]

煤气

gasoline qìyóu [chee-yoh]

气油

gas station jiāyóu zhàn [jyah-yoh jahn]

加油站

gate dàmén [dah-mun]

大门

(at airport) dēngjīkǒu [dung-jee-koh]

登机口

gay tóngxìngliàn [toong-hsing-lyen]

同性恋

general (adj) yì bān [yee bahn]

一般

gents' toilet nán cèsuǒ [nahn tsur-swor]

男厕所

genuine (antique etc) zhēnzhèng [jun-jung]

真正

German (adj) Déguó [dur-gwor]

德国

(language) Déyǔ [dur-yew]

德语

Germany Déguó

德国

get (fetch) qǔ [chew]

取

could you get me another one, please? qǐng nǐ zài gěi wǒ yí ge hǎo ma? [ching nee dzai gay wor yee gur how mah]

请你再给我一个好吗？

how do I get to-...? qù-... zěnme zǒu? [chew-... dzun-mur dzoh]

去 … 怎么走？

do you know where I can get them? nǐ zhīdao wǒ zài nǎr néng mǎi dào ma? [jee-dow wor dzai nar nung mai dow mah]

你知道我在哪儿能买到吗？

dialogue

can I get you a drink? hē diǎnr shénme ma? [hur dyenr shun-mur mah]

no, I'll get this one, what would you like? zhèi huí wǒ lái mǎi, nǐ xiǎng hē shénme? [jay hway wor – hsyahng hur]

a glass of Maotai (lái) yì bēi Máotáijiǔ [bay]

get back huílai [hway-lai]
回来

get in (arrive) dàodá [dow-dah]
到达

get off: where do I get off? wǒ zài nár xià chē? [wor dzai nar hsyah chur]
我在哪儿下车?

get on (to train etc) shàng chē [shahng chur]
上车

get out (of car etc) xià chē [hsyah-chur]
下车

get up (in the morning) qǐchuáng [chee-chwahng]
起床

gift lǐwù [lee-woo]
礼物

gift shop lǐwù shāngdiàn [shahng-dyen]
礼物商店

ginger shēngjiāng [shung-jyang]
生姜

girl nǚ háir [nyew]
女孩儿

girlfriend nǚ péngyou [pung-yoh]
女朋友

give gěi [gay]
给

can you give me some change? qǐng gěi wǒ líng qián, hǎo ma? [ching gay wor ling chyen how mah]
请给我零钱好吗?

I gave ... to him wǒ bǎ ... sòng gěi tā [wor bah ... soong gay tah]
我把 ... 送给他

will you give this to-...? qǐng bǎ zhèige sònggěi ...? [ching bah jay-gur soong-gay]
请把这个送给 ... ?

give back huán [hwahn]
还

glad gāoxìng [gow-sing]
高兴

glass (material) bōli [bor-lee]
玻璃

(for drinking) bōli bēi [bay]
玻璃杯

a glass of wine yì bēi jiǔ
一杯酒

glasses yǎnjìng [yahn-jing]
眼镜

gloves shǒutào [shoh-tow]
手套

glue jiāoshuǐr [jyow-shwayr]
胶水儿

go qù [chew]
去

we'd like to go to the
Summer Palace wǒmen
xiǎng qù Yíhéyuán [wor-mun
hsyahng]
我们想去颐和园

where are you going? nǐ qù
nǎr?
你去哪儿？

where does this bus go? zhèi
liàng chē qù nǎr? [jay lyang
chur]
这辆车去哪儿？

let's go! wǒmen zǒu ba! [wor-
mun dzoh bah]
我们走吧

she's gone tā yǐjing zǒule [tah
yee-ying zoh-lur]
她已经走了

where has he gone? tā dào
nǎr qù le? [dow]
他到哪儿去了？

I went there last week wǒ shì
shàng xīngqī qù nàr de [wor
shur shahng hsing-chee]
我是上星期去那儿的

go away líkāi
离开

go away! zǒu kāi! [dzoh]
走开

go back (return) huí [hway]
回

go down (the stairs etc) xià
[hsyah]
下

go in jìn
进

go out (in the evening) chūqu
[choo-chew]
出去

do you want to go out
tonight? nǐ jīntiān wǎnshang
xiǎng chūqù ma? [jin-tyen
wahn-shahng hsyahng – mah]
你今天晚上想出去吗？

go through chuān [chwahn]
穿

go up (the stairs etc) shàng
[shahng]
上

God shàngdì
上帝

gold (metal) huángjīn [hwahng-
jin]
黄金

(colour) jīnsè [jin-sur]
金色

good hǎo [how]
好

good! hǎo!
好

it's no good bù hǎo
不好

goodbye zàijiàn [dzai-jyen]
再见

good evening nǐ hǎo [how]
你好

good morning nǐ zǎo [zow]
你早

good night wǎn'ān [wahn-ahn]
晚安

goose é [ur]
鹅

gorge xiá [hsyah]
峡

got: we've got to leave
wǒmen déi zǒu le [wor-mun
day zoh lur]
我们得走了

have you got any-...? nǐ yǒu
... ma? [yoh ... mah]
你有 ... 吗？

government zhèngfǔ [jung-foo]
政府

gradually jiànjiàn de [jyen-jyen
dur]
渐渐地

grammar yǔfǎ [yew-fah]
语法

gram(me) kè [kur]
克

granddaughter (daughter's
daughter) wàisūnnǚr [wai-sun-
nyewr]
外孙女儿
(son's daughter) sūnnǚr
孙女儿

grandfather (maternal) wàigōng
[wai-goong]
外公
(paternal) yéye [yur-yur]
爷爷

grandmother (maternal) wàipó
[wai-por]
外婆
(paternal) nǎinai
奶奶

grandson (daughter's son) wài
sūnzi [sun-dzur]
外孙子
(son's son) sūnzi
孙子

grapefruit pútáoyòu [poo-tow-
yoh]
葡萄柚

grapes pútáo [poo-tow]
葡萄

grass cǎo [tsow]
草

grateful gǎnjī [gahn-jee]
感激

great (excellent) hǎojíle [how-
jee-lur]
好极了

a great success jùdà
chéngjiù [joo-dah chung-jyoh]
巨大成就

greedy (for money etc) tānxīn
[tahn-hsin]
贪心
(for food) chán [chahn]
馋

green lǜsè(de) [lyew-sur(-dur)]
绿色的

greengrocer's càidiàn [tsai-
dyen]
菜店

grey huīsè(de) [hway-sur(-dur)]
灰色的

grilled kǎo [kow]
烤

grocer's záhuòdiàn [dzah-hwor-dyen]
杂货店

ground: on the ground zài dì shàng [dzai dee shahng]
在地上

ground floor yī lóu [loh]
一楼

group (tourist etc) cānguāntuán [tsahn-gwahn-twahn]
参观团

(study, work etc) xiǎozǔ [hsyow-dzyew]
小组

guarantee (noun) bǎozhèng [bow-jung]
保证

is it guaranteed? bǎo bù bǎoxiū? [bow – hsyoh]
保不保修？

guest kèrén [kur-run]
客人

guesthouse bīnguǎn [bing-wahn]
宾馆

guide (tour guide) dǎoyóu [dow-yoh]
导游

guidebook dǎoyóu shǒucè [shoh-tsur]
导游手册

guided tour yǒu dǎoyóu de yóulǎn [yoh – dur yoh-lahn]
有导游的游览

guitar jítā [jee-tah]
吉他

gum (in mouth) chǐyín [chur-yin]
齿龈

gym tǐyùguǎn [tee-yoo-gwahn]
体育馆

H

hair tóufa [toh-fah]
头发

haircut lǐfà [lee-fah]
理发

hairdresser's lǐfàdiàn [dyen]
理发店

hairdryer diànchuīfēng [dyen-chway-fung]
电吹风

hair spray pēnfàjì [pun-fah-jee]
喷发剂

half* (adj) bàn [bahn]
半

(noun) yí bàn
一半

half an hour bàn xiǎoshí [hsyow-shur]
半小时

half a litre bàn shēng [shung]
半升

about half that nàme duō yí bàn [nah-mur dwor]
那么多一半

half board bàn shísù [shur-soo]
半食宿

half-bottle bàn píng
半瓶

half fare bànfèi [bahn-fay]
半费

half price bànjià [bahn-jyah]
半价

ham huǒtuǐ [hwor-tway]
火腿

hamburger hànbǎobāo [hahn-bow-bow]
汉堡包

hand shǒu [shoh]
手

handbag shǒutíbāo [shoh-tee-bow]
手提包

handkerchief shǒujuànr [shoh-jwahnr]
手绢儿

hand luggage shǒutí xíngli [shoh-tee hsing-lee]
手提行李

happen fāshēng [fah-shung]
发生

what's happening? zěnme huí shìr? [dzun-mur hway shur]
怎么回事儿？

what has happened? fāshēng le shénme shìr la? [fah-shung lur shun-mur lah]
发生了什么事儿啦？

happy kuàilè [kwai-lur]
快乐

I'm not happy about this wǒ duì zhèige bù mǎnyì [wor dway jay-gur boo mahn-yee]
我对这个不满意

harbour gǎngkǒu [gahng-koh]
港口

hard yìng
硬

(difficult) nán [nahn]
难

hardly: hardly ever hěn shǎo [hun show]
很少

hard seat yìngxí [ying-hshee]
硬席

hardware shop wǔjīn (shāng) diàn [woo-jin (shahng) dyen]
五金（商）店

hat màozi [mow-dzur]
帽子

hate (verb) hèn [hun]
恨

have* yǒu [yoh]
有

can I have a-...? (asking for

something) qǐng gěi wǒ-... hǎo
ma? [ching gay wor-... how]

请给我 ... 好吗？

(ordering food) qǐng lái-..., hǎo
ma? [ching]

请来 ... 好吗？

(in shop) wǒ xiǎng mǎi-... [wor
hsyahng]

我想买 ...

do you have-...? nǐmen
yǒu-... ma? [nee-mun yoh-...
mah]

你们有 ... 吗？

what'll you have? nǐ xiǎng hē
shénme? [hsyahng hur
shun-mur]

你想喝什么？

I have to leave now wǒ děi
zǒu le [wor day dzoh lur]

我得走了

do I have to-...? wǒ děi-...
ma?

我得 ... 吗？

hayfever huāfěnrè [hwah-fun-
rur]

花粉热

he* tā [tah]

他

head tóu [toh]

头

headache tóuténg [toh-tung]

头疼

hear tīngjian [ting-jyen]

听见

dialogue

can you hear me? nǐ néng
tīngjiàn ma? [nung ting-jyen
mah]

**I can't hear you, could
you repeat that?** duìbuqǐ,
tīngbujiàn, nǐ néng zài
shuō yí biàn ma? [dway-boo-
chee ting-boo-jyen – dzai shwor
yee byen]

hearing aid zhùtīngqì [joo-ting-
chee]

助听器

heart xīnzàng [hsin-dzahng]

心脏

heart attack xīnzàngbìng
[–bing]

心脏病

heat rè [rur]

热

heater sànrèqì [sahn-rur-chee]

散热器

heating nuǎnqì [nwahn-chee]

暖器

heavy zhòng [joong]

重

heel (of foot) jiǎogēn
[jyow-gun]

脚跟

(of shoe) xié hòugēn [hsyeh]

鞋后跟

could you heel these? qǐng
gěi wǒ dǎ hòugēn, hǎo ma?

[ching gay wor dah – how mah]
请给我打后跟好吗？

heelbar xiūxiépù [hsyoh-hsyeh-poo]
修鞋铺

helicopter zhíshēng fēijī [jur-shung fay-jee]
直升飞机

hello nǐ hǎo [nee how]
你好

(answer on phone) wéi [way]
喂

help bāngzhù [bahng-joo]
帮助

help! jiùmìng! [jyoh-ming]
救命

can you help me? nǐ néng bù néng bāngbāng wǒ? [nung bahng-bahng wor]
你能不能帮帮我？

thank you very much for your help xièxie nǐde bāngmáng [hsyeh-hsyeh nee-dur]
谢谢你的帮忙

helpful bāngle bú shǎo máng [bahng-lur boo show mahng]
帮了不少忙

hepatitis gānyán [gah-nyen]
肝炎

her* tā [tah]
她

that's her towel nà shì tāde máojīn [nah shur tah-dur mow-jin]
那是她的毛巾

herbs (for cooking) zuóliào [dzwor-lyow]
作料

(medicinal) cǎoyào [tsow-yow]
草药

here zhèr [jer]
这儿

here is/are-... zhèr shì ... [shur]
这儿是 ...

here you are gěi nǐ [gay]
给你

hers* tāde [tah-dur]
她的

that's hers zhè shì tāde [jur shur]
这是她的

hey! hēi! [hay]
嘿

hi! (hello) ní hǎo! [how]
你好

high gāo [gow]
高

hill shān [shahn]
山

him* tā [tah]
他

hip túnbù [tun-boo]
臀部

hire (bike, car) zū [dzoo]
租

(guide, interpreter) gù
顾

for hire chūzū [choo-dzoo]
出租

where can I hire a bike? zài

nǎr néng zū dào zìxíngchē?
[dzai nar nung zoo dow dzi-hsing-chur]

在哪儿能租到自行车？

his* tāde [tah-dur]

他的

hit (verb) dǎ [dah]

打

hitch-hike dā biànchē [byen-chur]

搭便车

hobby shìhào [shur-how]

嗜好

hole dòng [doong]

洞

holiday (public) jiàqī [jyah-chee]

假期

(festival) jiérì [jyeh-ree]

节日

on holiday dùjià [doo-jyah]

度假

home jiā

家

at home (in my house etc) zài jiā [dzai]

在家

we go home tomorrow (to country) wǒmen míngtian huí guó [wor-mun ming-tyen hway gwor]

我们明天回国

honest chéngshí [chung-shur]

诚实

honey fēngmì [fung-mee]

蜂蜜

honeymoon mìyuè [mee-yew-eh]

蜜月

Hong Kong Xiānggǎng [hsyahng-gahng]

香港

hope xīwàng [hshee-wahng]

希望

I hope so wǒ xīwàng shì zhèi yàng [wor – shur jay yang]

我希望是这样

I hope not wǒ xīwàng bú shì zhèi yàng

我希望不是这样

hopefully xīwàng rúcǐ [hshee-wahng roo-tsur]

希望如此

horrible kěpà [kur-pah]

可怕

horse mǎ [mah]

马

horse riding qí mǎ [chee]

骑马

hospital yīyuàn [yee-yew-ahn]

医院

hospitality hàokè [how-kur]

好客

thank you for your hospitality xièxie nínde shèngqíng kuǎndài [hsyeh-hsyeh nin-dur shung-ching kwahn-dai]

谢谢您的盛情款待

hot rè [rur]

热

(spicy) là [lah]
辣

I'm hot wǒ juéde hěn rè [wor jyew-eh-dur hun rur]
我觉得很热

it's hot today jīntiān hěn rè [jin-tyen]
今天很热

hotel (small) lǚguǎn [lyew-gwahn]
旅馆

(luxury) fàndiàn [fahn-dyen]
饭店

hour xiǎoshí [hsyow-shur]
小时

house fángzi [fahng-dzur]
房子

how zěnme [dzun-mur]
怎么 ?

how many? (if answer is likely to be more than ten) duōshao? [dwor-show]
多少 ?

(if answer is likely to be ten or less) jǐge? [jee-gur]
几个 ?

how do you do? nǐ hǎo [how]
你好 ?

dialogues

how are you? nǐ hǎo ma? [mah]
fine, thanks, and you?

hěn hǎo, nǐ ne? [hun – nur]

how much is it? duōshao qián? [chyen]

17 yuan shí qī kuài [shur chee kwai]
I'll take it wǒ mǎi [wor]

humid cháoshī [chow-shur]
潮湿

hungry è [ur]
饿

are you hungry? nǐ èle ma? [ur-lur mah]
你饿了吗 ?

hurry: **I'm in a hurry** wǒ hěn jí de [wor hun jee dur]
我很急的

there's no hurry mànmàn lái [mahn-mahn]
慢慢来

hurry up! kuài diǎnr! [kwai dyenr]
快点儿

hurt (verb) téng [tung]
疼

it really hurts zhēn téng [jun tung]
真疼

husband zhàngfu [jahng-foo]
丈夫

I

I wǒ [wor]
我

ice bīng
冰

with ice jiā bīngkuàir [jyah bing-kwair]
加冰块儿

no ice, thanks bù jiā bīngkuàir, xièxie [boo jyah bing-kwair hsyeh-hsyeh]
不加冰块儿谢谢

ice cream bīngqílín [bing-chee-lin]
冰淇淋

ice-cream cone dànjuǎnr bīngqílín [dahn-jyew-ahnr]
蛋卷儿冰淇淋

ice lolly bīnggùnr [bing-gunr]
冰棍儿

idea zhǔyi [joo-yee]
主意

idiot shǎguā [shah-gwah]
傻瓜

if rúguǒ [roo-gwor]
如果

ill bìngle [bing-lur]
病了

I feel ill wǒ juéde bù shūfu [wor jyew-eh-dur]
我觉得不舒服

illness jíbìng
疾病

imitation (leather etc) fǎng [fahng]
仿

immediately mǎshàng [mah-shahng]
马上

important zhòngyào [joong-yow]
重要

it's very important hěn zhòngyào [hun joong-yow]
很重要

it's not important bú zhòngyào
不重要

impossible bù kěnéng [kur-nung]
不可能

impressive (building, view) xióngwěi [hsyoong-way]
雄伟

improve tígāo [tee-gow]
提高

I want to improve my Chinese wǒ xiǎng tígāo wǒde Hànyǔ shuǐpíng [wor hsyahng – wor-dur hah-yew shway-ping]
我想提高我的汉语水平

in*: it's in the centre zài zhōngjiān [dzai joong-jyen]
在中间

in my car zài wǒde chē lǐ [wor-dur chur lee]
在我的车里

in London zài Lúndūn
在伦敦

in two days from now liǎng
tiān zhī hòu [tyen jur hoh]
两天之后

in five minutes wǔ fēn
zhōng (zhī) nèi [fun joong (jur)
nay]
五分钟（之）内

in May zài wǔyuè
在五月

in English yòng Yīngyǔ
用英语

in Chinese yòng Hànyǔ
用汉语

is Mr Li in? Lǐ xiānsheng zài
ma? [hsyahng-shung dzai mah]
李先生在吗？

inch yīngcùn [ying-tsun]
英寸

include bāokuò [bow-kwor]
包括

does that include meals? zhè
bāokuò fàn qián ma? [jur – fahn
chyen mah]
这包括饭钱吗？

is that included? nèige yě
bāokuò zài nèi ma? [nay-gur
yur]
那个也包括在内吗？

inconvenient bù fāngbiàn
[fahng-byen]
不方便

India Yìndù [yin-doo]
印度

Indian (adj) Yìndù
印度

indigestion xiāohuà bù liáng
[hsyow-hwah boo lyang]
消化不良

Indonesia Yìndùníxīyà [yin-
doo-nee-hshee-yah]
印度尼西亚

indoor pool shìnèi
yóuyǒngchí [shur-nay yoh-
yoong-chur]
室内游泳池

indoors shìnèi [shur-nay]
室内

inexpensive piányi [pyen-yee]
便宜

infection gǎnrǎn [gahn-rahn]
感染

infectious chuánrǎn [chwahn-
rahn]
传染

inflammation fāyán [fah-yen]
发炎

informal (clothes) suíbiàn [sway-
byen]
随便

(occasion) fēi zhèngshì [fay jung-
shur]
非正式

information xiāoxi [hsyow-
hshee]
消息

do you have any information
about-...? nǐ yǒu guānyú ...
de xiāoxi ma? [nee yoh gwahn-

yew dur – mah]

你有关于 ... 的消息吗？

information desk wènxùnchù
[wun-hsyewn-choo]

问讯处

injection dǎzhēn [dah-jun]

打针

injured shòushāng [shoh-shahng]

受伤

she's been injured tā
shòushāng le [tah – lur]

她受伤了

inner tube (for tyre) nèitāi [nay–]

内胎

innocent wúgū

无辜

insect kūnchóng [kun-choong]

昆虫

insect bite chóngzi yǎo de
[choong-dzur yow dur]

虫子咬的

do you have anything for
insect bites? yǒu zhì chóng
yǎo de yào ma? [yoh jur choong
yow dur yow mah]

有治虫咬的药吗？

insect repellent qūchóngjì
[chew-choong-jee]

驱虫剂

inside* zài-... lǐ [dzai-... lee]

在 ... 里

inside the hotel zài lǚguǎn
lǐmiàn

在旅馆里面

let's sit inside wǒmen jìnqù

zuò ba [wor-mun jin-chew dzwor
bah]

我们进去坐吧

insist: I insist wǒ jiānchí [wor
jyen-chur]

我坚持

instant coffee sùróng kāfēi
[soo-roong kah-fay]

速溶咖啡

insulin yídǎosù [yee-dow-soo]

胰岛素

insurance bǎoxiǎn [bow-hsyen]

保险

intelligent cōngming [tsoong-
ming]

聪明

interested: I'm interested in-...
wǒ duì-... hěn gǎn xìngqù
[wor dway-... hun gahn
hsing-chew]

我对 ... 很感兴趣

interesting yǒu yìsi [yoh yee-sur]

有意思

that's very interesting hěn
yǒu yìsi [hun]

很有意思

international guójì
[gwor-jee]

国际

Internet guójì wǎngluò [gwor-
jee wahng-luo]

国际网罗

interpreter fānyì [fahn-yee]

翻译

intersection (US) shízì lùkǒu

[shur-dzur loo-koh]

十字路口

interval (at theatre) mùjiān xiūxi
[moo-jyen hsyoh-hshee]

幕间休息

into: I'm not into-... wǒ duì ...
bù gǎn xìngqù [wor dway ... boo
gahn hsing-chew]

我对 ... 不感兴趣

introduce jièshào [jyeh-show]

介绍

may I introduce-...? wǒ lái
jièshào yíxià, zhèi wèi
shì-... [wor – yee-hsyah jay-way
shur]

我来介绍一下这位是 ...

invitation yāoqǐng
[yow-ching]

邀请

invite yāoqǐng

邀请

Ireland Ài'ěrlán [ai-er-lahn]

爱尔兰

Irish Ài'ěrlán [ai-er-lahn]

爱尔兰

I'm Irish wǒ shì Ài'ěrlán rén
[wor shur ai-er-lahn run]

我是爱尔兰人

iron (for ironing) yùndǒu [yewn-
doh]

熨斗

can you iron these for me?
qǐng nǐ bāng wǒ yùnyùn zhè
xiē yīfu, hǎo ma? [ching nee
bahng wor yun-yun jur hsyeh yee-

foo how mah]

请你帮我熨熨这些衣
服好吗？

is* shì [shur]

是

island dǎo [dow]

岛

it tā [tah]

它

it is-..., it was ... shì-... [shur]

是 ...

is it-...? shì-... ma? [mah]

是 ... 吗？

where is it? zài nǎr? [dzai]

在哪儿？

Italian (adj) Yìdàlì [yee-dah-lee]

意大利

Italy Yìdàlì

意大利

itch: it itches yǎng

痒

J

jacket jiākè [jyah-kur]

茄克

jade yù [yew]

玉

jam guǒjiàng [gwor-jyang]

果酱

January yīyuè [yee-yew-eh]

一月

Japan Rìběn [ree-bun]

日本

jar guànzi [gwahn-dzur]
罐子

jasmine tea mòlìhuā chá [mor-lee hwah chah]
茉莉花茶

jaw xiàba [hsyah-bah]
下巴

jazz juéshì yuè [jyeweh-shur yeweh]
爵士乐

jealous jìdù
忌妒

jeans niúzǎikù [nyoh-dzai-koo]
牛仔裤

jetty mǎtóu [mah-toh]
码头

jeweller's zhūbǎo (shāng)diàn [joo-bow (shahng-)dyen]
珠宝（商）店

jewellery zhūbǎo
珠宝

Jewish Yóutàirén de [yoh-tai-run dur]
犹太人的

job gōngzuò [goong-dzwor]
工作

jogging pǎobù [pow-boo]
跑步

to go jogging qù pǎobù [chew]
去跑步

joke wánxiào [wahn-hsyow]
玩笑

journey lǚxíng [lyew-sing]
旅行

have a good journey! yílù shùnfēng! [shun-fung]
一路顺风

jug guàn [gwahn]
罐

a jug of water yí guànr shuǐ
一罐儿水

July qīyuè [chee-yew-eh]
七月

jumper tàoshān [tow-shahn]
套衫

junction (road) jiāochākǒu [jyow-chah-koh]
交叉口

June liùyuè [lyoh-yew-eh]
六月

just (only just) jǐnjǐn
仅仅

(with numbers) zhǐ [jur]
只

just two zhǐ yào liǎngge [yow]
只要两个

just for me jiù wǒ yào [jyoh wor]
就我要

just here jiù zài zhèr [dzai jer]
就在这儿

not just now xiànzài bùxíng [hsyen-dzai boo-hsing]
现在不行

we've just arrived wǒmen gāng dào [wor-mun gahng dow]
我们刚到

K

keep liú [lyoh]
留
keep the change búyòng
zhǎo le [boo-yoong jow lur]
不用找了
can I keep it? wǒ kěyi
liúzhe ma? [wor kur-yee lyoh-jur
mah]
我可以留着吗？
please keep it qǐng liúzhe ba
[ching – bah]
请留着吧
kettle shuǐhú [shway-hoo]
水壶
key yàoshi [yow-shur]
钥匙
the key for room 201,
please qǐng gěi wǒ èr líng
yāo fáng de yàoshi [ching
gay wor er ling yow fahng dur
yow-shur]
请给我二零一房的钥匙
keyring yàoshi quān [yow-shur
choo-en]
钥匙环
kidneys (in body) shènzàng
[shun-dzahng]
肾脏
(food) yāozi [yow-dzur]
腰子
kill shā [shah]
杀

kilo gōngjīn [goong-jin]
公斤
kilometre gōnglǐ [goong-lee]
公里
how many kilometres is it
to-...? qù ... yǒu duōshao
gōnglǐ? [chew ... yoh dow-show]
去 ... 有多少公里？
kind (type) zhǒng [joong]
种
that's very kind nǐ zhēn hǎo
[nee jun how]
你真好

dialogue

which kind do you want? nǐ
yào nǎ yí zhǒng? [yow nah]
I want this/that kind wǒ
yào zhèi/nèi yì zhǒng [wor
yow jay/nay]

king guówáng [gwor-wahng]
国王
kiosk shòuhuòtíng [shoh-hwor-
ting]
售货亭
kiss wěn [wun]
吻
kitchen chúfáng [choo-fahng]
厨房
Kleenex® zhǐjīn [jur-jin]
纸巾
knee xīgài [hshee-gai]
膝盖

knickers sānjiǎokù [sahn-jyow-koo]
三角裤

knife dāozi [dow-dzur]
刀子

knock (verb) qiāo [chyow]
敲

knock over (object) dǎ fān [dah fahn]
打翻

(pedestrian) zhuàng dǎo [jwahng dow]
撞倒

know (somebody) rènshi [run-shur]
认识

(something, a place) zhīdao [jur-dow]
知道

I don't know wǒ bù zhīdao
我不知道

I didn't know that nà wǒ bù zhīdao [nah]
那我不知道

do you know where I can buy-...? nǐ zhīdao wǒ zài nǎr néng mǎi dào ...? [wor dzai nar nung mai dow]
你知道我在哪儿能买到 ... ?

Korean (adj) Cháoxiān [chow-hsyen]
朝鲜

L

lacquerware qīqì [chee-chee]
漆器

ladies' room, ladies' toilets nǚ cèsuǒ [nyew tsur-swor]
女厕所

ladies' wear nǚzhuāng [nyew-jwahng]
女装

lady nǚshì [nyew-shur]
女士

lager píjiǔ [pee-jyoh]
啤酒

lake hú [hoo]
湖

lamb (meat) yángròu [yang-roh]
羊肉

lamp dēng [dung]
灯

lane (motorway) chēdào [chur-dow]
车道

(small road) hútòng [hoo-toong]
胡同

language yǔyán [yew-yen]
语言

language course yǔyán kè [kur]
语言课

Laos Lǎowō [low-wor]
老挝

large dà [dah]
大

last (final) zuìhòu [dzway-hoh]

最后

last week shàng xīngqī
[shahng hsing-chee]

上星期

last Friday shàng xīngqī wǔ

上星期五

last night zuótiān wǎnshang
[dzwor-tyen wahn-shahng]

昨天晚上

**what time is the last train to
Beijing?** qù Běijīng de zuìhòu
yì bān huǒchē jǐ diǎn kāi?
[chew – dur dzway-hoh yur bahn
hwor-chur jee dyen]

去北京的最后一班火
车几点开？

late (at night) wǎn [wahn]

晚

(delayed) chí [chur]

迟

sorry I'm late duìbuqǐ, wǒ lái
wǎnle [dway-boo-chee wor lai
wahn-lur]

对不起我来晚了

the train was late huǒchē lái
wǎnle [hwor-chur]

火车来晚了

we must go – we'll be late
wǒmen děi zǒule láibujíle
[wor-mun day dzoh-lur lai-boo-jee-lur]

我们得走了来不及了

it's getting late bù zǎole
[dzow-lur]

不早了

later hòulái [hoh-lai]

后来

I'll come back later wǒ guò
yìhuǐr zài lái [wor gwor yee-
hwayr dzai]

我过一会儿再来

see you later huítóujiàn
[hway-toh-jyen]

回头见

later on hòulái

后来

latest zuìhòu [dzway-hoh]

最后

(most recent) zuìjìn
[dzway-jin]

最近

by Wednesday at the latest
zuìwǎn xīngqīsān

最晚星期三

laugh (verb) xiào [hsyow]

笑

laundry (clothes) xǐyī [hshee-yee]

洗衣

(place) xǐyīdiàn [–dyen]

洗衣店

lavatory cèsuǒ [tsur-swor]

厕所

law fǎlǜ [fah-lyew]

法律

lawyer lǜshī [lyew-shur]

律师

laxative xièyào [hsyeh-hyow]

泄药

lazy lǎn [lahn]

懒

lead: where does this road lead to? zhè tiáo lù tōng nǎr qù? [jur tyow loo toong nar chew]

这条路通哪儿去？

leak: the roof leaks wūdǐng lòule [woo-ding loh-lur]

屋顶漏了

learn xuéxí [hsyew-eh-hshee]

学习

least: not in the least yìdiǎn dōu bù [yee-dyenr doh bu]

一点儿都不

at least zhìshǎo [jee-show]

至少

leather pígé [pee-gur]

皮革

leave (depart) zǒu [dzoh]

走

I am leaving tomorrow wǒ míngtian zǒu [wor ming-tyen]

我明天走

when does the bus for Beijing leave? qù Běijīng de qìchē jǐ diǎn kāi? [chew – dur chee-chur jee dyen]

去北京的汽车几点开？

may I leave this here? wǒ néng bǎ zhèige liú zài zhèr ma? [wor nung bah jay-gur lyoh dzai jer mah]

我能把这个留在这儿吗？

he left yesterday tā shì zuótiān líkāi de [tah shur dzwor-tyen lee-kai dur]

他是昨天离开的

I left my coat in the bar wǒ bǎ wǒde dàyī liú zài jiǔbājiān [bah wor-dur dah-yee lyoh dzai jyoh-bah-jyen]

我把我的大衣留在酒吧间

there's none left shénme dōu búshèng [shun-mur doh boo-shung]

什么都不剩

left zuǒ [dzwor]

左

on the left zài zuǒbiānr [dzai dzwor-byenr]

在左边儿

to the left wǎng zuǒ [wahng]

往左

turn left wǎng zuǒ guǎi [gwai]

往左拐

left-handed zuópiězi [dzwor-pyeh-dzur]

左撇子

left luggage (office) xíngli jìcúnchù [hsing-lee jee-tsun-choo]

行李寄存处

leg tuǐ [tway]

腿

lemon níngméng [ning-mung]

柠檬

lemonade níngméng qìshuǐr [chee-shwayr]

柠檬汽水儿

lemon tea níngméngchá
[–chah]

柠檬茶

lend jiè [jyeh]

借

will you lend me your-...?
qǐng ba nǐde ... jiè gěi wǒ
[ching bah nee-dur ... jyeh gay wor]

请把你的 ... 借给我？

lens (of camera) jìngtóu [jing-toh]

镜头

less shǎo [show]

少

less than ... bǐ ... shǎo

比 ... 少

less expensive than ... bǐ ...
piányi [pyen-yee]

比 ... 便宜

lesson kè [kur]

课

let: will you let me know? nǐ
dào shíhou gàosu wǒ, hǎo
ma? [dow shur-hoh gow-soo wor
how mah]

你到时候告诉我好吗？

I'll let you know wǒ dào
shíhou gàosu nǐ

我到时候告诉你

let's go for something to eat
chīfàn, ba [chur-fahn bah]

吃饭吧

let off: will you let me off
at-...? wǒ zài-... xià, xíng ma?
[dzai-... hsyah hsing]

我在 ... 下行吗？

letter xìn [hsin]

信

do you have any letters for
me? yǒu xìn, ma? [yoh hsin
mah]

有信吗？

letterbox xìnxiāng [hsin-
hsyahng]

信箱

library túshūguǎn [too-shoo-
gwahn]

图书馆

lid gàir [gair]

盖儿

lie (tell untruth) shuōhuǎng
[shwor-hwahng]

说谎

lie down tǎng [tahng]

躺

life shēnghuó [shung-hwor]

生活

lifebelt jiùshēngquān [jyoh-
shung-choo-en]

救生圈

lifeguard jiùshēngyuán [jyoh-
shung-yew-ahn]

救生员

life jacket jiùshēngyī [jyoh-
shung-yee]

救生衣

lift (in building) diàntī
[dyen-tee]

电梯

could you give me a lift? nǐ
néng bù néng ràng wǒ dāge

chē? [nung – rahng wor dah-gur chur]

你能不能让我搭个车？

light (noun) dēng [dung]

灯

(not heavy) qīng [ching]

轻

do you have a light? (for cigarette) nǐ yǒu huǒ ma? [nur yoh hwor mah]

你有火吗？

light bulb dēngpào [dung-pow]

灯泡

I need a new light bulb wǒ xūyào yíge xīn dēngpào [wor hsyow-yow yee-gur hsin dung-pow]

我需要一个新灯泡

lighter (cigarette) dǎhuǒjī [dah-hwor-jee]

打火机

lightning shǎndiàn [shahn-dyen]

闪电

like xǐhuan [hshee-hwahn]

喜欢

I like it wǒ xǐhuan [wor]

我喜欢

I don't like it wǒ bù xǐhuan

我不喜欢

I like you wǒ xǐhuan nǐ

我喜欢你

do you like-...? nǐ xǐhuan-... ma? [mah]

你喜欢 ... 吗？

I'd like a beer wǒ xiǎng hē

yìpíng píjiǔ [hsyahng hur yee-ping]

我想喝一瓶啤酒

I'd like to go swimming wǒ xiǎng qù yóuyǒng

我想去游泳

would you like a drink? nǐ xiǎng hē diǎnr shénme ma? [hur dyenr shun-mur]

你想喝点儿什么吗？

would you like to go for a walk? nǐ xiǎng bu xiǎng qù zǒuyizǒu? [chew dzoh-yee-dzoh]

你想不想去走一走？

what's it like? tā xiàng shénme? [tah]

它象什么？

I want one like this wǒ yào tónglèide [yow toong-lay-dur]

我要同类的

line xiàn [hsyen]

线

could you give me an outside line? qǐng gěi wǒ wàixiàn, hǎo ma? [ching gay wor wai-hsyen how dzwaymah]

请给我外线好吗？

lips zuǐchún [dzway]

嘴唇

lip salve chúngāo [chun-gow]

唇膏

lipstick kǒuhóng [koh-hoong]

口红

listen tīng

听

litre shēng [shung]

升

little xiǎo [hsyow]

小

just a little, thanks jiù yìdiǎnr, xièxie [jyoh yee-dyenr hsyeh-hsyeh]

就一点儿谢谢

a little milk yìdiǎnr níunǎi [nyoh-nai]

一点儿牛奶

a little bit more duō yìdiǎnr [dwor yee-dyenr]

多一点儿

live (verb) zhù [joo]

住

we live together wǒmen zhù zài yìqǐ [wor-mun joo dzai yee-chee]

我们住在一起

dialogue

where do you live? nǐ zhù zài nǎr? [joo dzai]

I live in London wǒ zhù zài Lúndūn [wor]

lively (person) huópo [hwor-por]

活泼

(town) rènao [rur-now]

热闹

liver (in body, food) gān [gahn]

肝

lobby (in hotel) qiántīng [chyen-ting]

前厅

lobster lóngxiā [loong-hsyah]

龙虾

local dìfangde [dee-fahng-dur]

地方的

lock suǒ [swor]

锁

it's locked suǒshang le [swor shahng lur]

锁上了

lock out: I've locked myself out wǒ bǎ zìjǐ suǒ zài ménwài le [wor bah dzur-jee swor dzai mun-wai lur]

我把自己锁在门外了

locker (for luggage etc) xiǎochúguì [hsyow-choo-gway]

小橱柜

London Lúndūn

伦敦

long cháng [chahng]

长

how long does it take? yào duōcháng shíjian? [yow dwor-chahng shur-jyen]

要多长时间？

how long will it take to fix it? bǎ zhèige dōngxi xiūlí hǎo yào duōcháng shíjian? [bah jay-gur doong-hshee hsyoo-lee hao]

把这个东西修理好要多长时间？

a long time hěn cháng shíjian

[hun]
很长时间

one day/two days longer yí/
liǎng tiān duō [tyen dwor]
一／两天多

long-distance call chángtú
diànhuà [chahng-too dyen-hwah]
长途电话

look: I'm just looking, thanks
wǒ zhǐshi kànyikàn, xièxie
[wor jur-shur kahn-yee-kahn hsyeh-
hsyeh]
我只是看一看谢谢

you don't look well kànqǐlái,
nǐ shēntǐ bù shūfu [kahn-chee-
lai nee shun-tee boo shoo-foo]
看起来你身体不舒服

look out! xiǎoxīn! [hsyow-hsin]
小心

can I have a look? kěyi
kànkan ma? [kur-yee kahn-kahn
mah]
可以看看吗？

look after zhàokàn [jow-kahn]
照看

look at kàn [kahn]
看

look for zhǎo [jow]
找

I'm looking for-... wǒ zhǎo ...
[wor jow]
我找 ...

look forward to pànwàng
[pahn-wahng]
盼望

I'm looking forward to it wǒ
pànwàng [wor]
我盼望

loose (handle etc) sōng [soong]
松

lorry kǎchē [kah-chur]
卡车

lose diū [dyoh]
丢

I'm lost wǒ mílùle [wor mee-
loo-lur]
我迷路了

I've lost my bag wǒ bǎ
dàizi diūle [bah dai-dzur dyoh-
lur]
我把带子丢了

lost property (office) shīwù
zhāolǐng chù [shur-woo jow-ling
choo]
失物招领处

lot: a lot, lots hěnduō [hun-
dwor]
很多

not a lot bù duō
不多

a lot of people hěnduō rén
[run]
很多人

a lot bigger dà de duō [dah dur]
大得多

I like it a lot wǒ hén xǐhuan
[wor hun hshee-hwahn]
我很喜欢

loud dàshēng de [dah-shung dur]
大声的

lounge (in house) kètīng [kur-ting]
客厅
(in hotel) xiūxishì [hsyoh-hshee-shur]
休息室
love (noun) liàn'ài [lyen-ai]
恋爱
(verb) ài
爱
I love China wǒ ài Zhōngguó [wor ai joong-gwor]
我爱中国
lovely (person) kěài [kur-ai]
可爱
(thing) hěn hǎo [hun how]
很好
low (bridge) dī
低
(prices) piányide [pyen-yee-dur]
便宜的
luck yùnqi [yewn-chee]
运气
good luck! zhù nǐ shùnlì! [joo nee shun-lee]
祝你顺利
luggage xíngli [hsing-lee]
行李
luggage trolley xínglichē [–chur]
行李车
lunch wǔfàn [woo-fahn]
午饭
luxurious háohuá [how-hwah]
豪华

luxury (comfort etc) gāojí [gow-jee]
高级
(extravagance) shēchǐ [shur-chee]
奢侈
lychee lìzhī [lee-jur]
荔枝

M

machine jīqì [jee-chee]
机器
magazine zázhì [dzah-jur]
杂志
maid (in hotel) nǚ fúwùyuán [nyew foo-woo-yew-ahn]
女服务员
mail (noun) yóujiàn [yoh-jyen]
邮件
(verb) jì
寄
is there any mail for me? yǒu wǒde xìn ma? [yoh wor-dur hsin mah]
有我的信吗？
see **postal service**
mailbox xìnxiāng [hsin-hsyahng]
信箱
main zhǔyào de [joo-yow dur]
主要的
main course zhǔcài [joo-tsai]
主菜
main post office dà yóujú [dah

yoh-joo]

大邮局

main road dàlù [dah-loo]

大路

make (brand name) pái

牌

(verb) zhìzào [jur-dzow]

制造

I make it 10 yuan, OK? wǒ

suàn shí kuài qián, hǎo ma?

[wor swahn shur kwai chyen how

mah]

我算十块钱好吗？

what is it made of? zhè shì

yòng shénme zào de? [jur shur

yoong shun-mur dzow dur]

这是用什么造的？

make-up huàzhuāngpǐn [hwah-

jwahng-pin]

化妆品

Malaysia Mǎláixīyà [mah-lai-

hshee-yah]

马来西亚

man nánrén [nahn-run]

男人

manager jīnglǐ

经理

can I see the manager? kěyǐ

jiànjian jīnglǐ ma? [kur-yee jyen-

jyen – mah]

可以见见经理吗？

Mandarin Pǔtōnghuà [poo-

toong-hwah]

普通话

mandarin orange gānzi [gahn-

dzur]

柑子

many hěn duō [hun dwor]

很多

not many bù duō

不多

map dìtú

地图

March sānyuè [sahn-yew-eh]

三月

margarine rénzào huángyóu

[run-zow hwahng-yoh]

人造黄油

market shìchǎng [shur-chahng]

市场

married: I'm married wǒ

jiéhūnle [wor jyeh-hun-lur]

我结婚了

are you married? nǐ jiéhūnle

ma? [nee jyeh-hun-lur mah]

你结婚了吗？

martial arts wǔshù

武术

mascara jiémáogāo [jyeh-mow-

gow]

睫毛膏

match (sport) bǐsài

比赛

football match zúqiú sài [dzoo-

chyoh]

足球赛

matches huǒchái [hwor-]

火柴

material (fabric) bù

布

matter: it doesn't matter méi guānxi [may gwahn-hshee]
没关系

what's the matter? zěnmele? [dzun-mur-lur]
怎么了？

mattress chuángdiàn [chwahng-dyen]
床垫

May wǔyuè [woo-yew-eh]
五月

may: may I have another one? qǐng zài lái yīge [ching dzai lai yee-gur]
请再来一个

may I come in? wǒ néng jìnlái ma? [wor nung jin-lai mah]
我能进来吗？

may I see it? wǒ néng kàn ma? [kahn]
我能看吗？

may I sit here? wǒ néng zuò zhèr ma? [zwor jer]
我能坐这儿吗？

maybe kěnéng [kur-nung]
可能

me* wǒ [wor]
我

that's for me zhè shì wǒde [jer shur wor-dur]
这是我的

send it to me qǐng sòng gěi wǒ [ching soong gay]
请送给我

me too wǒ yě [yur]
我也

meal fàn [fahn]
饭

dialogue

did you enjoy your meal?
chīde hái hǎo ma? [chur-dur hai how mah]
it was excellent, thank you
hěn hǎo, xièxie [hun how hsyeh-hsyeh]

mean: what do you mean? nǐ zhǐde shì shénme? [nee jur-dur shur shun-mur]
你指的是什么？

dialogue

what does this word mean?
zhèige cír shì shénme yìsi?
[jay-gur tsur – yee-sur]
it means-... in English yòng yīngwen shì ... de yìsi
[yoong ying-wun – dur]

meat ròu [roh]
肉

medicine (Western) xīyào [hshee-yow]
西药

(Chinese) zhōngyào [joong-yow]
中药

medium (adj: size) zhōngděng
[joong-dung]

中等

medium-rare (steak) bànshēng
de [bahn-shung dur]

半生的

medium-sized zhōnghào
[joong-how]

中号

meet pèngjiàn [pung-jyen]

碰见

nice to meet you jiàndào nǐ
hěn gāoxìng [jyen-dow nee hun
gow-hsing]

见到你很高兴

where shall I meet you? wǒ
zài nǎr jiàn nǐ? [wor dzai-nar
jyen]

我在哪儿见你？

meeting huì(yì) [hway-yee]

会（议）

melon guā [gwah]

瓜

men nánde [nahn-dur]

男的

mend (machine, bicycle) xiūlǐ
[hsyoh-lee]

修理

(clothes) féngbǔ [fung-boo]

缝补

could you mend this for me?
qǐng gěi wǒ xiūlǐ yíxià hǎo
ma? [ching gay wor – yee-hsyah
how mah]

请给我修理一下好吗？

men's room nán cèsuǒ [nahn
tsur-swor]

男厕所

menswear nánzhuāng [nahn-
jwahng]

男装

mention shuōdào [shwor-dow]

说到

don't mention it búyòng kèqi
[boo-yoong kur-chee]

不用客气

menu càidānr [tsai-dahnr]

菜单儿

may I see the menu, please?
qǐng lái càidānr, hǎo ma?
[ching lai tsai-dahnr – how mah]

请来菜单儿好吗？

see menu reader page 244

message xìnr [hsinr]

信儿

are there any messages for
me? yǒu wǒde xìn shénmede
ma? [yoh wor-dur hsin shun-mur-
dur mah]

有我的信什么的吗？

I want to leave a message
for-... wǒ xiǎng gěi ... liúge
xìnr [hsyahng gay ... lyoh-gur]

我想给 ... 留个信儿

metal jīnshǔ [jin-shoo]

金属

metre mǐ

米

midday zhōngwǔ [joong-woo]

中午

at midday zhōngwǔ
中午

middle*: in the middle zài
zhōngjiān [dzai joong-jyen]
在中间

in the middle of the night yèlǐ
[yur-lee]
夜里

the middle one zhōngjiānde
[joong-jyen-dur]
中间的

midnight bànyè [bahn-yur]
半夜

at midnight bànyè [bahn-yur]
半夜

might: I might ... yěxǔ ... [yur-
hsoo]
也许

I might not ... yěxǔ bù ...
也许不 ...

mild (taste) wèidàn
[wei-dahn]
味淡

(weather) nuǎnhuo [nwahn-hwor]
暖和

mile yīnglǐ
英里

milk niúnǎi [nyoh-nai]
牛奶

millimetre háomǐ [how-mee]
毫米

mind: never mind méi guānxi
[may gwahn-hshee]
没关系

I've changed my mind wǒ

gǎibiàn zhǔyì le [wor gai-byen
joo-yee lur]
我改变主意了

dialogue

do you mind if I open the
window? wǒ kāi chuāng,
xíngbùxíng? [chwahng hsing-
boo-hsing]

no, I don't mind xíng
[hsing]

mine*: it's mine shì wǒde [shur
wor-dur]
是我的

mineral water kuàngquánshuǐr
[kwahng-choo-en-shwayr]
矿泉水儿

Ming Tombs shísānlíng [shur-
sahn-ling]
十三陵

minute fēn(zhōng) [fun(-joong)]
分（钟）

in a minute yìhuǐr [yee-hwayr]
一会儿

just a minute děng yìhuǐr
[dung]
等一会儿

mirror jìngzi [jing-dzur]
镜子

Miss xiǎojiě [hsyow-jyeh]
小姐

miss: I missed the bus wǒ méi
gǎnshàng chē [wor may gahn-

shahng chur]

我没赶上车

missing: my-... is missing
wǒde ... diūle [wor-dur ... dyoh-lur]

我的 ... 丢了

there's a suitcase missing
yíge yīxiāng diūle [yee-gur yee-hsyahng dyoh-lur]

一个衣箱丢了

mist wù

雾

mistake cuò(wù) [tswor–]

错（误）

I think there's a mistake zhèr yǒuge cuòr [jer yoh-gur]

这儿有个错儿

sorry, I've made a mistake
dùibùqǐ, wǒ nòngcuòle [dway-boo-chee wor noong-tswor-lur]

对不起我弄错了

misunderstanding wùhuì [woo-hway]

误会

mobile phone shǒutí diànhuà [shoh-tee dyen-hwah]

手提电话

modern xiàndài [hsyen-dai]

现代

moisturizer cāliǎnyóu [tsah-lyen-yoh]

擦脸油

moment: I won't be a moment
jiù yìfēn zhōng [jyoh yee-fun joong]

就一分钟

monastery (Buddhist) sìyuàn [sur-yew-ahn]

寺院

Monday xīngqīyī [hsing-chee-yee]

星期一

money qián [chyen]

钱

Mongolia Ménggǔ [mung-goo]

蒙古

Mongolian (adj) Ménggǔ

蒙古

monk sēng [sung]

僧

month yuè [yew-eh]

月

monument jìniànbēi [jin-yen-bay]

纪念碑

moon yuèliang [yew-eh-lyang]

月亮

more* gèng duō [gung dwor]

更多

can I have some more water, please? qǐng zài lái diǎnr shuǐ? [ching dzai lai shway]

请再来点儿水？

more expensive gèng guì [gung gway]

更贵

more interesting than ... bǐ ... gèng yǒu xìngqù [yoh hsing-chew]

比 ... 更有兴趣
more than 50/100 wǔshí/
yìbǎi duō
五十／一百多
more than that one bǐ nèige
duō [nay-gur]
比那个多
a lot more duōde duō [dwor-
dur]
多得多

dialogue

would you like some more?
nǐ hái yào diānr shénme
ma? [yow dyenr shun-mur mah]
no, no more for me, thanks
búyào, xièxie [boo-yow
hsyeh-hsyeh]
how about you? nǐ ne?
[nee-nur]
**I don't want any more,
thanks** wǒ bú zàiyàole,
xièxie [wor boo dzai-yow-lur]

morning zǎoshang [dzow-
shahng]
早上
this morning jīntiān zǎoshang
[jin-tyen dzow-shahng]
今天早上
in the morning zǎoshang
[dzow-shahng]
早上

mosquito wénzi [wun-dzur]
蚊子
mosquito net wénzhàng [wun-
jahng]
蚊帐
mosquito repellent qūwénjì
[chew-wun-jee]
驱蚊剂
**most*: I like this one most of
all** wǒ zuì xǐhuān zhèige [wor
dzway hshee-hwahn jay-gur]
我最喜欢这个
most of the time dàbùfen
shíjiān [dah-boo-fun shur-jyen]
大部分时间
most tourists dà duōshù
lǚyóuzhe [dah dwor-shoo]
大多数旅游者
mostly dàduō [dah-dwor]
大多
mother mǔqīn [moo-chin]
母亲
mother-in-law pópo [por-por]
婆婆
motorbike mótuōchē [mor-
twor-chur]
摩托车
motorboat qìtǐng [chee-ting]
汽艇
mountain shān [shahn]
山
in the mountains zài shānlǐ
[dzai shahn-lee]
在山里
mountaineering dēngshān

[dung-shahn]

登山

mouse lǎoshǔ [low-shoo]

老鼠

moustache xiǎo húzi [hsyow hoo-dzur]

小胡子

mouth zuǐ [dzway]

嘴

move: he's moved to another room tā bāndào lìngwài yì jiān qùle [tah bahn-dow ling-wai yee jyen choo-lur]

他搬到另外一间去了

could you move it? qǐng nín nuó yíxià, hǎo ma? [ching nin nwor yee-hsyah how mah]

请您挪一下好吗？

could you move up a little? qǐng wǎng qián núo yíxià, hǎo ma? [wahng chyen nwor yee-hsyah]

请往前挪一下好吗？

movie diànyǐng [dyen-ying]

电影

movie theater diànyǐng yuàn [dyen-ying yew-ahn]

电影院

Mr xiānsheng [hsyen-shung]

先生

Mrs fūren [foo-run]

夫人

Ms nǚshì [nyew-shur]

女士

much duō [dwor]

多

much better/worse hǎo/huài de duō [dur]

好／坏得多

not (very) much bù hěn duō

不很多

I don't want very much wǒ búyào tài duō [wor boo-yow]

我不要太多

mug (for drinking) bēi [bay]

杯

I've been mugged wǒ gěi rén qiǎngle [gay run chyang-lur]

我给人抢了

mum māma [mah-mah]

妈妈

museum bówùguǎn [bor-woo-gwahn]

博物馆

mushrooms mógu [mor-goo]

蘑菇

music yīnyuè [yin-yew-eh]

音乐

Muslim (adj) mùsīlín [moo-sur-lin]

穆斯林

must*: I must wǒ bìxū [wor bee-hsyew]

我必须

I mustn't drink alcohol wǒ búhuì hē jiǔ [wor-boo-hway hur jyoh]

我不会喝酒

my* wǒde [wor-dur]
我的
myself: I'll do it myself wǒ zìjǐ
lái [wor dzur-jee]
我自己来
by myself wǒ yíge rén [yee-gur
run]
我一个人

N

nail (finger) zhǐjiā [jur-jyah]
指甲
(metal) dīngzi [ding-dzur]
钉子
nail varnish zhǐjiā yóu [jur-jyah
yoh]
指甲油
name míngzi [ming-dzur]
名子
my name's John wǒde
míngzi jiào John [wor-dur
– jyow]
我的名子叫John
what's your name? nǐ
jiào shénme? [nee –
shun-mur]
你叫什么？
what is the name of this
street? zhèi tiáo lù jiào
shénme? [jay tyow]
这条路叫什么？
napkin cānjīn [tsahn-jin]
餐巾

nappy niàobù [nyow-boo]
尿布
narrow (street) zhǎi [jai]
窄
nasty (person) ràng rén tǎoyàn
[rahng run tow-yen]
让人讨厌
(weather, accident) zāotòule
[dzow-toh-lur]
糟透了
national (state) guójiā [gwor-
jyah]
国家
(nationwide) quánguó [choo-en-
gwor]
全国
nationality guójí [gwor-jee]
国籍
(for Chinese minorities) shǎoshù
mínzú [show-shoo min-dzoo]
少数民族
natural zìrán [dzur-rahn]
自然
near jìn
近
near the ... lí-... hěnjìn [hun-
jin]
离 ... 很近
is it near the city centre?
lí-shì zhōngxīn jìn ma? [shur
joong-hsin jin mah]
离市中心近吗？
do you go near the Great
Wall? nǐ zài-Chángchéng
fùjìn tíngchē ma? [nee dzai

chahng-chung foo-jin ting-chur
mah]

你在长城附近停车吗？

where is the nearest-...?
zuìjìn de-... zài nǎr? [dzway-jin
dur-... dzai nar]

最近的 ... 在哪儿？

nearby fùjìn [foo-jin]

附近

nearly chàbuduō [chah-boo-dwor]

差不多

necessary bìyào(de) [bee-yow(-dur)]

必要（的）

neck bózi [boh-dzur]

脖子

necklace xiàngliàn [hsyahng-lyen]

项链

necktie lǐngdài

领带

need: I need-... wǒ xūyào-... [wor hsyew-yow]

我需要

do I need to pay? wǒ yīnggāi
fùqián ma? [foo-chyen mah]

我应该付钱吗？

needle zhēn [jun]

针

neither: neither (one) of them
liǎngge dōu bù [lyang-gur doh]

两个都不

Nepal Níbó'er [nee-bor-er]

尼泊尔

Nepali (adj) Níbó'er

尼泊尔

nephew zhízi [jur-dzur]

侄子

net (in sport) wǎng [wahng]

网

network map jiāotōngtú [jyow-toong-too]

交通图

never (not ever) cónglái bù [tsoong-lai]

从来不

(not yet) hái méiyou [may-yoh]

还没有

dialogue

**have you ever been to
Beijing?** nǐ qùguo Běijīng
méiyou? [chew-gwor – may-yoh]

**no, never, I've never
been there** cónglái méiqù
[tsoong-lai may-chew]

new xīn [hsin]

新

news (radio, TV etc) xīnwén [hsin-wun]

新闻

newspaper bào(zhǐ) [bow(-jur)]

报（纸）

New Year xīnnián [hsin-nyen]

新年

Chinese New Year chūnjié

[chun-jyeh]

春节

Happy New Year! xīnnián hǎo! [how]

新年好

(Chinese) gōnghè xīnxǐ! [goong-hur hsin-hshee]

恭贺新禧

New Year's Eve: Chinese New Year's Eve chúxī [choo-hshee]

除夕

New Zealand Xīnxīlán [hsin-see-lahn]

新西兰

New Zealander: I'm a New Zealander wǒ shì xīnxīlánren [-run]

我是新西兰人

next xià yíge [hsyah yee-gur]

下一个

the next street on the left zuǒbiānr díyì tiáo lù [dzwor-byenr dee-yee tiao]

左边儿第一条路

at the next stop xià yízhàn [hsyah yee-jahn]

下一站

next week xià(ge) xīngqī [hsyah(-gur) hsing-chee]

下（个）星期

next to ... zài-... pángbiān [dzai-... pahng-byen]

在 ... 旁边

nice (food) hǎochī [how-chur]

好吃

(looks, view etc) hǎokàn [how-kahn]

好看

(person) hǎo [how]

好

niece zhínǚ [jin-yew]

侄女

night yè [yur]

夜

at night yèli [yur-lee]

夜里

good night wǎn ān [wahn ahn]

晚安

dialogue

do you have a single room for one night? yǒu yìtiān de dānrén jiān ma? [yoh yee-tyen dur dahn-run jyen mah]

yes, madam yǒu [yoh]

how much is it per night? yìwǎn yào duōshaoqián? [yee-wahn yow dwor-show-chyen]

it's 30 yuan for one night yìwǎn yào sānshí kuài qián [sahn-shur – chyen]

thank you, I'll take it xíng [hsing]

nightclub yèzǒnghuì [yur-dzoong-hway]

夜总会

no* bù

不

I've no change wǒ méiyou líng qián [wor may-yoh – chyen]

我没有零钱

no way! bù xíng! [hsing]

不行

oh no! (upset) tiān na! [tyen nah]

天哪

nobody méirén [may-run]

没人

there's nobody there méirén zài nàr [dzai]

没人在那儿

noise zàoyīn [dzow-yin]

噪音

noisy: it's too noisy tài chǎole [chow-lur]

太吵了

non-alcoholic bù hán jiǔjīng de [hahn jyoh-jing dur]

不含酒精的

none shénme yě méiyou [shun-mur yur may-yoh]

什么也没有

noon zhōngwǔ [joong-woo]

中午

at noon zhōngwǔ

中午

no-one méirén [may-run]

没人

nor: nor do I wǒ yě bù [wor yur]

我也不

normal zhèngcháng(de) [jung-chahng(-dur)]

正常（的）

north běi [bay]

北

in the north běibian [bay-byen]

北边

to the north wǎng běi [wahng]

往北

north of Rome Luómǎ běi

罗马北

northeast dōngběi [doong-bay]

东北

northern běibiān [bay-byen]

北边

Northern Ireland Běi Ài'ěrlán [bay ai-er-lahn]

北爱尔兰

North Korea Běi Cháoxiǎn [bay chow-hsyen]

北朝鲜

northwest xīběi [hshee-bay]

西北

Norway Nuówēi [nwor-way]

挪威

Norwegian (adj, language) Nuówēiyǔ

挪威语

nose bízi [bee-dzur]

鼻子

not* bù

不

no, I'm not hungry wǒ búè [wor bway]

我不饿

I don't want any, thank you
búyào, xièxie [boo-yow hsyeh-
hsyeh]

不要谢谢

it's not necessary búbìyào

不必要

I didn't know that wǒ bù
zhīdao [wor boo jur-dow]

我不知道

not that one, this one búyào
nèige, yào zhèige [nay-gur yow
jay-gur]

不要那个要这个

note (banknote) chāopiào [chow-
pyow]

钞票

notebook bǐjìběn [bee-jee-bun]

笔记本

nothing méiyou shénme [may-
yoh shun-mur]

没有什么

nothing for me, thanks wǒ
shénme dōu bú yào, xièxie
[wor – doh boo yow hsyeh-hsyeh]

我什么都不要谢谢

nothing else, thanks qítade
búyào, xièxie [chee-tah-dur boo-
yow]

其他的不要谢谢

novel (noun) xiǎoshuō [hsyow-
shwor]

小说

November shíyīyuè [shur-yee-
yew-eh]

十一月

now xiànzài [hsyen-dzai]

现在

number hàomǎ [how-mah]

号码

(figure) shùzì [shoo-dzur]

数字

I've got the wrong number
wǒ dǎcuòle [wor dah-tswor-lur]

我打错了

what is your phone number?
nǐde diànhuà hàomǎ shì
duōshao? [nee-dur dyen-hwah
shur dwor-show]

你的电话号码是多少？

number plate chēpái [chur-pai]

车牌

nurse hùshi [hoo-shur]

护士

nut (for bolt) luósī [lwor-sur]

螺丝

nuts (chestnuts) lìzi [lee-dzur]

栗子

(hazelnuts) zhēnzi [jun-dzur]

榛子

(walnuts) hétao [hur-tow]

核桃

O

occupied (US) yǒurén [yoh-run]

有人

o'clock* diǎnzhōng [dyen-
joong]

点钟

October shíyuè [shur-yew-eh]
十月

odd (strange) qíguài [chee-gwai]
奇怪

of* de [dur]
的

off (lights, machine) guān shangle
[gwahn shahng-lur]
关上了

it's just off ... (street etc) lí ...
bùyuán [boo-ywahn]
离 ... 不远

we're off tomorrow wǒmen
míngtian zǒu [wor-mun ming-tyen dzoh]
我们明天走

office (place of work)
bàngōngshì [bahn-goong-shur]
办公室

often jīngcháng [jing-chahng]
经常

not often bù jīngcháng [boo jing-chahng]
不经常

how often are the buses?
yíge zhōngtóu duōshao
qìchē? [yee-gur joong-toh dwor-show chee-chur]
一个钟头多少汽车？

oil (for car) yóu [yoh]
油

vegetable oil càiyóu [tsai-yoh]
菜油

oily (food) yóunì [yoh-nee]
油腻

ointment yàogāo [yow-gow]
药膏

OK hǎo [how]
好

are you OK? hái hǎo ma?
[mah]
还好吗？

I feel OK hěn hǎo [hun]
很好

is that OK with you? xíng bù
xíng? [hsing]
行不行？

is it OK to-...? wó kěyi ...?
[wor kur-yee]
我可以 ... ？

that's OK, thanks xíngle
xièxie [hsing-lur hsyeh-hsyeh]
行了谢谢

is this train OK for-...? zhè
liè huǒchē qù ... ma? [jer lyeh
hwor-chur chew ... mah]
这列火车去 ... 吗？

old (person) lǎo [low]
老

(thing) jiù [jyoh]
旧

dialogue

how old are you? nín
duō dà niánling? [dwor dah
nyen-ling]
(to an old person) nín duō dà
niánjì le? [dwor dah nyen-jee
lur]

(to a child) ni jǐsuì le? [jee-sway lur]

I'm 25 wǒ èrshíwǔ suì [wor – sway]

and you? nǐ ne? [nur]

old-fashioned guòshí(de) [gwor-shur(-dur)]
过时（的）

(person) shǒujiù(de) [shoh-jyoh(-dur)]
守旧（的）

old town (old part of town) jiùchéng [jyoh-chung]
旧城

omelette chǎojīdàn [chow-jee-dahn]
炒鸡蛋

on*: on ... (on top of) zài-... shàngmian [dzai-... shahng-myen]
在 ... 上面

on the street zài-lùshàng
在路上

on the beach zài-hǎitān shàng
在海滩上

is it on this road? zài-zhètiaolù ma? [jur-tyow-loo mah]
在这条路吗？

on the plane zài-feījī shàng
在飞机上

on Saturday xīngqī liù [lyoh]
星期六

on television zài diànshìshang
在电视上

I haven't got it on me wǒ méi dài zài shēnshang [wor may dai dzai shun-shahng]
我没带在身上

this one's on me (drink) wǒ fùqián [wor foo-choo-en]
我付钱

the light wasn't on dēng méi kāi [dung may]
灯没开

what's on tonight? jīntiān wǎnshang yǒu shénme huódòng? [jin-tyen wahn-shahng you shun-mur hwor-dong]
今天晚上有什么活动？

once (one time) yícì [yee-tsur]
一次

at once (immediately) mǎshàng [mah-shahng]
马上

one* yī [yur]
一

the white one báisè de [bai-sur dur]
白色的

one-way ticket dānchéng piào [dahn-chung pyow]
单程票

onion yángcōng [yang-tsoong]
洋葱

only zhǐ yǒu [jur yoh]
只有

only one zhǐ yǒu yíge [yee-

gur]
只有一个

it's only 6 o'clock cái liùdiǎn [tsai lyoh-dyen]
才六点

I've only just got here wǒ gāng dào le [wor gahng dow lur]
我刚到了

on/off switch kāiguān [kai-gwahn]
开关

open (adj) kāi(de) [kai(-dur)]
开（的）

(verb) kāi
开

when do you open? nǐmen shénme shíhou kāiménr? [nee-mun shun-mur shur-hoh kai-munr]
你们什么时候开门儿？

I can't get it open wǒ dǎbúkāi [wor dah-boo--kai]
我打不开

in the open air zài shìwài [dzai shur-wai]
在室外

opening times yíngyè shíjiān [ying-yur shur-jyen]
营业时间

opera gējù [gur-jyew]
歌剧

operation (medical) shǒushù [shoh-shoo]
手术

operator (telephone) zǒngjī [dzoong-jee]
总机

opposite: the opposite direction xiāngfǎn de fāngxiàng [hsyahng-fahn dur fahng-hsyahng]
相反的方向

the bar opposite zài duìmianr de jiǔba [dzai dway-myenr dur jyoo-bah]
在对面儿的酒吧

opposite my hotel zài wǒ fàndiàn duìmianr
在我饭店对面儿

optician yǎnjìngdiàn [yen-jing-dyen]
眼镜店

or (in statement) huòzhě [hwor-jur]
或者

(in question) háishi [hai-shur]
还是

orange (fruit) júzi [joo-dzur]
橘子

(colour) júhuángsè [jyew-sur]
橘黄色

orange juice (fresh) xiānjúzhī [hsyen-jyew-jur]
鲜橘汁

(fizzy) júzi qìshuǐ [jyew-dzur chee-shway]
橘子汽水

(diluted) júzishuǐr [jyew-dzur-shwayr]
橘子水儿

order: can we order now? (in

restaurant) wǒmen kěyǐ diǎncài
ma? [wor-mun kur-yee dyen-tsai
mah]

我们可以点菜吗？

I've already ordered, thanks
yǐjing diǎn le, xièxie [yee-jing
dyen lur hsyeh-hsyeh]

已经点了谢谢

I didn't order this wǒ méiyǒu
diǎn zhège cài [wor may-yoh
dyen jay-gur tsai]

我没有点这个菜

out of order huàile [hwai-lur]

坏了

ordinary pǔtōng [poo-toong]

普通

other qítā [chee-tah]

其他

the other one lìng yíge [yee-
gur]

另一个

the other day zuìjìn
[dzway-jin]

最近

I'm waiting for the others wǒ
děngzhe qíyúde [wor dung-jer
chee-yoo-dur]

我等着其余的

do you have any others?
(other kinds) hái yǒu biéde ma?
[yoh byeh-dur mah]

还有别的吗？

otherwise yàobùrán [yow-boor-
ahn]

要不然

our/ours* wǒmende [wor-mun-
dur]

我们的

out: he's out tā chūqule [tah
choo-chew-lur]

他出去了

three kilometres out of town
lí shìqū sān gōnglǐ [shur-chew
– goong-lee]

离市区三公里

outdoors lùtiān [loo-tyen]

露天

outside* wàimian
[wai-myen]

外面

can we sit outside? wǒmen
kěyǐ dào wàimian qù zuò ma?
[wor-mun kur-yee dow wai-myen
chew dzwor mah]

我们可以到外面去坐
吗？

oven kǎoxiāng [kow-syang]

烤箱

over: over here zài zhèr [dzai
jer]

在这儿

over there zài nàr [dzai nàr]

在那儿

over 500 wǔbǎi duō [dwor]

五百多

it's over wánle [wahn-lur]

完了

**overcharge: you've
overcharged me** nǐ duōshōule
wǒde qián [dwor-shoh-lur wor-

dur chyen]

你多收了我的钱

overland mail lùshang yóudì [loo-shahng yoh-dee]

陆上邮递

overnight (travel) guòyè [gwor-yur]

过夜

overtake chāoguò [chow-gwor]

超过

owe: how much do I owe you? yígòng duōshao qián? [yee-goong dwor-show chyen]

一共多少钱？

own: my own-... wǒ zìjǐde-... [wor dzur-jur-dur]

我自己的 ...

are you on your own? jiù nǐ yíge rén ma? [jyoh nee yee-gur run mah]

就你一个人吗？

I'm on my own jiù wǒ yíge rén [jyoh wor yee-gur run]

就我一个人

P

pack (verb) shōushi [shoh-shur]

收拾

package (parcel) bāoguǒ [bow-gwor]

包裹

packed lunch héfàn [hur-fahn]

盒饭

packet: a packet of cigarettes yìbāo yān [yee-bow yen]

一包烟

paddy field dàotián [dow-tyen]

稻田

page (of book) yè [yur]

页

could you page Mr-...? nǐ néng jiào yíxia-... xiānsheng ma? [nung jyow yee-hsyah-... hsyen-shung mah]

你能叫一下 ... 先生吗？

pagoda tǎ [tah]

塔

pain téng [tung]

疼

I have a pain here wǒ zhèr téng [wor jer]

我这儿疼

painful téng

疼

painkillers zhǐténgyào [jur-tung-yow]

止疼药

painting huà [hwah]

画

(oil) yóuhuà [yoh-hwah]

油画

(Chinese) guóhuà [gwor-hwah]

国画

pair: a pair of-... yíduìr-... [yee-dwayr]

一对儿 ...

Pakistani (adj) Bājīsītǎn [bah-jee-sur-tahn]

巴基斯坦

palace gōngdiàn [goong-dyen]

宫殿

pale cāngbái [tsahng-bai]

苍白

pale blue dàn lánsè [dahn lahn-sur]

淡蓝色

panda dà xióngmāo [dah hsyoong-mow]

大熊猫

pants (underwear: men's) kùchǎ [koo-chah]

裤衩

(women's) xiǎo sānjiǎokù [hsyow sahn-jyow-koo]

小三角裤

(US: trousers) kùzi [koo-dzur]

裤子

pantyhose liánkùwà [lyen-koo-wah]

连裤袜

paper zhǐ [jur]

纸

(newspaper) bàozhǐ [bow-jur]

报纸

a piece of paper yìzhāng zhǐ [yee-jahng jur]

一张纸

paper handkerchiefs zhǐjīn [jur-jin]

纸巾

parcel bāoguǒ [bow-gwor]

包裹

pardon (me)? (didn't understand/hear) nǐ shuō shénme? [shwor shun-mur]

你说什么？

parents fùmǔ

父母

park (noun) gōngyuán [goong-yew-ahn]

公园

(verb) tíngchē [ting-chur]

停车

can I park here? wǒ néng zài zhèr tíngchē ma? [wor nung dzai-jer ting-chur mah]

我能在这儿停车吗？

parking lot tíngchē chǎng [ting-chur chahng]

停车场

part (noun) bùfen

部分

partner (boyfriend, girlfriend etc) bànr [bahnr]

伴儿

party (group) tuántǐ [twahn-tee]

团体

(celebration) wǎnhuì [wahn-hway]

晚会

passenger chéngkè [chung-kur]

乘客

passport hùzhào [hoo-jow]

护照

past*: in the past guòqu [gwor-chew]

过去

just past the information office gāng jīngguò wènxùnchù [gahng jing-gwor wun-hsun-choo]

刚经过问讯处

path xiǎolù [hsyow-loo]

小路

pattern tú'àn [too-ahn]

图案

pavement rénxíng dào [run-hsing dow]

人行道

pavilion tíngzi [ting-dzur]

亭子

pay (verb) fù qián [foo(-chyen)]

付钱

can I pay, please? suànzhàng ba? [swahn-jahng bah]

算帐吧？

it's already paid for zhèige yǐjīng fùqián le [jay-gur yee-jing foo-chyen lur]

这个已经付钱了

dialogue

who's paying? shúi fùqián? [shway foo-chyen]

I'll pay wǒ fùqián [wor foo-chyen]

no, you paid last time, I'll pay bù, nǐ shì zuìhòu yícì fùde, wǒ fùqián [shur dzway-hoh yee-tsur foo-dur]

payphone jìfèi diànhuà [jee-fay dyen-hwah]

计费电话

peaceful ānjìng [ahn-jing]

安静

peach táozi [tow-dzur]

桃子

peanuts huāshēng [hwah-shung]

花生

pear lí

梨

peculiar (taste, custom) guài [gwai]

怪

pedestrian crossing rénxíng héngdào [run-hsing hung-dow]

人行横道

Peking Opera Jīngjù [jing-jew]

京剧

pen gāngbǐ [gahng-bee]

钢笔

pencil qiānbǐ [chyen-bee]

铅笔

penfriend bíyǒu [bee-yoh]

笔友

penicillin pánníxīlín [pahn-nee-see-lin]

盘尼西林

penknife qiānbǐdāo [chyen-bee-dow]

铅笔刀

pensioner lǐng yánglǎojīn de rén [yang-low-jin dur run]

领养老金的人

people rénmín [run-min]

人民

the other people in the hotel
fàndiàn li de qítā kèrén [lee dur
chee-tah ker-run]

饭店里的其他客人

too many people rén tài duō
le [run tai dwor-lur]

人太多了

**People's Republic of
China** Zhōnghuá Rénmín
Gònghéguó [joong-hwah run-
min goong-hur-gwor]

中华人民共和国

pepper (spice) hújiāo [hoo-
jyow]

胡椒

(vegetable, red) shìzijiāo [shur-
dzur-jyow]

柿子椒

per: per night měi wǎn [may
wahn]

每晚

how much per day? yìtiān
yào duōshao qián? [yee-tyen
yow dwor-show chyen]

一天要多少钱？

... per cent bǎifēn zhī-... [bai-
fun jur]

百分之 ...

perfect wánměi [wahn-may]

完美

perfume xiāngshuǐr [hsyahng-
shwayr]

香水儿

perhaps kěnéng [kur-nung]

可能

perhaps not kěnéng bù

可能不

period (of time) shíqī
[shur-chee]

时期

(menstruation) yuèjīng [yew-eh-
jing]

月经

permit (noun) xǔkě zhèng
[hsyew-kur jung]

许可证

person rén [run]

人

personal stereo fàngyīnjī
[fahng-yin-jee]

放音机

petrol qìyóu [chee-yoh]

汽油

petrol can yóutǒng [yoh-toong]

油桶

petrol station jiāyóu zhàn [jyah-
yoh jahn]

加油站

pharmacy yàodiàn [yow-dyen]

药店

Philippines Fēilǜbīn [fay-lew-bin]

菲律宾

phone (noun) diànhuà [dyen-
hwah]

电话

(verb) dǎ diànhuà [dah]

打电话

phone book diànhuà bù [dyen-hwah]

电话簿

phone box diànhuàtíng

电话亭

phonecard diànhuàkǎ [dyen-hwah-kah]

电话卡

phone number diànhuà hàomǎ [how-mah]

电话号码

photo zhàopiàn [jow-pyen]

照片

could you take a photo of us, please? qǐng gěi wǒ zhàozhāng xiàng [ching gay-wor jow-jahng hsyahng]

请给我照张相

phrasebook duìhuà shǒucè [dway-hwah shoh-tsur]

对话手册

piano gāngqín [gahng-chin]

钢琴

pickpocket páshǒu [pah-shoh]

扒手

pick up: will you be there to pick me up? nǐ lái jiē wó hǎo ma? [ni lai jyeh wor how mah]

你来接我好吗？

picnic (noun) yěcān [yur-tsahn]

野餐

picture (painting) huà [hwah]

画

(photo) zhàopiàn [jow-pyen]

照片

piece kuàir [kwair]

块儿

a piece of-... yíkuàir-... [yee-kwair]

一块儿 ...

pig zhū [joo]

猪

pill bìyùnyào [bee-yewn-yow]

避孕药

I'm on the pill wǒ chī bìyùnyào [wor chur bee-yew-nyow]

我吃避孕药

pillow zhèntou [jun-toh]

枕头

pillow case zhěntào [jun-tow]

枕套

pin (noun) biézhēn [byeh-jun]

别针

pineapple bōluó [bor-lwor]

菠萝

pineapple juice bōluózhī [bor-lwor-jur]

菠萝汁

pink fěnhóng [fun-hoong]

粉红

pipe (for smoking) yāndǒu [yen-doh]

烟斗

(for water) guǎnzi [gwahn-dzur]

管子

pity: it's a pity zhēn kěxī [jun kur-hshee]

真可惜

place (noun) dìfāng [dee-fahng]
地方
at your place zài nǐde jiā [dzai nee-dur jyah]
在你的家
plane fēijī [fay-jee]
飞机
by plane zuò fēijī [dzwor]
坐飞机
plant zhíwù [jur-woo]
植物
plasters xiàngpí gāo [syang-pee gow]
橡皮膏
plastic sùliào [soo-lyow]
塑料
plastic bag sùliàodài
塑料袋
plate pánzi [pahn-dzur]
盘子
platform zhàntái [jahn-tai]
站台
which platform is it for Beijing? wǎng Běijīng de huǒchē cóng jǐhào zhàntái kāichū? [wahng – dur hwor-chur tsoong jee-how jahn-tai kai-choo]
往北京的火车从几号站台开出？
play (verb) wánr [wahnr]
玩儿
(noun: in theatre) huàjù [hwah-jew]
话剧
pleasant lìngrén yúkuài [ling-

run yew-kwai]
令人愉快
please qǐng [ching]
请
yes, please hǎo, xièxie [how hsyeh-hsyeh]
好谢谢
could you please-...? qǐng nín-..., hǎo ma? [mah]
请您 … 好吗？
please don't qǐng nín-bù
请您不
pleased: pleased to meet you hěn gāoxìng jiàndào nǐ [hun gow hsing jyen dow]
很高兴见到你
pleasure: my pleasure méi shìr [may shur]
没事儿
plenty: plenty of-... xǔduō-... [hsyew-dwor]
许多
there's plenty of time hǎo duō shíjian [how dwor shur-jyen]
好多时间
that's plenty, thanks gòule, xièxie [goh-lur hsyeh-hsyeh]
够了谢谢
plug (electrical) chātóu [chah-toh]
插头
(in sink) sāizi [sai-dzur]
塞子
plum lǐzi [lee-dzur]
李子

plumber guǎnzigōng [gwahn-dzur-goong]
管子工

p.m. xiàwǔ [hsyah-woo]
下午

pocket kǒudàir [koh-dair]
口袋儿

point: two point five èr diǎn wǔ [dyen]
二点五

there's no point bù zhíde [jur-dur]
不值得

poisonous yǒudúde [yoh-doo-dur]
有毒的

police jǐngchá [jing-chah]
警察

call the police! kuài jiào jǐngchá! [kwai jyow jing-chah]
快叫警察

policeman jǐngchá [jing-chah]
警察

police station pàichūsuǒ [pai-choo-swor]
派出所

polish (for shoes) xiéyóu [hsyeh-yoh]
鞋油

polite kèqi [kur-chee]
客气

polluted wūrǎnle de [woo-rahn-lur dur]
污染了的

pool (for swimming) yóuyǒngchí [yoh-yoong-chur]
游泳池

poor (not rich) qióng [chyoong]
穷

(quality) lièzhì [lyeh-jur]
劣质

pop music liúxíng yīnyuè [lyoh-hsing yin-yew-eh]
流行音乐

pop singer liúxíng gēshǒu [gur-shoh]
流行歌手

pork zhūròu [joo-roh]
猪肉

port (for boats) gángkǒu [gahng-koh]
港口

porter (in hotel) ménfáng [mun-fahng]
门房

possible kěnéng [kur-nung]
可能

is it possible to-...? kěyǐ...ma? [yoh]
可以 … 吗？

as-... as possible jǐn kěnéng
尽可能

post (noun: mail) yóujiàn [yoh-jyen]
邮件

(verb) jì [jee]
寄

could you post this letter for me? qǐng bāng wǒ bǎ zhèifēng xìn jìzǒu, hǎo ma?

[ching bahng wor bah jay-fung hsin jee-dzoh how mah]

请帮我把这封信寄走好吗？

postbox xìnxiāng [hsin-hsyahng]

信箱

postcard míngxìnpiàn [ming-hsin-pyen]

名信片

poster zhāotiē [jow-tyeh]

招贴

poste restante dàilǐng yóujiàn [yoh-jyen]

待领邮件

post office yóujú [yoh-jew]

邮局

potato tǔdòu [too-doh]

土豆

potato chips (US) zhá tǔdòupiànr [jah too-doh-pyenr]

炸土豆片儿

pound (money) yīngbàng [ying-bahng]

英镑

(weight) bàng [bahng]

磅

power cut tíngdiàn [ting-dyen]

停电

power point diànyuán chāzuò [dyen-yew-ahn chah-dzwor]

电源插座

practise: I want to practise my Chinese wǒ xiǎng liànxí jiǎng

Zhōngwén [wor hsyahng lyen-hshee jyang joong-wun]

我想练习讲中文

prawn crackers xiābǐng [hsyah-bing]

虾饼

prawns duìxiā [dway-hsyah]

对虾

prefer: I prefer-... wǒ gèng xǐhuan-... [wor gung see-hwahn]

我更喜欢 ...

pregnant huáiyùn [hwai-yewn]

怀孕

prescription (for medicine) yàofāng [yow-fahng]

药方

present (gift) lǐwù

礼物

president (of country) zóngtǒng [dzoong-toong]

总统

pretty piàoliang [pyow-lyang]

漂亮

it's pretty expensive tài guìle [gway-lur]

太贵了

price jiàgé [jyah-gur]

价格

prime minister shǒuxiàng [shoh-hsyahng]

首相

printed matter yìnshuāpǐn [yin-shwah-pin]

印刷品

prison jiānyù [jyen-yew]
监狱

private sīrén(de) [sur-run(-dur)]
私人（的）

private bathroom sīrén(de)yùshì [–yoo-shur]
私人（的）浴室

probably dàgài [dah-gai]
大概

problem wèntí [wun-tee]
问题

no problem! méi wèntí! [may]
没问题

programme (theatre) jiémùdānr [jyeh-moo-dahnr]
节目单儿

pronounce: how is this pronounced? zhèige zì zěnme fāyīn? [jay-gur dzur dzun-mur fah-yin]
这个字怎么发音？

Protestant xjīnjiàotú [hsin-jyow-too]
新教徒

public convenience gōnggòng cèsuǒ [goong-goong tsur-swor]
公共厕所

public holiday gōngjià [goong-jyah]
公假

pull lā [lah]
拉

pullover tàoshān [mow-bay-hsin]
套衫

puncture (noun) pǎoqì [pow-chee]
跑气

purple zǐ [dzur]
紫

purse (for money) qiánbāo [chyen-bow]
钱包

(US: handbag) shǒutíbāo [shoh-tee-bow]
手提包

push tuī [tway]
推

put fàng [fahng]
放

where can I put-...? wǒ bǎ-... fàng zai nǎr? [wor bah–– dzai]
我把 ... 放在哪儿？

could you put us up for the night? wǒmen kěyi zài zhèr guò yíyè ma? [wor-mun kur-yee – jer gwor yee-yur mah]
我们可以在这儿过一夜吗？

pyjamas shuìyī [shway-yee]
睡衣

Q

quality zhìliàng [jur-lyang]
质量

quarter sì fēn zhī yī [sur fun jur yee]
四分之一

question wèntí [wun-tee]
问题

queue (noun) duì [dway]
队

quick kuài [kwai]
快

that was quick zhēn kuài [jun]
真快

what's the quickest way there? něitiáo lù zuì jìn? [nay-tyow loo zway]
哪条路最近？

quickly hěn kuài di [hun kwai]
很快的

quiet (place, hotel) ānjìng [ahn-jing]
安静

quite (fairly) xiāngdāng [hsyahng-dahng]
相当

that's quite right duì jíle [dway-jee-lur]
对极了

quite a lot xiāngdāng duō [hsyahng-dahng dwor]
相当多

R

rabbit (meat) tùzi [too-dzur]
兔子

race (for runners, cars) bǐsài [bee-sai]
比赛

racket (tennis, squash) qiúpāi [chyoh-pai]
球拍

radiator (in room) nuǎnqì [nwahn-chee]
暖器

(of car) sànrèqì [sahn-rur-chee]
散热器

radio shōuyīnjī [shoh-yin-jee]
收音机

on the radio zài shōuyīnjīlǐ [dzai – lee]
在收音机里

rail: by rail zuò huǒchē [dzwor hwor-chur]
坐火车

railway tiělù [tyeh-loo]
铁路

rain (noun) yǔ [yew]
雨

in the rain zài yǔli [dzai yew-lee]
在雨里

it's raining xià yǔ le [hsyah yew lur]
下雨了

raincoat yǔyī [yew-yee]
雨衣

rape (noun) qiángjiān [chyang-jyen]
强奸

rare (uncommon) xīyǒu [hshee-yoh]
稀有

(steak) nèn diǎnr [nun dyenr]

嫩点儿

rash (on skin) pízhěn [pee-jun]

皮疹

rat láoshǔ [low-shoo]

老鼠

rate (for changing money) duìhuànlǜ [dway-hwahn-lyew]

兑换率

rather: it's rather good búcuò [boo-tswor]

不错

I'd rather-... wǒ nìngkě... [wor ning-kur]

我宁可 ...

razor (wet) tìxúdāo [tee-hsyew-dow]

剃须刀

(electric) diàntìdāo [dyen-tee-dow]

电剃刀

razor blades tìxú dāopiàn [tee-hsyew dow-pyen]

剃须刀片

read (book) kànshū [kahn-shoo]

看书

(newspaper) kànbào [kahn-bow]

看报

ready zhǔnbèi hǎole [jun-bay how-lur]

准备好了

are you ready? zhǔnbèi hǎole ma? [mah]

准备好了吗 ?

I'm not ready yet wǒ hái

méi hǎo ne [wor hai may how nur]

我还没好呢

dialogue

when will it be ready?
(repair etc) shénme shíhou
xiūwánle? [shun-mur shur-hoh
hsyoh-wahn-lur]
it should be ready in a
couple of days liǎngtiān jiù
hǎole [lyang-tyen jyoh how-lur]

real (genuine) zhēn de [jun dur]

真的

really zhēnde [jun-dur]

真的

I'm really sorry zhēn duìbuqǐ [jun dway-boo-chee]

真对不起

that's really great bàngjíle [bahng-jee-lur]

棒极了

really? (doubt) shì ma? [shur mah]

是吗 ?

(polite interest) zhēnde ma? [mah]

真的吗 ?

reasonable (prices etc) hélǐ [hur-lee]

合理

receipt shōujù [shoh-jyew]

收据

recently zuìjìn [dzway-jin]
最近

reception (in hotel) fúwùtái [foo-woo-tai]
服务台

(for guests) zhāodàihuì [jow-dai-hway]
招待会

reception desk zǒng fúwùtái [dzoong foo-woo-tai]
总服务台

receptionist fúwùyuán [foo-woo-yew-ahn]
服务员

recognize rènshi [run-shur]
认识

recommend: could you recommend-...? qǐng nín tuījiàn-..., hǎo ma? [ching nin tway-jyen-... how mah]
请您推荐 ... 好吗 ?

red hóngsède [hoong-sur-dur]
红色的

red wine hóng pútaojiǔ [hoong poo-tow-jyoh]
红葡萄酒

refund (noun) tuìkuǎn [tway-kwahn]
退款

can I have a refund? qǐng nín ba qián tuì gěi wǒ hǎo ma? [ching nin bah chyen tway gay wor how mah]
请您把钱退给我好吗 ?

region dìqū [dee-chew]
地区

registered: by registered mail guàhàoxìn [gwah-how-hsin]
挂号信

registration number chēhào [chur-how]
车号

religion zōngjiào [dzoong-jyow]
宗教

remember: I don't remember wǒ jìbudé le [wor jee-boo-dur lur]
我记不得了

I remember wǒ jìdé [wor jee-dur]
我记得

do you remember? nǐ jìde ma? [nee jee-dur mah]
你记得吗 ?

rent (noun: for apartment etc) fángzū [fahng-dzoo]
房租

(verb: car etc) chūzū [choo-dzoo]
出租

to rent chūzū
出租

I'd like to rent a bike wǒ xiǎng zū yīliàng zìxíng chē [wor hsyahng dzoo yee-lyang dzur-hsing chur]
我想租一辆自行车

repair (verb) xiūlǐ [hsyoh-lee]
修理

can you repair it? nǐ kěyi

xiūxiu ma? [kur-yee hsyoh-hsyoh mah]

你可以修修吗？

repeat chóngfù [choong-foo]

重复

could you repeat that? qǐng nǐ zài shuō yíbiàn, hǎo ma? [ching nee dzai shwor yee-byen how mah]

请你再说一遍好吗？

reservation yùdìng [yew-ding]

预订

I'd like to make a reservation for a train ticket wǒ xiǎng yùdìng huǒchēpiào [wor hsyahng yew-ding hwor-chur-pyow]

我想预订火车票

dialogue

I have a reservation wǒ yǐjing yùdìng le [yee-jing –lur]

yes sir, what name, please? hǎo, nín guì xìng? [how nin gway hsing]

reserve (verb) yùdìng [yew-ding]

预订

dialogue

can I reserve a table for tonight? wǒ kěyi dìng ge

jīntiān wǎnshang de zuò ma? [kur-yee ding gur jin-tyen wah-shahng dur dzwor mah]

yes madam, for how many people? hǎo, yígòng jǐge rén? [how yee-goong jee-gur run]

for two liǎngge rén [lyang-gur run]

and for what time? jǐdiǎn zhōng? [jee-dyen joong]

for eight o'clock bā diǎn zhōng [bah dyen]

and could I have your name, please? hǎo, nín guì xìng? [how nin gway hsing]

rest: I need a rest wǒ xūyào xiūxi yíxià [wor hsyew-yow hsyoh-hshee yee-hsyah]

我需要休息一下

the rest of the group tāmen biéde rén [tah-mun byeh-dur]

他们别的人

restaurant cāntīng [tsahn-ting]

餐厅

(big) fàndiàn [fahn-dyen]

饭店

(small) fànguǎnr [fahn-gwahnr]

饭馆儿

(Western-style) xīcāntīng [hshee-tsahn-ting]

西餐厅

restaurant car cānchē [tsahn-

chur]
餐车

rest room cèsuǒ [tsur-swor]
厕所

retired: I'm retired wǒ tuìxiūle
[wor tway-hsyoh-lur]
我退休了

return: a return to-... dào-... de
láihui piào [dow-... dur lai-hway
pyow]
到 ... 的来回票

return ticket láihui piào
来回票

reverse charge call duìfāng
fùkuǎn [dway-fahng
foo-kwahn]
对方付款

revolting ràng rén ěxīn [rahng
run ur-hsin]
让人恶心

rice (cooked) mǐfàn [mee-fahn]
米饭

(uncooked) dàmǐ [dah-mee]
大米

rice bowl fànwǎn [fahn-wahn]
饭碗

rice field dàotián [dow-tyen]
稻田

rice wine míjiǔ [mee-jyoh]
米酒

rich (person) yǒuqián [yoh-chyen]
有钱

ridiculous kěxiàode [kur-hsyow-
dur]
可笑的

right (correct) duì [dway]
对

(not left) yòu(biānr) [yoh(-byenr)]
右（边儿）

you were right nǐ duìle [nee
dway-lur]
你对了

that's right duì le
对了

this can't be right zhè búduì
[jur boo-dway]
这不对

right! duì!
对

is this the right road for-...?
qù-..., zhème zǒu duì ma?
[chew-... jur-mur dzoh dway mah]
去 ... 这么走对吗？

on the right zài yòubiānr
[dzai]
在右边儿

turn right wǎng yòu guǎi
[wahng yoh gwai]
往右拐

ring (on finger) jièzhi [jyeh-jur]
戒指

I'll ring you wǒ géi nǐ dǎ
diànhuà [wor gay nee dah dyen-
hwah]
我给你打电话

ring back zài dǎ diànhuà [dzai]
再打电话

ripe (fruit) shú [shoo]
熟

rip-off: it's a rip-off zhè shì

qiāozhúgàng [jur shur chyow-joo-gahng]

这是敲竹杠

rip-off prices qiāozhúgàng de jiàr [chyow-joo-gahng dur jyahr]

敲竹杠的价儿

risky màoxiǎn [mow-hsyen]

冒险

river hé [hur]

河

RMB rénmínbì [run-min-bee]

人民币

road lù [loo]

路

is this the road for-...? zhèi tiáo lù wǎng ... qù? [jay tyow loo wahng ... chew]

这条路往 ... 去？

rob: I've been robbed wǒ bèi rén qiǎngle [wor bay run chyang-lur]

我被人抢了

rock yánshí [yen-shur]

岩石

(music) yáogǔn yuè [yow-gun yew-eh]

摇滚乐

on the rocks (with ice) jiā bīngkuàir [jyah bing-kwair]

加冰块儿

roll (bread) miànbāo juǎnr [myen-bow jyew-ahnr]

面包卷儿

roof fángdǐng [fahng-ding]

房顶

room (hotel) fángjiān [fahng-jyen]

房间

(space) kōngjiān [koong-jyen]

空间

in my room zài wǒ fángjiānli [dzai]

在我房间里

room service sòng fàn fúwù [soong fahn foo-woo]

送饭服务

rope shéngzi [shung-dzur]

绳子

roughly (approximately) dàyuē [dah-yew-eh]

大约

round: it's my round gāi wǒ mǎi le [gai wor mai lur]

该我买了

round trip ticket láihuí piào [lai-hway pyow]

来回票

route lùxiàn [loo-hsyen]

路线

what's the best route? něitiáo lùxiàn zuì hǎo? [nay-tyow loo-hsyen dzway how]

哪条路线最好？

rubber (material) xiàngjiāo [hsyahng-jyow]

橡胶

(eraser) xiàngpí [hsyahng-pee]

橡皮

rubbish (waste) lājī [lah-jee]

垃圾

(poor-quality goods) fèiwù
[fay-woo]

废物

rubbish! (nonsense) fèihuà! [fay-
hwah]

废话

rucksack bèibāo [bay-bow]

背包

rude bù lǐmào [lee-mow]

不礼貌

ruins fèixū [fay-hsyew]

废墟

rum lángmújiǔ [lahng-moo-
jyoh]

朗姆酒

  rum and Coke® kěkoukělè jiā
lángmújiǔ [kur-koh-kur-lur jyah
lahng-moo-jyoh]

可口可乐加朗姆酒

run (verb: person) pǎo [pow]

跑

  how often do the buses run?
gōnggòng qìchē duócháng
shíjian yítàng? [goong-goong
chee-chur dwor-chahng shur-jyen
yee-tahng]

公共汽车多长时间一
趟？

Russia Éguó [ur-gwor]

俄国

Russian (adj) Éguó

俄国

S

saddle (for horse) ānzi
[ahn- dzur]

鞍子

safe (not in danger) píng'ān

平安

  (not dangerous) ānquán [ahn-
choo-en]

安全

safety pin biézhēn [byeh-jun]

别针

sail (noun) fān [fahn]

帆

salad shālà [shah-lah]

沙拉

salad dressing shālà yóu [yoh]

沙拉油

sale: for sale chūshòu [choo-
shoh]

出售

salt yán [yahn]

盐

same: the same yíyàng [yee-
yang]

一样

  the same as this gēn zhèige
yíyàng [gun jay-gur yee-yang]

跟这个一样

  the same again, please qǐng
zài lái yíge [ching dzai lai yee-
gur]

请再来一个

  it's all the same to me wǒ wú

suǒwèi [wor woo swor-way]

我无所谓

sandals liángxié [lyang-hsyeh]

凉鞋

sandwich sānmíngzhì [sahn-ming-jur]

三明治

sanitary napkins/towels wèishēngjīn [way-shung-jin]

卫生巾

Saturday xīngqiliù [hsing-chee-lyoh]

星期六

say (verb) shuō [shwor]

说

how do you say-...-in Chinese? yòng Zhōngwén zěnme shuō-...? [yoong-joong-wun dzun-mur shwor]

用中文怎么说 ... ?

what did he say? tā shuō shénme? [tah – shun-mur]

他说什么 ?

he said tā shuō [tah]

他说

could you say that again? qǐng zài shuō yíbiān [ching dzai – yee-byen]

请再说一遍

scarf (for neck) wéijīn [way-jin]

围巾

(for head) tóujīn [toh-jin]

头巾

scenery fēngjǐng [fung-jing]

风景

schedule (US: train) lièchē shíkè biǎo [lyeh-chur shur-kur byow]

列车时刻表

scheduled flight bānjī [bahn-jee]

班机

school xuéxiào [hsyew-eh-hsyow]

学校

scissors: a pair of scissors yìbá jiǎnzi [yee-bah jyen-dzur]

一把剪子

scotch wēishìjì [way-shur-jee]

威士忌

Scotch tape® tòumíng jiāodài [toh-ming jyow-dai]

透明胶带

Scotland Sūgélán

苏格兰

Scottish Sūgélán [soo-gur-lahn]

苏格兰

I'm Scottish wǒ shi Sūgélánren [wor shur –run]

我是苏格兰人

scrambled eggs chǎo jīdàn [chow jee-dahn]

炒鸡蛋

sea hǎi

海

by the sea zài hǎibiānr [dzai hai-byenr]

在海边儿

seafood hǎiwèi [hai-way]

海味

seal (for printing name) túzhāng

[too-jahng]

图章

seasick: I feel seasick wǒ yūnchuánle [wor yewn-chwahn-lur]

我晕船了

I get seasick wǒ yūnchuán [wor yewn-chwahn]

我晕船

seat zuòwei [dzwor-way]

座位

is this seat taken? yǒu rén ma? [yoh run mah]

有人吗？

second (adj) dìèrge [dee-er-gur]

第二个

(of time) miǎo [myow]

秒

just a second! zhè jiù dé! [jur jyoh dur]

这就得

second class (travel etc) èr děng [er dung]

二等

(hard sleeper) yìngwò [ying-wor]

硬卧

second-hand jiù(de) [jyoh(-dur)]

旧（的）

see kànjian [kahn-jyen]

看见

can I see? wǒ kěyi kànkan ma? [wor kur-yee kahn-kahn mah]

我可以看看吗？

have you seen-...? nǐ

kàndàole-...-ma? [kahn-dow-lur mah]

你看到了 … 吗？

I saw him this morning wǒ jīntian zǎoshang kànjian tā le [wor jin-tyen dzow-shahng kahn-jyen tah lur]

我今天早上看见他了

see you! zàijiàn! [dzai-jyen]

再见

I see (I understand) wǒ míngbai le [wor ming-bai lur]

我明白了

self-service zìzhù [dzur-joo]

自助

sell mài

卖

do you sell-...? nǐ mài bu mài-...?

你卖不卖 … ？

Sellotape® tòumíng jiāobù [toh-ming jyow-boo]

透明胶布

send sòng [soong]

送

(by post) jì

寄

I want to send this to England wǒ xiǎng ba zhèige jì dào Yīngguó qù [wor syahng bah jay-gur jee dow ying-gwor chew]

我想把这个寄到英国去

senior citizen lǎoniánren [low-nyen-run]

老年人

separate fēnkāi [fun-kai]
分开

separately (pay, travel) fēnkāi de
分开地

September jiǔyuè [jyoh-yew-eh]
九月

serious (problem, illness)
yánzhòng(de) [yen-joong(-dur)]
严重（的）

service charge (in restaurant)
xiǎofèi [hsyow-fay]
小费

serviette cānjīn [tsahn-jin]
餐巾

set menu fènrfàn [funr-fahn]
份儿饭

several jǐge [jee-gur]
几个

sew féng [fung]
缝

could you sew this-...-back
on? qǐng nín bāng wǒ bǎ
zhèige-...-fénghuíqù, hǎo
ma? [ching nin bahng wor bah jay-
gur ... fung-hway-chew how mah]
请您帮我把这个 ... 缝回
去好吗？

sex (male/female) xìngbié [hsing-
byeh]
性别

sexy xìnggǎn [hsing-gahn]
性感

shade: in the shade zài
yīnliáng chù [dzai yin-lyang]
在阴凉处

shake: let's shake hands
wǒmen wòwo shǒu ba [wor-
mun wor-wor shoh bah]
我们握握手吧

shallow (water) qiǎn [chyen]
浅

shame: what a shame! zhēn
kěxī! [jun kur-hshee]
真可惜

shampoo (noun) xǐfàqì [hshee-
fah-chee]
洗发剂

share (verb: room, table etc)
héyòng [hur-yoong]
合用

sharp (knife) jiānruì
[jyen-rway]
尖锐

(pain) ruì [rway]
锐

shaver diàndòng tìxū dāo
[dyen-doong tee-hsyew dow]
电动剃须刀

shaving foam guā hú pàomò
[gwah hoo pow-mor]
刮胡泡沫

shaving point diàntìdāo
chāxiāo [dyen-tee-dow chah-
hsyow]
电剃刀插销

she* tā [tah]
她

is she here? tā zài ma? [dzai
mah]
她在吗？

sheet (for bed) bèidān [bei-dahn]
被单

shelf jiàzi [jyah-dzur]
架子

shellfish bèilèi [bay-lay]
贝类

ship chuán [chwahn]
船

by ship zuò chuán [dzwor]
坐船

shirt chènyī [chun-yee]
衬衣

shock: I got an electric shock from the-...-wǒ pèngzhe...-ér chùdiàn [wor pung-jur – dyen]
我碰着 ... 而触电

shocking jīngrénde [jing-run-dur]
惊人的

shoe xié [hsyeh]
鞋

a pair of shoes yìshuāng xié [yee-shwahng]
一双鞋

shoelaces xiédài [hsyeh-dai]
鞋带

shoe polish xiéyóu [hsyeh-yoh]
鞋油

shoe repairer xiūxiéjiàng [hsyoh-hsyeh-jyang]
修鞋匠

shop shāngdiàn [shahng-dyen]
商店

shopping: I'm going shopping wǒ qù mǎi dōngxi [wor chew mai doong-hshee]
我去买东西

shore (of sea, lake) àn [ahn]
岸

short (person) ǎi [ai]
矮

(time, journey) duǎn [dwahn]
短

shorts duǎnkù [dwahn-koo]
短裤

should: what should I do? wǒ gāi zěnme bàn? [wor gai dzun-mur bahn]
我该怎么办？

you should-...-nǐ yīnggāi-...-[ying-gai]
你应该 ...

you shouldn't-...-nǐ bù yīnggāi-...
你不应该 ...

he should be back soon guò yíhuìr, tā yīng zài huílai [gwor yee-hwayr tah ying dzai hway-lai]
过一回儿他应再回来

shoulder jiānbǎng [jyen-bahng]
肩膀

shout (verb) hǎn [hahn]
喊

show (in theatre) biǎoyǎn [byow-yahn]
表演

could you show me? nǐ néng ràng wǒ kànkan ma? [nung

rahng wor kahn-kahn mah]

你能让我看看吗？

shower (of rain) zhènyǔ [jun-yew]

阵雨

(in bathroom) línyù [lin-yew]

淋浴

with shower dài línyù

带淋浴

shrine shénkān [shun-kahn]

神龛

shut (verb) guān [gwahn]

关

when do you shut? nǐmen jídiǎn guānménr? [nee-mun jee-dyen gwahn-munr]

你们几点关门儿？

when does it shut? jídiǎn guānménr? [jee-dyen]

几点关门儿？

they're shut guānménr le [lur]

关门儿了

I've shut myself out wǒ bǎ zìjǐ guān zài wàitou le [wor bah dzur-jee gwahn dzai wai-toh lur]

我把自己关在外头了

shut up! zhù zuǐ! [joo dzway]

住嘴

shy hàixiū [hai-hsyoh]

害羞

sick (ill) yǒubìng [yoh-bing]

有病

I'm going to be sick (vomit) wǒ yào ǒutù [wor yow oh-too]

我要呕吐

side: the other side of the street zài jiē duìmian [dzai jyeh dway-myen]

在街对面

sidewalk rénxíng dào [run-hsing dow]

人行道

sight: the sights of-...--...-de fēngjǐng [fung-jing]

... 的风景

sightseeing: we're going sightseeing wǒmen qù yóulǎn [wor-mun chew yoh-lahn]

我们去游览

silk sīchóu [sur-choh]

丝绸

Silk Road sīchóu zhī lù [jur]

丝绸之路

silly chǔn

蠢

silver (noun) yín(zi) [yin-dzur]

银（子）

similar xiāngjìn de [hsyahng-jin dur]

相近

simple (easy) jiǎndān [jyen-dahn]

简单

since: since last week zìcóng shàngge xīngqī yǐlái [dzur-tsoong shahng-gur hsing-chee yee-lai]

自从上个星期以来

since I got here zìcóng wǒ lái yǐhòu [dzur-tsoong wor lai yee-hoh]

自从我来以后

sing chànggē [chahng-gur]

唱歌

Singapore Xīnjiāpō [hsin-jyah-por]

新加坡

singer gēchàngjiā [gur-chahng-jyah]

歌唱家

single: a single to-...-yìzhāng qù-...-de dānchéngpiào [yee-jahng chew-...-dur dahn-chung-pyow]

一张去 ... 的单程票

I'm single wǒ shì dúshēn [wor shur dahn-shun]

我是独身

single bed dānrén chuáng [dahn-run chwahng]

单人床

single room dānrén jiān [jyen]

单人间

single ticket (dānchéng) piào [pyow]

（单程）票

sink (in kitchen) shuǐchí [shway-chur]

水池

sister (elder) jiějie [jyeh-jyeh]

姐姐

(younger) mèimei [may-may]

妹妹

sit: can I sit here? wǒ kěyǐ zuò zhèr ma? [wor kur-yee dzwor

jer mah]

我可以坐这儿吗？

is anyone sitting here? yǒu rén zài zhèr ma? [yoh run]

有人在这儿吗？

sit down zuòxià [dzwor-hsyah]

坐下

sit down! qǐng zuò! [ching]

请坐

size chǐcùn [chur-tsun]

尺寸

skin (human) pífu

皮肤

(animal) pí

皮

skinny shòu [shoh]

瘦

skirt qúnzi [chewn-dzur]

裙子

sky tiān [tyen]

天

sleep (verb) shuìjiào [shway-jyow]

睡觉

did you sleep well? nǐ shuì de hǎo ma? [shway dur how mah]

你睡得好吗？

sleeper (on train) wòpù [wor-poo]

卧铺

(soft) ruǎnwò [rwahn-wor]

软卧

(hard) yìngwò [ying-wor]

硬卧

sleeping bag shuìdài [shwaydai]

睡袋

sleeping car wòpù chēxiāng [wor-poo chur-hsyahng]

卧铺车厢

sleeve xiùzi [hsyoh-dzur]

袖子

slide (photographic) huàndēngpiānr [hwahn-dung-pyenr]

幻灯片儿

slip (garment) chènqún [chun-chewn]

衬裙

slow màn [mahn]

慢

slow down! màn diǎnr! [dyenr]

慢点儿

slowly màn

慢

very slowly hěn màn [hun]

很慢

small xiǎo [hsyow]

小

smell: it smells (bad) yǒu wèir le [yoh wayr lur]

有味儿了

smile (verb) xiào [hsyow]

笑

smoke (noun) yān [yahn]

烟

do you mind if I smoke? wǒ kěyǐ zài zhèr chōu yān ma? [wor kur-yee dzai jer choh yahn mah]

我可以在这儿抽烟吗？

I don't smoke wǒ bú huì chōu yān [hway]

我不会抽烟

do you smoke? nǐ chōu yān ma?

你抽烟吗？

snack diǎnxīn [dyen-hsin]

点心

sneeze (noun) dǎ pēntì [da pun-tee]

打喷嚏

snow (noun) xuě [hsyew-eh]

雪

so: it's so good nàme [nah-mur]

那么好

it's so expensive nàme guì

那么贵

not so much méi nàme duō [may – dwor]

没那么多

not so bad méi nàme huài

没那么坏

so-so búguò rúcǐ [boo-gwor roo-tsur]

不过如此

soap féizào [fay-dzow]

肥皂

soap powder xǐyīfěn [hshee-yee-fun]

洗衣粉

sock duǎnwà [dwahn-wah]

短袜

socket chāzuò [chah-dzwor]

插座

soda (water) sūdá [soo-dah]

苏打

sofa shāfā [shah-fah]

沙发

soft (material etc) ruǎn [rwahn]

软

soft drink qìshuǐr

[chee-shwayr]

汽水儿

soft seat ruǎnzuò

[rwahn-dzwor]

软座

sole (of shoe) xiédǐ [hsyeh-dee]

鞋底

(of foot) jiáodǐ [jyow-dee]

脚底

could you put new soles on
these? qǐng nín huàn shuāng
xīn xiédǐ, hǎo ma? [ching nin
hwahn shwahng hsin – how mah]

请你换双新鞋底好吗？

some: can I have some water?
qǐng lái yídiǎnr shuǐ, hǎo ma?
[ching lai yee-dyenr – how mah]

请来一点儿水好吗？

can I have some apples?
qǐng lái yíxiē píngguǒ, hǎo
ma? [yee-hsyeh]

请来一些苹果好吗？

somebody, someone mǒurén
[moh-run]

某人

something mǒushì [moh-shur]

某事

I want something to eat wǒ

xiǎng chī diǎn dōngxī [wor
hsyahng chur dyen doong-hshee]

我想吃点东西

sometimes yǒushíhhou [yoh-
shur-hoh]

有时候

somewhere mǒudì [moh-dee]

某地

I need somewhere to stay wǒ
yào zhǎoge zhùchù [wor yow
jow-gur]

我要找个住处

son érzi [er-dzur]

儿子

song gē [gur]

歌

son-in-law nǔxu [nyoo-hsoo]

女婿

soon (after a while) yìhuǐr [yee-
hwayr]

一会儿

(quickly) kuài [kwai]

快

I'll be back soon wǒ yìhuǐr
jiù huílai [wor yee-hwayr jyoh
hway-lai]

我一会儿就回来

as soon as possible yuè kuài
yuè hǎo [yew-eh – how]

越快越好

sore: it's sore téng [tung]

疼

sore throat sǎngzǐténg [sahng-
dzur-tung]

嗓子疼

sorry: (I'm) sorry duìbuqǐ
[dway-boo-chee]
对不起

sorry? (didn't understand) nǐ
shuō shénme? [shwor shun-mur]
你说什么？

sort: what sort of-...? shénme
yàng de-...? [dur]
什么样的 ... ？

soup tāng [tahng]
汤

sour (taste) suān [swahn]
酸

south nán [nahn]
南

  in the south nánfāng [nahn-
  fahng]
  南方

South Africa Nánfēi [nahn-fay]
南非

South African (adj) Nánfēi
南非

  I'm South African wǒ shì
  Nánfēirén [wor shur –run]
  我是南非人

South China Sea Nánhǎi
[nahn-haï]
南海

southeast dōngnán [doong-
nahn]
东南

southern nánde [nahn-dur]
南的

South Korea nán Cháoxiān
[nahn chow-hsyen]

南朝鲜

southwest xīnán [hsin-ahn]
西南

souvenir jìniànpǐn
[jin-yen-pin]
纪念品

soy sauce jiàngyóu [jyahn-gyoh]
酱油

Spain Xībānyá [hshee-bahn-yah]
西班牙

Spanish (adj) Xībānyáde [hshee-
bahn-yah-dur]
西班牙的

speak: do you speak English?
nín huì jiǎng Yīngyǔ ma?
[hway jyang ying-yew mah]
您会讲英语吗？

I don't speak-...-wǒ búhuì
jiǎng-...-[wor boo-hway]
我不会讲 ...

can I speak to-...? (in person)
máfan nín zhǎo yíxia ... hǎo
ma? [mah-fahn nin jow yee-
hsyah-...-how]
麻烦您找一下 ... 好吗？

dialogue

can I speak to Mr Wang?
Wáng xiānsheng zàibúzài?
[hsyahng-shung dzai-boo-dzai]
who's calling? nǐ shì
nǎwéi? [shur nar-way]
it's Patricia wǒ shì Patricia
[wor]

I'm sorry, he's not in, can I take a message? duìbuqǐ, tā búzài, yàobúyào liú gexìn? [dway-boo-chee tah boo-dzai yow-boo-yow lyoh gur-hsin]

no thanks, I'll call back later xièxie, guò yíhuìr wǒ zài dǎ [hsyeh-hsyeh gwor yee-hwayr wor dzai dah]

please tell him I called qǐng gàosu tā wǒ dǎ le diànhuà [ching gow-soo tah wor dah lur dyen-hwah]

spectacles yǎnjìng [yenjing]
眼镜

spend huāfèi [hwah-fay]
花费

spoke (in wheel) fútiáo [foo-tyow]
辐条

spoon sháozi [show-dzur]
勺子

sport yùndòng [yewn-doong]
运动

sprain: I've sprained my-...-wǒde ... niǔ le [wor-dur-... nyoh lur]
我的 ... 扭了

spring (season) chūntiān [chun-tyen]
春天

in the spring chūntian
春天

square (in town) guángchǎng

[gwahng-chahng]
广场

stairs lóutī [loh-tee]
楼梯

stamp (noun) yóupiào [yoh-pyow]
邮票

dialogue

a stamp for England, please mǎi yìzhāng jì Yīngguó de yóupiào [mai yee-jahng jee ying-gwor dur]
what are you sending? nǐ jì shénme? [shun-mur]
this postcard zhèizhāng míngxìnpiàn [jay-jahng ming-hsin-pyen]

star xīngxing [hsing-hsing]
星星

start kāishǐ [kai-shur]
开始

when does it start? jǐdiǎn kāishǐ? [jee-dyen]
几点开始？

the car won't start chē fādòngbùqǐlái [chur fah-doong-boo-chee-lai]
车发动不起来

starter (food) lěngpánr [lung-pahnr]
冷盘儿

station (train) huǒchē zhàn

[hwor-chur jahn]

火车站

(city bus) qìchē zǒng zhàn
[chee-chur dzoong]

汽车总站

(long-distance bus) chángtú
qìchēzhàn [chahng-too chee-
chur-jahn]

长途汽车站

(underground) dì tiě zhàn [tyeh
jahn]

地铁站

statue sùxiàng [soo-hsyahng]

塑像

stay: where are you staying?
nǐmen zhù zài nǎr? [nee-mun
joo dzai nar]

你们住在哪儿？

I'm staying at-...-wǒ zhù
zài-...-[wor joo dzai]

我住在 ...

I'd like to stay another two
nights wǒ xiǎng zài zhù liǎng
tiān [syahng dzai joo]

我想再住两天

steak niúpái [nyoh-pai]

牛排

steal tōu [toh]

偷

my bag has been stolen
wǒde bāo bèi tōule [wor-dur
bow bay toh-lur]

我的包被偷了

steamed zhēng [jung]

蒸

steamed roll huājuǎnr [hwah-
jwahnr]

花卷儿

steep (hill) dǒu [doh]

陡

step: on the steps zài táijiē
shang [dzai tai-jyeh shahng]

在台阶上

stereo lìtǐshēng [lee-tee-shung]

立体声

Sterling yīngbàng [ying-bahng]

英镑

steward (on plane) fúwùyuán
[nahn foo-woo-yew-ahn]

服务员

stewardess kōngzhōng
xiáojiě [koong-joong hsyow-jyeh]

空中小姐

still: I'm still here wǒ hái zài
[wor hai dzai]

我还在

is he still there? tā hái zài ma?
[tah – mah]

他还在吗？

keep still! bié dòng! [byeh
doong]

别动

sting: I've been stung wǒ gěi
zhēle [wor gay jur-lur]

我给蜇了

stockings chángtǒngwà
[chahng-toong-wah]

长统袜

stomach wèi [way]

胃

stomach ache wèiténg [way-tung]

胃疼

stone (rock) shítou [shur-toh]

石头

stop (verb) tíng

停

please, stop here (to taxi driver etc) qǐng tíng zài zhèr [ching ting dzai jer]

请停在这儿

do you stop near-...? zài-...-fùjìn tíng ma? [mah]

在 ... 附近停吗？

stop it! tíngzhǐ! [ting-jur]

停止

storm bàofēngyǔ [bow-fung-yew]

暴风雨

straight (whisky etc) chún

纯

it's straight ahead yìzhí cháoqián [yee-jur chow-chyen]

一直朝前

straightaway mǎshàng [mah-shahng]

马上

strange (odd) qíguài de [chee-gwai dur]

奇怪的

stranger shēngrén [shun-grun]

生人

strap dàir

带儿

strawberry cǎoméi [tsow-may]

草莓

stream xiǎoxī [hsyow-hshee]

小溪

street jiē(dào) [jyeh(-dow)]

街（道）

on the street zài jiēshang [dzai jyeh-shahng]

在街上

streetmap jiāotōngtú [jyow-toong-too]

交通图

string shéngzi [shung-dzur]

绳子

strong (person) qiángzhuàng [chyang-jwahng]

强壮

(material) jiēshi [jyeh-shur]

结实

(drink, taste) nóng [noong]

浓

stuck: it's stuck kǎle [kah-lur]

卡了

student xuésheng [hsyew-eh-shung]

学生

stupid bèn [bun]

笨

suburb jiāoqū [jyow-chew]

郊区

subway (US) dìtiě [dee-tyeh]

地铁

suddenly tūrán [too-rahn]

突然

sugar táng [tahng]
糖

suit (noun) tàozhuāng [tow-jwahng]
套装

it doesn't suit me (jacket etc) wǒ chuān bù héshì [wor chwahn boo hur-shur]
我穿不合适

it suits you nǐ chuān héshì
你穿合适

suitcase shǒutíxiāng [shoh-tee-hsyahng]
手提箱

summer xiàtian [hsyah-tyen]
夏天

in the summer xiàtian
夏天

sun tàiyáng
太阳

sunbathe shài tàiyáng
晒太阳

sunblock (cream) fángshàirǔ [fahng-shai-roo]
防晒乳

sunburn rìzhì [rur-shur]
日炙

Sunday xīngqītiān [hsing-chee-tyen]
星期天

sunglasses tàiyángjìng [tai-yang-jing]
太阳镜

sunny: it's sunny yángguāng chōngzú [yang-gwahng choong-dzoo]
阳光充足

sunset rìluò [rur-lwor]
日落

sunshine yángguāng [yang-gwahng]
阳光

sunstroke zhòngshǔ [joong-shoo]
中暑

suntan lotion fángshài jì [fahng-shai]
防晒剂

suntan oil fángshàiyóu [–yoh]
防晒油

super hǎojíle [how-jee-lur]
好极了

supermarket chāojí shìchǎng [chow-jee shur-chahng]
超级市场

supper wǎnfàn [wahn-fahn]
晚饭

supplement (extra charge) fùjiāfèi [foo-jyah-fay]
附加费

sure: are you sure? zhēnde ma? [jun dur mah]
真的吗？

sure! dāngrán! [dahn-grahn]
当然

surname xìng [hsing]
姓

swearword zāngzìr [dzahng-

dzur]
脏字儿

sweater máoyī [mow-yee]
毛衣

sweatshirt (chángxiù) hànshān [chahng-hsyoh hahn-shahn]
（长袖）汗衫

Sweden Ruìdiǎn [rway-dyen]
瑞典

Swedish (adj) Ruìdiǎnyǔ
瑞典语

sweet (taste) tián [tyen]
甜

(noun: dessert) tiánshí [tyen-shur]
甜食

sweets tángguǒ [tahng-gwor]
糖果

swim (verb) yóuyǒng [yoh-yoong]
游泳

I'm going for a swim wǒ qù yóuyǒng [wor chew yoh-yoong]
我去游泳

let's go for a swim zánmen qù yóuyǒng ba [zahn-mun]
咱们去游泳吧

swimming costume yóuyǒngyī [yoh-yoong-yee]
游泳衣

swimming pool yóuyǒng chí [chur]
游泳池

swimming trunks yóuyǒngkù

[yoh-yoong-koo]
游泳裤

switch (noun) kāiguān [kai-gwahn]
开关

switch off guān [gwahn]
关

switch on kāi [kai]
开

swollen zhǒng [joong]
肿

T

table zhuōzi [jwor-dzur]
桌子

a table for two liǎngrén zhuō [lyang-run]
两人桌

tablecloth zhuōbù [jwor-boo]
桌布

table tennis pīngpāngqiú [ping-pahng-chyoh]
乒乓球

tailor cáifeng [tsai-fung]
裁缝

Taiwan Táiwān [tai-wahn]
台湾

Taiwanese (adj) Táiwān(de) [–dur]
台湾（的）

take ná [nah]
拿

(somebody somewhere) lǐng

领

(something somewhere) dài

带

(accept) jiēshòu [jyeh-shoh]

接受

can you take me to the-...?
qǐng dài wǒ dào-...? [ching dai wor dow]

请带我到 … ？

do you take credit cards? nǐ shòu xìnyòngkǎ ma? [shoh hsin-yoong-kah mah]

你受信用卡吗？

fine, I'll take it hǎo, xíngle [how hsing-lur]

好行了

can I take this? (leaflet etc) kěyi ná ma? [kur-yee nah]

可以拿吗？

how long does it take? yào duōcháng shíjiān? [yow dwor-chahng shur-jyen]

要多长时间？

it takes three hours yào sānge zhōngtóu [yow sahng-gur joong-toh]

要三个钟头

is this seat taken? zhèr yǒu rén ma? [jer yoh run mah]

这儿有人吗？

talk (verb) shuōhuà [shwor-hwah]

说话

tall gāo [gow]

高

tampons wèishēngjīn [way-shung-jin]

卫生巾

tap shuǐlóng tóu [shway-loong toh]

水龙头

tape (cassette) cídài [tsur-dai]

磁带

taste (noun) wèir [wayr]

味儿

can I taste it? kěyǐ chángchang ma? [kur-yee chahng-chahng mah]

可以尝尝吗？

taxi chūzū qìchē [choo-dzoo chee-chur]

出租汽车

will you get me a taxi? qǐng nín bāng wǒ jiào liàng chūzūchē, hǎo ma? [ching nin bahng wor jyow lyang choo-dzoo-chur how mah]

请您帮我叫辆出租车好吗？

where can I find a taxi? zài nǎr kěyǐ zhǎodao chūzū qìchē? [dzai nar kur-yee jow-dow]

在哪儿可以找到出租汽车？

dialogue

to the airport/to the Xian Hotel, please qǐng dài

151

wǒ dào fēijīchǎng/Xiān
fàndiàn [dow –
fay-jee-chahng]

how much will it be?
duōshao qián? [dwor-show
chyen]

30 yuan sānshí kuài qián
[sahn-shur kwai]

**that's fine right here,
thanks** jiù zài zhèr, xièxie
[jyoh dzai jer hsyeh-hsyeh]

taxi driver chūzū sījī [choo-dzoo
sur-jee]
出租司机
taxi rank chūzūchē diǎnr
[dyenr]
出租车点儿
tea (drink) chá [chah]
茶
tea for one/two, please qǐng
lái yí/liǎngge rén de chá [ching
– run dur]
请来一／两个人的茶
teach: could you teach me?
nín kěyi jiāojiao wǒ ma? [kur-
yee jyow-jyow wor mah]
您可以教教我吗？
teacher lǎoshī [low-shur]
老师
team duì [dway]
队
teaspoon cháchí [chah-chur]
茶匙
tea towel cāwǎnbù [tsah-wahn-

boo]
擦碗布
teenager qīngshàonián [ching-
show-nyen]
青少年
telegram diànbào
[dyen-bow]
电报
telephone diànhuà [dyen-
hwah]
电话
see **phone**
television diànshì [dyen-shur]
电视
tell: could you tell him-...?
qǐng nín gàosu tā-..., hǎo ma?
[ching nin gow-soo tah-...-how
mah]
请您告诉他 ... 好吗？
temperature (weather) qìwēn
[chee-wun]
气温
(fever) fāshāo [fah-show]
发烧
temple (Buddhist) sì [sur]
寺
(Taoist) guàn [gwahn]
观
tennis wǎngqiú [wahng-
chyoh]
网球
term (at university, school) xuéqī
[hsyew-eh-chee]
学期
terminus (rail) zhōngdiǎnzhàn

[joong-dyen-jahn]
终点站
terrible zāogāo [dzow-gow]
糟糕
that's terrible tài zāogāo le
[lur]
太糟糕了
terrific bàngjíle [bahng-jee-lur]
棒极了
text (message) duǎnxìn
[dwahn-hsin]
短信
Thailand Tàiguó [tai-gwor]
泰国
than* bǐ
比
even more-...-than-...-bǐ-...
-gèngduō [gung-...-dwor]
比 ... 更多
smaller than bǐ-...-xiǎo
[hsyow]
比 ... 小
thank: thank you xièxie [hsyeh-hsyeh]
谢谢
thank you very much fēicháng
gǎnxiè [fay-chahng gahn-hsyeh]
非常感谢
thanks for the lift xièxie nín
ràng wǒ dāle chē [rahng wor
dah-lur chur]
谢谢您让我搭了车
no, thanks xièxie, wǒ bú yào
[boo yow]
谢谢我不要

dialogue

thanks xièxie
that's OK, don't mention it
bú kèqi [kur chee]

that* nèige [nay-gur]
那个
that one nèi yíge [yee-gur]
那一个
I hope that-...-wǒ
xīwàng-...-[wor hshee-wahng]
我希望 ...
that's nice nà zhèng hǎo
[nah jung-how]
那正好
is that-...? nà shì-...-ma?
[shur-...-mah]
那是 ... 吗？
that's it (that's right) duìle
[dway-lur]
对了
the*
theatre jùyuàn
[jyew-yew-ahn]
剧院
their/theirs* tāmende [tah-mun-dur]
他们的
them* tāmen [tah-mun]
他们
then (at that time) nèi shíhou
[nay shur-hoh]
那时候

(after that) ránhòu [rahn-hoh]
然后

there nàr
那儿

over there zài nàr [dzai]
在那儿

up there zài shàngtou [dzai shahng-toh]
在上头

is/are there-...? yǒu-...-ma? [yoh-...-mah]
有 ... 吗？

there is/are-...-yǒu-...
有 ...

there you are (giving something) gěi nǐ [gay]
给你

Thermos® flask rèshuǐpíng [rush-way-ping]
热水瓶

these* zhèixie [jay-hsyeh]
这些

they* tāmen [tahmun]
他们

thick hòu [hoh]
厚

(stupid) bèn [bun]
笨

thief zéi [dzay]
贼

thigh dàtuǐ [dah-tway]
大腿

thin (person) shòu [shoh]
瘦

(object) xì [hshee]
细

thing (matter) shìr [shur]
事儿

(object) dōngxi [doong-hshee]
东西

my things wǒde dōngxi
我的东西

think xiǎng [hsyahng]
想

I think so wǒ xiǎng shì zhèiyang [wor hsyahng shur jay-yang]
我想是这样

I don't think so wǒ bú zhèiyang xiǎng [jay-yang]
我不这样想

I'll think about it wǒ kǎolǜ yíxia [kow-lyew yee-hsyah]
我考虑一下

third class sānděng [sahn-dung]
三等

(hard seat) yìngzuò [ying-dzwor]
硬座

thirsty: I'm thirsty wǒ kǒukě [wor koh-kur]
我口渴

this* zhèige [jay-gur]
这个

this one zhèige
这个

this is my wife zhè shì wǒ qīzi [jur shur wor chee-dzur]
这是我妻子

154

is this-...? zhèi shìbúshì-...?
[shur-boo-shur]

这是不是 ... ？

those* nèixie [nay-hsyeh]

那些

thread (noun) xiàn [hsyen]

线

throat sǎngzi [sahng-dzur]

嗓子

throat lozenges rùnhóu piàn
[run-hoh pyen]

润喉片

through jīngguò [jing-gwor]

经过

does it go through-...? (train,
bus) jīngguò-...-ma? [mah]

经过 ... 吗 ？

throw/throw away rēng
[rung]

扔

thumb dàmúzhǐ [dah-moo-jur]

大拇指

thunderstorm léiyǔ [lay-yew]

雷雨

Thursday xīngqīsì [hsing-chee-
sur]

星期四

Tibet Xīzàng [hshee-dzahng]

西藏

Tibetan (adj) Xīzàngde [hshee-
dzahng]

西藏的

ticket piào [pyow]

票

a return to Xian wǎng Xīān
de láihuí piào [wahng – dur
lai-hway]

coming back when?
nèitiān yào huílái? [shur nay-
tyen yow]

today/next Tuesday
jīntian/xiàge xīngqīer

that will be 30 yuan sānshí
kuài qián [chyen]

ticket office (bus, rail)
shòupiàochù [shoh-pyow-choo]

售票处

tie (necktie) lǐngdài

领带

tight (clothes etc) xiǎo [hsyow]

小

it's too tight tài xiǎo le [lur]

太小了

tights liánkùwà [lyen-koo-wah]

连裤袜

time* shíjiān [shur-jyen]

时间

what's the time? jǐdiǎn le?
[jee-dyen lur]

几点了 ？

this time zhèicì [jay-tsur]

这次

last time shàngcì [shahng-tsur]

上次

next time xiàcì [hsyah]

下次

three times sāncì
三次

timetable (train) lièchē shíkè
biǎo [lyeh-chur shur-kur byow]
列车时刻表

tin (can) guàntou [gwahn-toh]
罐头

tinfoil xīzhǐ [hshee-jur]
锡纸

tin-opener guàntou qǐzi
[gwahn-toh chee-dzur]
罐头起子

tiny yìdiánrdiǎnr [yee-dyenr-
dyenr]
一点儿点儿

tip (to waiter etc) xiǎo fèi [hsyow
fay]
小费

tire (US) lúntāi [lun-tai]
轮胎

tired lèi [lay]
累

I'm tired wǒ lèi le [wor lay lur]
我累了

tissues zhǐjīn [jur-jin]
纸巾

to*: to Shanghai/London dào
Shànghǎi/Lúndūn [dow]
到上海／伦敦

to China/England qù
Zhōngguó/Yīnggélán [chew]
去中国／英格兰

to the post office qù yóujú
去邮局

toast (bread) kǎo miànbāo [kow

myen-bow]
烤面包

today jīntian [jin-tyen]
今天

toe jiáozhǐtou [jyow-jur-toh]
脚指头

together yìqǐ [yee-chee]
一起

we're together (in shop etc)
wǒmen shì yíkuàir de [wor-
mun shur yee-kwair dur]
我们是一块儿的

toilet cèsuǒ [tsur-swor]
厕所

where is the toilet? cèsuǒ zài
nǎr? [dzai]
厕所在哪儿？

I have to go to the toilet wǒ
děi qù fāngbian fāngbian [wor
day chew fahng-byen]
我得去方便方便

toilet paper wèishēngzhǐ [way-
shung-jee]
卫生纸

tomato xīhóngshì [hshee-hoong-
shur]
西红柿

tomato juice fānqié zhī [fahn-
chyeh jur]
番茄汁

tomorrow míngtian [ming-tyen]
明天

tomorrow morning míngtian
zǎoshang [dzow-shahng]
明天早上

the day after tomorrow
hòutian [hoh-tyen]
后天

tongue shétou [shur-toh]
舌头

tonic (water) kuàngquánshuǐ
[kwahng-choo-en-shway]
矿泉水

tonight jīntian wǎnshang [jin-
tyen wahn-shahng]
今天晚上

too (also) yě [yur]
也

(excessively) tài
太

too hot tài rè [rur]
太热

too much tài duō [dwor]
太多

me too wǒ yě [wor]
我也

tooth yá [yah]
牙

toothache yáténg [yah-tung]
牙疼

toothbrush yáshuā [yah-shwah]
牙刷

toothpaste yágāo [yah-gow]
牙膏

top: on top of-... -zài ...
shàngtou [dzai-...-shahng-toh]
在 ... 上头

at the top zài dǐngshang [ding-
shahng]
在顶上

torch shǒudiàntǒng [shoh-dyen-
toong]
手电筒

total (noun) zǒnggòng [dzoong-
goong]
总共

tour (noun) lǚxíng [lyew-hsing]
旅行

is there a tour of-...? yǒu
méiyou wǎng-...-de lǚxíng?
[yoh may-yoh wahng-...-dur]
有没有往 ... 的旅行？

tour guide dǎoyóu [dow-yoh]
导游

tourist lǚyóu zhě [lyew-yoh jur]
旅游者

tour operator lǚxíng shè [lyew-
hsing shur]
旅行社

towards cháozhe [chow-jur]
朝着

towel máojīn [mow-jin]
毛巾

town chéngzhèn [chung-jun]
城镇

in town (zài) chéngli [(dzai)
chung-lee]
（在）城里

out of town (zài) chéngwài
[chung-wai]
（在）城外

town centre shì zhōngxīn [shur
joong-hsin]
市中心

town hall shì zhèngfǔ dàlóu

〖shur-jung-foo〗

市政府大楼

toy wánjù 〖wahn-jyew〗

玩具

track (US) zhàntái 〖jahn-tai〗

站台

tracksuit yùndòngfú 〖yewn-doong-foo〗

运动服

traditional chuántǒng 〖chwahn-toong〗

传统

train huǒchē 〖hwor-chur〗

火车

by train zuò huǒchē 〖dzwor hwor-chur〗

坐火车

dialogue

is this the train for Shanghai? zhèliè huǒchē qù Shànghǎi ma? 〖jur-lyeh hwor-chur chew – mah〗

sure qù 〖chew〗

no, you want that platform there búqù, nǐ yào dào nèige zhàntái qù 〖boo-chew nee yow dow nay-gur jahn-tai〗

trainers (shoes) lǚyóuxié 〖lyew-yoh-hsyeh〗

旅游鞋

train station huǒchēzhàn

〖hwor-chur-jahn〗

火车站

tram yǒuguǐ diànchē 〖yoh-gway dyen-chur〗

有轨电车

translate fānyì 〖fahn-yee〗

翻译

could you translate that?

qǐng nín fānyì yíxia, hǎo ma? 〖ching nin fahn-yee yee-hsyah how mah〗

请您翻译一下好吗？

translator fānyì 〖fahn-yee〗

翻译

trash lājī 〖lah-jee〗

垃圾

travel lǚxíng 〖lyew-hsing〗

旅行

we're travelling around

wǒmen zài lǚxíng 〖wor-mun dzai lyew-hsing〗

我们在旅行

travel agent's lǚxíngshè 〖lyew-hsing-shur〗

旅行社

traveller's cheque lǚxíng zhīpiào 〖lyew-hsing jur-pyow〗

旅行支票

tray chápán 〖chah-pahn〗

茶盘

tree shù 〖shoo〗

树

trim: just a trim, please (to hairdresser) qǐng zhǐ xiūxiu biānr 〖ching jur hsyoh-hsyoh byenr]

请只修修边儿

trip: I'd like to go on a trip
to-...-wǒ xiǎng dào-...-qù
[wor hsyahng dow-...-chew]

我想到 ... 去

trouble (noun) máfan [mah-fahn]

麻烦

I'm having trouble with-...-w
ǒde-...-yùdàole diǎnr máfan
[wor-duh-... yew-dow-lur dyenr]

我的 ... 遇到了点儿麻烦

trousers kùzi [koo-dzur]

裤子

true zhēnde [jun-dur]

真的

that's not true bú duì [dway]

不对

trunk (US: of car) xínglixiāng
[hsing-lee-hsyahng]

行李箱

trunks (swimming) yóuyǒngkù
[yoh-yoong-koo]

游泳裤

try (verb) shì [shur]

试

can I try it? kěyi shìyishì ma?
[kur-yee shur-yee-shur mah]

可以试一试吗？

try on: can I try it on? kěyi
shìyishì ma?

可以试一试吗？

T-shirt T xùshān [tee hsoo
shahn]

T 恤衫

Tuesday xīngqièr [hsing-chee-
er]

星期二

tunnel suīdào [sway-dow]

隧道

turn: turn left wǎng zuó guǎi
[wahng dzwor gwai]

往左拐

turn right wǎng yòu guǎi

往右拐

turn off: where do I turn off?
wǒ děi zài nǎr guǎiwān? [wor
day dzai nar gwai-wahn]

我得在哪儿拐弯？

can you turn the heating off?
qǐng ba nuǎnqì guānshang
[ching bah nwahn-chee-gwahn-
shahng]

请把暖器关上？

turn on: can you turn the
heating on? qǐng ba nuǎnqì
dǎkāi yíxià [dah-kai
yee-hsyah]

请把暖器打开一下？

turning (in road) zhuǎnwānr
[jwahn-wahnr]

转弯儿

TV diànshì [dyen-shur]

电视

twice liǎngcì [lyang-tsur]

两次

twice as much duō yíbèi
[dwor yee-bay]

多一倍

twin beds liǎngge

dānrénchuáng 〖lyang-gur dahn-run-chwahng〗

两个单人床

twin room shuāngrén fángjiān 〖shwahng-run fahng-jyen〗

双人房间

twist: I've twisted my ankle wǒde jiǎobózi niǔle 〖wor-dur jyow-bor-dzur nyoh-lur〗

我的脚脖子扭了

type (noun) zhǒng 〖joong〗

种

another type of-...-lìng yìzhǒng-...-〖ling yee-joong〗

另一种 ...

typical diǎnxíng 〖dyen-hsing〗

典型

tyre lúntāi

轮胎

U

ugly nánkàn 〖nahn-kahn〗

难看

UK Yīngguó 〖ying-gwor〗

英国

umbrella yǔsǎn 〖yew-sahn〗

雨伞

uncle (father's elder brother) bófù

伯父

(father's younger brother) shūshu 〖shoo-shoo〗

叔叔

(mother's brother) jiùjiu 〖jyoh-

jyoh〗

舅舅

under-...-(in position) zài-...-xià 〖dzai-...-hsyah〗

在 ... 下

(less than) shǎoyú-...-〖show-yew〗

... 少于

underdone (meat) bàn shēng bù shú 〖bahn shung boo shoo〗

半生不熟

underground (railway) dìtiě 〖dee-tyeh〗

地铁

underpants kùchǎ 〖koo-chah〗

裤衩

understand: I understand wǒ dǒng le 〖wor doong lur〗

我懂了

I don't understand wǒ bù dǒng

我不懂

do you understand? nǐ dǒngle, ma?

你懂了吗？

unemployed shīyè 〖shur-yur〗

失业

unfashionable bù shímáo 〖boo shur-mow〗

不时髦

United States Měiguó 〖may-gwor〗

美国

university dàxué

[dah-hsyew-eh]

大学

unlock kāi

开

unpack dǎkāi [dah-kai]

打开

until-...-zhǐdào-...-wéizhǐ
[jur-dow-...-way-jur]

只到 ... 为止

unusual bù chángjiàn(de)
[chahng-jyen(-dur)]

不常见（的）

up shàng [shahng]

上

up there zài nàr [dzai]

在那儿

he's not up yet tā hái méi qǐlai
[tah hai may chee-lai]

他还没起来

what's up? zěnme huí shìr?
[dzun-mur hway shur]

怎么回事儿？

upmarket gāojí [gow-jee]

高级

upset stomach wèi bù shūfu
[way boo shoo-foo]

胃不舒服

upside down dàoguolai [dow-gwor-lai]

倒过来

upstairs lóushàng
[loh-shahng]

楼上

urgent jǐnjí(de) [jin-jee(-dur)]

紧急（的）

us* wǒmen [wor-mun]

我们

with us gēn wǒmen yìqǐ [gun
– yee-chee]

跟我们一起

for us wéi wǒmen [wei]

为我们

use (verb) yòng [yoong]

用

may I use-...? wǒ kěyi
yòng yíxia... ma? [wor
kur-yee yoong-yee-hsyah-...-mah]

我可以用一下 ... 吗？

useful yǒuyòng [yoh-yoong]

有用

usual (normal) píngcháng [ping-chahng]

平常

(habitual) yuánlái de [yew-ahn-lai
dur]

原来的

V

vacancy: do you have
any vacancies? (hotel)
zhèr yǒu kòng fángjiān
ma? [jer yoh koong fahng-jyen
mah]

这儿有空房间吗？

vacation (holiday) jiàqī [jyah-chee]

假期

on vacation xiūjià [hsyoh-jyah]
休假

vacuum cleaner xīchénqì [hshee-chun-chee]
吸尘器

valid (ticket etc) yǒuxiào [yoh-hsyow]
有效

how long is it valid for? duō cháng shíjiānnei yǒuxiào? [dwor chahng shur-jyen nay yoh-hsyow]
多长时间内有效？

valley shāngǔ [shahn-goo]
山谷

valuable (adj) bǎoguì(de) [bow-gway(-dur)]
宝贵（的）

can I leave my valuables here? wǒ kěyi bǎ guìzhòng de dōngxi fàng zài zhèr ma? [wor kur-yee bah gway-joong dur doong-hshee fahng dzai jer mah]
我可以把贵重的东西放在这儿吗？

van huòchē [hwor-chur]
货车

vary: it varies jīngcháng biàn [jing-chahng byen]
经常变

vase huāpíng [hwah-ping]
花瓶

vegetables shūcài [shoo-tsai]
蔬菜

vegetarian (noun) chīsùde [chur-soo-dur]
吃素的

very fēicháng [fay-chahng]
非常

very little hěn xiǎo [hun hsyow]
很小

I like it very much wǒ hěn xǐhuan [wor hun hshee-hwahn]
我很喜欢

via tújīng [toojing]
途经

Vietnam Yuènán [yew-eh-nahn]
越南

view jǐng
景

village cūnzi [tsun-dzur]
村子

vinegar cù [tsoo]
醋

visa qiānzhèng [chyen-jung]
签证

visit (verb: person) qù kàn [chew kahn]
去看

(place) cānguān [tsahn-gwahn]
参观

I'd like to visit-... wǒ xiǎng cānguān-...- [wor hsyahng]
我想参观 …

voice shēngyīn [shung-yin]
声音

voltage diànyā [dyen-yah]
电压

vomit ǒutù [oh-too]
呕吐

W

waist yāo [yow]

腰

wait děng [dung]

等

wait for me děngdeng wǒ
[wor]

等等我

don't wait for me búyòng
déng wǒ [boo-yoong]

不用等我

can I wait until my wife gets
here? wǒ néng děngdào wǒ
qīzi lái ma? [nung dung-dow wor
chee-dzur lai mah]

我能等到我妻子来吗？

can you do it while I wait?
shìbúshì lìděng kéqǔ? [shur-
boo-shur lee-dung kur-chew]

是不是立等可取？

could you wait here for me?
qǐng zài zhèr děng hǎo
ma? [ching dzai jer dung how
mah]

请在这儿等好吗？

waiter/waitress fúwùyuán [foo-
woo-yew-ahn]

服务员

waiter!/waitress!
fúwùyuán!

服务员

wake: can you wake me up
at 5.30? qǐng zài wǔdiǎnbàn

jiàoxíng wǒ, hǎo ma? [ching
dzai – jyow-hsing wor]

请在五点半叫醒我好
吗？

Wales Wēiěrshì [way-er-shur]

威尔士

walk: is it a long walk? yào
zǒu hén yuǎn ma? [yow dzoh
hun yew-ahn mah]

要走很远吗？

it's only a short walk zhǐ shì
liūdaliūda [jur shur
lyoh-dah–]

只是溜达溜达

I'll walk wǒ zǒuzhe qù [wor
dzoh-jur chew]

我走着去

I'm going for a walk wǒ
chūqu sànsan bù [choo-chew
sahn-sahn]

我出去散散步

wall qiáng [chyang]

墙

the Great Wall of China
Chángchéng [chahng-chung]

长城

wallet qiánbāo [chyen-bow]

钱包

want: I want a-...-wǒ yào
yíge-...-[wor yow yee-gur]

我要一个

I don't want any-...-wǒ bú
yào-...

我不要

I want to go home wǒ yào

huíjiā [hway-jyah]
我要回家
I don't want to wǒ bú yào
我不要
he wants to-...-tā
xiǎng-...-[tah hsyahng]
他想 …
what do you want? nǐ yào
shénme? [shun-mur]
你要什么？
ward (in hospital) bìngfáng [bing-
fahng]
病房
warm nuǎnhuo [nwahn-hwor]
暖和
was*: he/she was tā yǐqián shì
[tah yee-chyen shur]
他／她以前是
it was shì
是
wash (verb) xǐ [hshee]
洗
can you wash these? qǐng
xǐxi zhèixie, hǎo ma? [ching
hshee-hshee jay-hsyeh how mah]
请洗洗这些好吗？
washhand basin liǎnpén [lyen-
pun]
脸盆
washing (dirty clothes) dài xǐ de
yīfu [yow hshee dur yee-foo]
待洗的衣服
(clean clothes) yíxǐ de yīfu [yee-
hshee-how]
已洗的衣服

washing machine xǐyījī [hshee-
yee-jee]
洗衣机
washing powder xǐyīfěn
[–fun]
洗衣粉
wasp huángfēng [hwahng-fung]
黄蜂
watch (wristwatch) shóubiǎo
[shoh-byow]
手表
water shuǐ [shway]
水
may I have some water? qǐng
lái diánr shuǐ, hǎo ma? [ching
lai dyenr shway how mah]
请来点儿水好吗？
water melon xīguā [hshee-gwah]
西瓜
waterproof (adj) fángshuǐ
[fahng-shway]
防水
way: it's this way shì zhèitiáo
lù [shur jay-tyow]
是这条路
it's that way shì nèitiáo lù
[nay-tyow]
是那条路
is it a long way to-...?
dào-...-yuǎn ma? [dow-...-chew
yew-ahn mah]
到 … 远吗？
no way! bù kěnéng! [kur-nung]
不可能

dialogue

could you tell me the way to-...? qǐng nín gàosu wǒ, dào-...-zěnme zǒu, hǎo ma? [ching nin gow-soo wor dow-...-dzun-mur dzoh how mah]

go straight on until you reach the traffic lights yìzhí zǒu hónglùdēng [yee-jur dzoh hoong-loo-dung]

turn left wǎng zuǒ guǎi [wahng dzwor gwai]

take the first on the right yào yòubiānr dì yízhuǎn [yow yoh-byenr dee yee-jwahn]

see **where**

we* wǒmen [wor-mun]
我们

weak (person) ruò [rwor]
弱

(drink) dàn [dahn]
淡

weather tiānqi [tyen-chee]
天气

wedding hūnlǐ [hun-lee]
婚礼

wedding ring jiéhūn jièzhi [jyeh-hun jyeh-jur]
结婚戒指

Wednesday xīngqīsān [hsing-chee-sahn]
星期三

week xīngqī [hsing-chee]
星期

a week (from) today xiàge xīngqī de jīntian [hsyah-gur – dur jin-tyen]
下个星期的今天

a week (from) tomorrow xiàge xīngqi de míngtian [ming-tyen]
下个星期的明天

weekend zhōumò [joh-mor]
周末

at the weekend zhōumò
周末

weight zhòngliàng [joong-lyang]
重量

welcome: welcome to-...-huānyíng dào-...-[hwahn-ying dow]
欢迎到 ...

you're welcome (don't mention it) búyòng xiè [boo-yoong hsyeh]
不用谢

well: I don't feel well wǒ bù shūfu [wor boo shoo-foo]
我不舒服

she's not well tā bù shūfu [tah]
她不舒服

you speak English very well nǐ Yīngyǔ jiǎngde hěn hǎo [ying-yew jyang-dur hun how]
你英语讲得很好

well done! tài hǎole! [how-lur]
太好了

I would like this one as well

zhèige wǒ yě yào 〖 jay-gur wor yeh yow〗

这个我也要

well well! āiyā! 〖ai-yah〗

哎呀

dialogue

how are you? nín hǎo ma? 〖how mah〗

very well, thanks, and you? hén hǎo xièxie, nǐ ne? 〖hun how hsyeh-hsyeh nee-neh〗

well-done (meat) lànshú 〖lahn-shoo〗

烂熟

Welsh Wēi'ěrshì 〖way-er-shur〗

威尔士

I'm Welsh wǒ shì Wēi'ěrshìrén 〖wor shur –run〗

我是威尔士人

were*: we were wǒmen yǐqián shì 〖wor-mun yee-chyen shur〗

我们以前是

you were nǐmen shì 〖nee-mun〗

你们是

west xī 〖hshee〗

西

in the west xībiānr 〖hshee-byenr〗

西边儿

West (European etc) Xīfāng 〖hshee-fahng〗

西方

in the West Xīfāng

西方

western (adj) xī 〖hshee〗

西

Western (adj: European etc) xīfāng de 〖hshee-fahng dur〗

西方的

Western-style xīshì 〖hshee-shur〗

西式

Western-style food xīcān 〖hshee-tsahn〗

西餐

West Indian (adj) Xī Yìndù qúndǎo rén 〖hshee yin-doo chun-dow run〗

西印度群岛人

wet shī 〖shur〗

湿

what? shénme? 〖shun-mur〗

什么？

what's that? nà shì shénme? 〖nah shur〗

那是什么？

what should I do? wǒ yīnggāi zuò shénme? 〖wor ying-gai dzwor〗

我应该作什么？

what a view! kàn zhè jǐngr! 〖kahn jur〗

看这景儿

what bus do I take? wǒ gāi zuò něilù chē? 〖wor gai dzwor nay-loo chur〗

我该坐哪路车？

wheel lúnzi [lun-dzur]
轮子

wheelchair lúnyǐ [lun-yee]
轮椅

when? shénme shíhou? [shun-mur shur-hoh]
什么时侯？

when we get back wǒmen huílai de shíhou [wor-mun hway-lai dur]
我们回来的时侯

when's the train/ferry? huǒchē/dùchuán jídiǎn kāi? [hwor-chur/doo-chwahn jee-dyen]
火车／渡船几点开？

where? nǎr?
哪儿？

I don't know where it is wǒ bù zhīdao zài nàr [wor boo jur-dow dzai nar]
我不知道在那儿

dialogue

> **where is the Dragon temple?** lóng miào zài nǎr? [dzai]
> **it's over there** jiù zài nàr [jyoh]
> **could you show me where it is on the map?** qǐng zài dìtúshang zhǐshì gěi wǒ ba [ching – dee-too-shahng jur-shur gay wor bah]
> **it's just here** jiù zài zhèr

[jyoh – jer]
see **way**

which: which bus? něilù chē? [nay-loo chur]
哪路车？

dialogue

> **which one?** nǎ yíge? [nah yee-gur]
> **that one** nèige [nay-gur]
> **this one?** zhèige? [jay-gur]
> **no, that one** búshì, nèige [boo-shur]

while: while I'm here wǒ zài zhèr de shíhou [wor dzai jer dur shur-hoh]
我在这儿的时侯

whisky wēishìjì [way-shur-jee]
威士忌

white bái
白

white wine bái pútaojiǔ [poo-tow-jyoh]
白葡萄酒

who? shéi? [shay]
谁

who is it? shéi? [shway]
谁

**the man who-...-...-de nèige rén [dur nay-gur run]
… 的那个人

whole: the whole week

Wh

zhěngzheng yíge xīngqī [jung-jung yee-gur hsing-chee]

整整一个星期

the whole lot quánbù [choo-en-boo]

全部

whose: whose is this? zhèi shì shéide? [jay shur shay-dur]

这是谁的？

why? wèishénme? [way-shun-mur]

为什么？

why not? wèishénme bù?

为什么不？

wide kuān de [kwahn dur]

宽的

wife qīzi [chee-dzur]

妻子

will*: will you do it for me? qǐng gěi wǒ zuò yíxìa [ching gay wor dzwor yee-hsyah]

请给我作一下

wind (noun) fēng [fung]

风

window chuānghu [chwahng-hoo]

窗户

near the window kào chuānghu [kow]

靠窗户

in the window (of shop) zài chúchuāngli [dzai choo-chwahng-lee]

在橱窗里

window seat kào chuāng de zuòwei [kow chwahng dur dzwor-way]

靠窗的座位

windy: it's windy yǒufēng [yoh-fung]

有风

wine pútaojiǔ [poo-tow-jyoh]

葡萄酒

can we have some more wine? qǐng zài lái diǎnr pútaojiǔ, hǎo ma? [ching dzai lai dyenr – how mah]

请再来点儿葡萄酒好吗？

wine list jiǔdān [jyoh-dahn]

酒单

winter dōngtian [doong-tyen]

冬天

in the winter dōngtian

冬天

with* hé-...-yìqǐ [hur-...-yee-chee]

和 … 一起

I'm staying with-...-wǒ gēn-...-zhù zài yìqǐ [wor gun-...-joo dzai yee-chee]

我跟 … 住在一起

without méiyǒu [may-yoh]

没有

witness zhèngren [jung-run]

证人

wok guō [gwor]

锅

woman fùnǚ [foo-nyew]

妇女

wonderful hǎojíle [how-jee-lur]

好极了

won't*: it won't start bù dáhuǒ
[dah-hwor]

不打火

wood (material) mùtou [moo-toh]

木头

(forest) shùlín [shoo-lin]

树林

wool yángmáo [yang-mow]

羊毛

word cí [tsur]

词

work (noun) gōngzuò [goong-
dzwor]

工作

it's not working huàile [lur]

坏了

world shìjiè [shur-jyeh]

世界

worry: I'm worried wǒ bù ān
[wor bwahn]

我不安

worse: it's worse huàile [hway-
lur]

坏了

worst zuì huài [dzway hwai]

最坏

would: would you give this
to-...? qǐng nín bǎ zhèige
gěi-..., hǎo ma? [ching nin bah
jay gay-...-how mah]

请您把这个给 … 好吗？

wrap: could you wrap it up?
qǐng nín bāng wǒ bāo
yíxia, hǎo ma? [ching nin
bahng wor bow yee-hsyah how
mah]

请您帮我包一下好吗？

wrapping paper bāozhuāngzhǐ
[bow-jwahng-jur]

包装纸

wrist shǒuwànr [shoh-wahnr]

手腕儿

write xiě [hsyeh]

写

writing paper xìnzhǐ [hsin-jur]

信纸

wrong: this is the wrong train
wǒmen shàngcuò huǒchēle
[wor-mun chung-tswor-lur hwor-
chur-lur]

我们上错火车了

the bill's wrong zhàngdānr
cuòle [jahng-dahnr tswor-lur]

帐单儿错了

sorry, wrong number
duìbuqǐ, dǎcuòle [dway-boo-
chee dah-]

对不起打错了

sorry, wrong room duìbuqǐ,
zhàocuò fángjiān le
[jow-fahng-jyen]

对不起找错房间了

there's something wrong
with-...-...-yǒu máobìng [yoh
mow-bing]

… 有毛病

what's wrong? zěnmele?
[dzun-mur-lur]
怎么了？

Y

yacht fānchuán [fahn-chwahn]
帆船
Yangtze Gorge Chángjiāng
sānxiá [chahng-jyang sahn-syah]
长江三峡
Yangtze River Chángjiāng
长江
year nián [nyen]
年
yellow huángsè [hwahng-sur]
黄色
Yellow River Huáng Hé
[hwahng hur]
黄河
Yellow Sea Huánghǎi
黄海
yes* shìde [shur-dur]
是的
yesterday zuótian [dzwor-tyen]
昨天
  yesterday morning zuótian
  zǎoshang [dzow-shahng]
  昨天早上
  the day before yesterday
  qiántiān [chyen-tyen]
  前天
yet hái
还

dialogue

is it here yet? hái láile
méiyou? [lai-lur may-yoh]
no, not yet hái méilái
[may-lai]
you'll have to wait a little
longer yet nǐ hái yào děng
yídiǎnr [yow dung yee-dyenr]

yoghurt suānnǎi [swahn-nai]
酸奶
you* (sing) nǐ
你
(sing, pol) nín
您
(pl) nǐmen [nee-mun]
你们
this is for you zhèi shì gěi nǐ
de [jay shur gay nee dur]
这是给你的
with you gēn nǐ yìqǐ [gun nee
yee-chee]
跟你一起
young niánqīng [nyen-ching]
年轻
your/yours* (sing) nǐde
[nee-dur]
你的
(sing, pol) nínde [nin-dur]
您的

Z

zero líng
零
zip lāliàn 〖lah-lyen〗
拉链
could you put a new zip on?
qǐng nín bāng wǒ huànge xīn
lāliànr, hǎo ma? 〖ching nin bahng
wor hwahn-gur hsin – how mah〗
请您帮我换个新拉链
好吗？
zoo dòngwùyuán 〖doong-woo-
yew-ahn〗
动物园

Chinese

→

English

Colloquialisms

You might well hear the following expressions, but on no account should you use any of the stronger ones – they will cause great offence if used by a foreigner.

bèndàn! [bun-dahn] idiot!
chǔnhuò! [chun-hwor] idiot!
dàbízi! [dah-bee-dzur] big nose!
dà tuánjié [dah twahn-jyeh] ten-yuán note
fèihuà! [fay-hwah] rubbish!
gàile màorle [gai-lur mow-lur] absolutely the best
gǔn! [goon] go away!, get lost!
gǔnchūqù! [goon-choo-chyew] get out!
húndàn! [hoon-dahn] bastard!
juéle [jweh-lur] wonderful, unique
lǎowài! [low-wai] foreigner!
liǎobude [lyow-boo-dur] terrific, extraordinary
méizhìle [may-jur-lur] excellent
nǎli, nǎli [nah-lee] oh, it was nothing, you're welcome
suànle [swahn-lur] forget it
suíbiàn [sway-byen] as you wish
tāmāde! [tah-mah-dur] hell!, damn!
tài bàngle [bahng-lur] that's great
tài zāogāole [dzow-gow-lur] that's terrible
tài zāotòule [dzow-toh-lur] that's awful
xīpíshì [hshee-pee-shur] hippy
yángguǐzi! [yang-gway-dzur] foreign devil!
yāpíshì [yah-pee-shur] yuppie
yílù píng'ān [yee-loo ping-ahn] safe journey, bon voyage
yuánmù qiúyú [yew-ahn-moo choh-yoo] a waste of time (literally: climbing a tree to catch fish)
zāole! [dzow-lur] damn!, shit!
zhù zuǐ! [joo dzway] shut up!
zǒu kāi! [dzoh] go away!

A

ǎi short
Àiěrlán [ai-ur-lahn] Ireland; Irish
àizībìng [ai-dzur-bing] AIDS
àn [ahn] dark; shore
ānjìng [ahn-jing] quiet
ānquán [ahn-choo-en] safe
ānzuò [ahn-dzwor] saddle
Àodàlìyà [or-dah-lee-yah] Australia; Australian (adj)

B

ba [bah] particle at the end of a sentence to indicate a suggestion, piece of advice etc
bā eight
bǎ measure word* used for chairs, knives, teapots, tools or implements with handles, stems and bunches of flowers
bàba [bah-bah] father
bābǎi eight hundred
bái white
bǎidù ferry
báisè [bai-sur] white
bái tiān [tyen] day, daytime
bǎiwàn [bai-wahn] one million
bàn [bahn] half
bàndá [bahn-dah] half a dozen
bàngjíle [bahng-jee-lur] terrific
bàngōngshì [bahn-goong-shur] office
bāngzhù [bahng-joo] help
bànr [bahnr] partner, boyfriend; girlfriend

bànyè [bahn-yur] midnight; at midnight
báo [bow] thin
bàofēngyǔ [bow-fung-yew] storm
bàozhǐ [bow-jur] newspaper
bāoguǒ [bow-gwor] package, parcel
bāokuò [bow-kwor] include
bǎole [bow-lur] full
bǎozhèng [bow-jung] promise; guarantee
bǎozhǐ [bow-jur] tissue, Kleenex®
bāshí [bah-shur] eighty
bāyuè [bah-yew-eh] August
bēi [bay] cup, glass
běi north
Běi Ài'ěrlán [ai-er-lahn] Northern Ireland
bēizi [bay-dzur] cup
bèn [bun] stupid
běn measure word* used for books, magazines etc
bēngdài [bung-dai] bandage
bǐ [bee] than
bǐ-... gèng [gung] even more than-...
bǐ nèi duō diǎnr [nay dwor dyenr] more than that
biānjiè [byen-jyeh] border
biānjìng [byen-jing] border
biānr [byenr] side
biǎo [byow] form
biǎodì [byow-dee] cousin (male, younger than speaker)
biǎogē [byow-gur] cousin (male, older than speaker)
biáojiě [byow-jyeh] cousin

(female, older than speaker)

biǎomèi [byow-may] cousin
(female, younger than speaker)

biéde dìfang [byeh-dur dee-fahng]
somewhere else

biéde dōngxi [byeh-dur doong-
hshee] something else

bīng ice

bīngdòngde [–doong-dur]
frozen

bìngfáng [–fahng] ward

bīnguǎn [–wahn] hotel

bīngxiāng [–hsyang] fridge

bǐsài game; match; race

bìxū [bee-hsyew] must

bìyào(de) [bee-yow(-dur)]
necessary

bíyǒu [bee-yoh] penfriend

bízi [bee-dzur] nose

bōhào [bor-how] dial

bōli [bor-lee] glass (material)

bōli bēi [bay] glass (for drinking)

bówùguǎn [bor-woo-gwahn]
museum

bózi [boh-dzur] neck

bù [boo] no; not; material,
fabric

bù duō [dwor] not much

bù chángjiàn(de) [chahng-jyen(-
dur)] unusual

bú kèqi [kur-chee] you're
welcome, don't mention it

bùfen [boo-fun] part

bùhǎo [boo-how] bad

bù jiǔ [jyoh] soon

bù kěnéng [kur-nung]
impossible

bùliào [boo-lyow] cloth, fabric

bù lǐmào [lee-mow] rude

búshì [boo-shur] no, it is not
the case

búshi-... jiùshi-... [jyoh-shur]
either-... or-...

bùtóng [boo-toong] different;
difference

bùxíng [boo-sing] on foot

búyào! [boo-yow] don't!

búyàole [–lur] that's all;
nothing else

búyòng xiè [hsyeh] you're
welcome, don't mention it

C

cài [tsai] dish; meal

cái only

cānchē [tsahn-chur] buffet car

cánfèi [tsahn-fay] disabled

cáng [tsahng] hide

cāngbái [–bai] pale

cānguān [–wahn] visit

cāngying fly (noun)

cānjīn [tsahn-jin] napkin

cāntīng restaurant; dining
room

cǎo [tsow] grass

cǎoyào [tsow-yow] herbs
(medicinal)

céng [tsung] floor (in hotel etc)

cèsuǒ [tsur-swor] toilet, rest
room

chá [chah] tea (drink)

chà to (the hour)

chàbuduō [chah-boo-dwor]
almost, nearly

cháchí [chah-chur] teaspoon

cháhàotái [chah-how-tai]
directory enquiries

chán [chahn] greedy

cháng [chahng] long

chànggē [–gur] sing

chàngpiàn [–pyen] record (music)

chángtú chēzhàn [–too chur-jahn] long-distance bus station

chángtú diànhuà [dyen-hwah] long-distance call

chángtú qìchē [chee-chur] long-distance bus

chángtú qūhào [chew-how] dialling code

chāojí shìchǎng [chow-jee shur-chahng] supermarket

chǎole [chow-lur] noisy

chāopiào [chow-pyow] banknote, (US) bill

cháoshī [chow-shur] damp; humid

cháozhe [chow-jur] towards

chápán [chah-pahn] tray

cházi [chah-dzur] fork

chē [chur] city bus

chēfèi [chur-fay] fare

chēlún [chur-lun] wheel

chéngbǎo [chung-bow] castle

chéngjiā [–jyah] married

chéngkè [–kur] passenger

chénglǐ [–lee] in town, in the city

chéngshì [–shur] city, town

chéngshí honest

chéngzhèn [–jun] town

chènyī [chun-yee] shirt

chētāi [chur-tai] tyre

chēzhàn [chur-jahn] bus station; bus stop

chī [chur] eat

chí late

chǐcùn [chur-tsun] size

chīde [chur-dur] food

chīsùde [chur-soo-dur] vegetarian

chóngfù [choong-foo] repeat

chuán [chwahn] ship, boat

chuáncāng [–tsahng] cabin

chuáng [chwahng] bed

chuángdān [–dahn] sheet

chuángdiàn [–dyen] mattress

chuānghu [–hoo] window

chuānkǒng [chwahn-koong] puncture

chuánrǎn [–rahn] infectious

chuántǒng [–toong] traditional

chuánzhēn [–jun] fax

chúfáng [choo-fahng] kitchen

chūkǒu [choo-koh] exit

chúle-... yǐwài [choo-lur-... yee-wai] except-..., apart from-...

chǔn silly

chūnjié [chun-jyeh] Chinese New Year

chūntian [chun-tyen] spring; in the spring

chúxī [choo-hshee] New Year's Eve

chǔxù [choo-hsyew] deposit

chūzū [choo-dzoo] hire, rent

chūzūchē diǎnr [–chur dyenr] taxi rank

chūzū qìchē [chee-chur] taxi

cí [tsur] word

cídài [tsur-dai] tape, cassette

cóng [tsoong] from

cōngcong hurriedly

cónglái bù never (referring to the past or present)

cōngming clever, intelligent

cūnzhuāng [tsun-jwahng] village

cuò(wù) [tswor(-woo)] mistake, error; fault

D

dà [dah] big, large

dǎ hit

dàbó [dah-bor] brother-in-law (husband's elder brother)

dà bùfen shíjiān [dah boo-fun shur-jyen] most of the time

dǎcuòle [dah-tswor-lur] wrong number

dǎ diànhuà [dyen-hwah] phone, call

dàgài probably

dàhuì [dah-hway] conference

dáhuǒjī [dah-hwor-jee] cigarette lighter

dài take (something somewhere)

dàilái bring

dàilǐng yóujiàn [yoh-jyen] poste restante

dàitì instead

dàjíle [dah-jee-lur] enormous

dàlù main road

dàmǐ uncooked rice

dàn [dahn] weak; pale

dānchéngpiào [dahn-chung-pyow] single ticket, one-way ticket

dāndú alone

dāngrán [dahn-grahn] of course, certainly

dànián sānshí [dah-nyen sahn-shur] Chinese New Year's Eve

dānrén jiān [dahn-run jyen] single room

dānshēn [dahn-shun] single, unmarried

dànshì [dahn-shur] but

dānyuán [dahn-yew-ahn] flat, apartment

dǎo [dow] island

dāo knife

dào to; arrive

dào-... wéizhǐ [way-jur] until-...

dàodá [dow-dah] arrive

dàodá shíjiān [shur-jyen] arrival

dàotián [dow-tyen] paddy field, rice field

dǎoyóu [dow-yoh] tour guide

dāozi [dow-dzur] knife

dàrén [dah-run] adult

dàshēng de [dah-shung dur] loud

dàshíguǎn [dah-shur-gwahn] embassy

dàxióngmāo [hsyoong–mow] panda

dàxué [dah-hsyew-eh] university

dàyī [dah-yee] coat, overcoat

dàyuē [dah-yew-eh] roughly, approximately

dǎzhàng [dah-jahng] fight

de [dur] of (particle inserted between adjective and noun to denote possession)

dé get, obtain

de duō:-... de duō [dwor] much more-...

Déguó [dur-gwor] Germany; German (adj)

dēng [dung] light; lamp

děng wait

dēngjì [dung-jee] check-in

dēngjīkǒu [–koh] gate (at airport)

dēngjī pái boarding pass

dēngpào [dung-pow] lightbulb

dì [dee] floor

dì èr tiān [tyen] the day after

dī low

diàn [dyen] electric; electricity

-diǎn hour; o'clock

diànchí [dyen-chur] battery

diànchuīfēng [dyen-chway-fung] hairdryer

diàndòng tìxú dāo [dyen-doong tee-hsyew dow] shaver

diàngōng [dyen-goong] electrician

diànhuà [dyen-hwah] phone

diànhuà hàomǎ bù [how-mah] phone book

diànhuàtíng phone box

diànnǎo [dyen-now] computer

diǎnr [dyenr] a little bit

... diǎnr more-...

diànshì [dyen-shur] television

diàntī lift, elevator

diàntìdāo [dyen-tee-dow] electric shaver

diànxiàn [dyen-hsyen] wire; lead

diǎnxíng [dyen-hsing] typical

diànyā [dyen-yah] voltage

diànyǐng [dyen-ying] film, movie

diànyǐng yuàn [yew-ahn] cinema, movie theater

diànyuán chāzuò [dyen-yew-ahn chah-dzwor] power point

diànzi [dyen-dzur] cushion

diàochuáng [dyow-chwahng] cot

dìbā [dee-bah] eighth

dìdi younger brother

dì'èr(ge) [–gur] second

diézi [dyeh-dzur] dish, bowl; saucer

dìfāng [dee-fahng] place

dìjiǔ [dee-jyoh] ninth

dìliǎng [dee-lyang] second

dìliù [dee-lyoh] sixth

dìnghūnle [–hun-lur] engaged (to be married)

dǐngshang: zài dǐngshang [dzai ding-shahng] at the top

dìngzuò [–dzwor] reserve

dìqī [dee-chee] seventh

dìqū [dee-chew] region

dǐr [deer] bottom

dìsān [dee-sahn] third

dìshang [dee-shahng] on the ground

dìshí [dee-shur] tenth

dìsì [dee-sur] fourth

dísīkē [–kur] disco

dìtǎn [dee-tahn] carpet

dìtiě [dee-tyeh] underground, (US) subway

dìtiě zhàn [jahn] underground station, subway station

dìtú [dee-too] map

diū [dyoh] lose

dìwǔ [dee-woo] fifth

dìyī first

dìzhǐ [dee-jur] address

dǒng: nǐ dǒngle? [doong-lur] do you understand?

wǒ bù dǒng [wor] I don't understand

dōng [doong] east

dòng hole; puncture

dōngběi [–bay] northeast

dōngbiān [–byen] in the

east

dōngnán [–nahn] southeast

dōngshì [–shur] director

dōngtian [–tyen] winter; in the winter

dòngwù [–woo] animal

dòngwùyuán [–yew-ahn] zoo

dōngxi [–hshee] thing (object)

dōu [doh] both, all

dǒu steep

dú [doo] read

duǎn [dwahn] short

duǎnkù shorts

duànle [–lur] broken

duǎnwà [–wah] sock

duì [dway] right, correct; towards; with regard to; queue; side

duìbuqǐ [dway-boo-chee] sorry, excuse me

duìfāng fùkuǎn [–fahng foo-kwahn] collect call

duìhuàn [dway-hwahn] change (verb: money)

duìhuànlǜ [–lyew] exchange rate

duìjíle! [–jee-lur] exactly!

duìle yes, that's it, that's right

duō [dwor] much; more than

  duōde duō [–dur] a lot more

duōle:-... duōle [–lur] far more-...

duōshao? [dwor-show] how much?, how many? (if answer is likely to be more than ten)

duōxiè [–hsyeh] thank you very much

duō yíbèi [yee-bay] twice as

much

duō yìdiǎnr [yee-dyenr] a bit more

duōyòng chātóu [–yoong chah-toh] adapter

dúpǐn [doo-pin] drugs, narcotics

dǔzhùle [doo-joo-lur] blocked

E

è [ur] hungry

Éguó [ur-gwor] Russia; Russian (adj)

èr two

èrbǎi two hundred

èr děng [dung] second class

ěrduo [er-dwor] ear

ěrhuán [er-hwahn] earring

ěr lóng [loong] deaf

èrlóu [er-loh] first floor, (US) second floor

èrshí [er-shur] twenty

értóng [er-toong] children

èrwàn [er-wahn] twenty thousand

érxí [er-hshee] daughter-in-law

èryuè [er-yew-eh] February

érzi [er-dzur] son

ěxīn [ur-hsin] disgusting; nausea

F

Fǎguó [fah-gwor] France; French (adj)

fán [fahn] bored

fàn meal

fàndiàn [fahn-dyen] large restaurant; luxury hotel

fǎng [fahng] imitation

fàng put

fāngbiàn [–byen] convenient

fángdǐng roof; ceiling

fángfǔjì [–foo-jee] antiseptic

fángjiān [–jyen] room

fànguǎnr [fahn-gwahnr] small
restaurant

fāngxiàng [–hsyang] direction

fángzi [–dzur] building; house

fángzū [–dzoo] rent (noun)

fànwǎn [fahn-wahn] rice bowl

fānyì translate; translation;
translator

fāshēng [fah-shung] happen

fēi [fay] fly (verb)

fēicháng [fay-chahng] very,
extremely

fēijī [fay-jee] plane

zuò fēijī [dzwor] by air

fēijīchǎng [–chahng] airport

fèixū [fay-hsyew] ruins

féizào [fay-dzow] soap

fēi zhèngshì [jung-shur]
informal

fēn [fun] minute

fēng [fung] mad, insane; wind;
measure word* used for
letters

fēngjǐng [fung-jing] scenery;
sights

fēngshàn [fung-shahn] fan
(electrical)

fēngsú [fung-soo] custom

fěnhóng [fun-hoong] pink

fēnjī [fun-jee] extension

fēnkāi separate

fēnzhōng [fun-joong] minute

Fó [for] Buddha

Fójiào [for-jyow] Buddhism;
Buddhist

fù(qián) [foo(-chyen)] pay

fūfù couple (two people)

fùjiāfèi [foo-jyah-fay]
supplement, extra charge

fùjìn [foo-jin] nearby; near

fùmǔ parents

fùnǚ [foo-nyew] woman

fùqin [foo-chin] father

fūren [foo-run] Mrs

fúshǒu [foo-shoh] handle

fúwùtái [foo-woo-tie] reception

fúwùyuán [–yew-ahn]
receptionist

fùzá [foo-zah] complicated

G

gàir [gai-r] lid

gālí [gah-lee] curry

gān [gahn] dry; liver

gǎn catch up

gānbēi! [gahn-bay] cheers!

gāngbǐ [gahng-bee] pen

gǎngkǒu [–koh] port,
harbour

gānjìng [gahn-jing] clean

gǎnjué [gahn-jyew-eh] feel

gǎnmào [gahn-mow] cold
(illness)

gǎnrǎn [gahn-rahn] infection

gāo [gow] high; tall

gāodiǎndiàn [–dyen] cake shop

gāomíng [gow-ming] brilliant

gāoxìng [gow-hsing] pleased,
glad

hěn gāoxìng jiàndào nǐ [hun
– jyen dow] pleased to meet

you

ge [gur] general all-purpose measure word★

gē song

gēbo [gur-bor] arm

gēbozhǒu [-joh] elbow

gēchàngjiā [gur-chahng-jyah] singer

gēge [gur-gur] elder brother

gěi [gay] give; for

gējù [gur-jyew] opera

gēn [gun] with

gèng:-... gèng [gung] even more-...

gèng hǎo [how] better; even better

Gòngchándǎng [goong-chahn-dahng] Communist Party

Gòngchándǎngyuán [-yew-ahn] Communist Party member

gōngchǎng [-chahng] factory

gòngchánzhǔyì [-chahn-joo-yee] communism

gōngchǐ [-chur] metre

gōngdiàn [-dyen] palace

gōnggòng cèsuǒ [tsur-swor] public convenience

gōnggong pópo [por-por] wife's parents-in-law

gōnggòng qìchē [chee-chur] city bus

gōnggòng qìchē zhàn [jahn] bus stop

gōnggòng qìchē zǒngzhàn [dzoong-jahn] bus station

gōngjià [-jyah] public holiday

gōngjīn [-jin] kilogram

gōnglǐ kilometre

gōnglù motorway, (US) highway, (US) freeway

gōngsī [-sur] company, business, firm

gōngxǐ! gōngxǐ! [-hshee] congratulations!

gōngyuán [-yew-ahn] park

gōngzuò [-dzwor] job; work

gǒu [goh] dog

gòu(le) [-lur] enough

guài [gwai] peculiar

guān [gwahn] close, shut

guàn jug

guángchǎng [gwahng-chahng] square

Guǎngdōng [-doong] Cantonese (adj)

Guǎngdōnghuà [-hwah] Cantonese (language)

Guǎngdōng rén [run] Cantonese (person)

guānkǒu [gwahn-koh] pass (in mountains)

guānle [-lur] closed

guānménle [-mun-lur] closed

guānshang le [shahng] off, switched off

guàntou [-toh] can, tin

guānyú [-yew] about, concerning

gúdǒng [goo-doong] antique

gūgu aunt (father's sister)

guì(le) [gway(-lur)] expensive

guìzi [gway-dzur] cupboard

-guo [gwor] verb suffix indicating a past experience

guóhuà [-hwah] Chinese painting

guójí [–jee] nationality
guójì [–jee] international
guójiā [–jyah] country, nation; national, state
guòle [–lur] beyond
guòmǐn allergic
guòqu [–chew] in the past
guòshí(de) [–shur(-dur)] old-fashioned
guówài abroad
guòyè [–yur] overnight
gútou [goo-toh] bone
gùyì deliberately
gǔzhé [gyew-jur] fracture

H

hǎi sea
hái still
   hái hǎo ma? [how mah] are you OK?
hǎibiānr [hai-byenr] sea; seaside
hǎibīn coast
hǎiguān [hai-gwahn] Customs
háishi [hai-shur] or
hǎitān [hai-tahn] beach
hǎiwān [hai-wahn] bay
háizi [hai-dzur] child
hǎn [hahn] shout
hángbān [hahng-bahn] flight
hángbān hào [how] flight number
hángkōng [–koong] by airmail
hángkōng xìnfēng [hsin-fung] airmail envelope
Hànyǔ [hahn-yew] Chinese (spoken language)
hǎo [how] good; nice; all right, OK

hǎo, xièxie [hsyeh-hsyeh] yes, please
hǎochī [how-chur] delicious
háohuá [how-hwah] luxurious; posh
hǎojíle [how-jee-lur] great, wonderful, excellent
hǎokàn [how-kahn] attractive
hàomǎ [how-mah] number
hǎo yìdiǎnr [yee-dyenr] better
hé [hur] and; river
hé-... yìqǐ [yee-chee] together with-...
... hé-... dōu bù-... [doh boo] neither-... nor-...
hē drink (verb)
hēi [hay] black
hēi àn [ahn] dark
hélǐ [hur-lee] reasonable
hěn [hun] very
hěnduō [hun-dwor] a lot, lots; many
hěnkuài de [kwai] quickly
hézi [hur-dzur] box
hēzuìle [hur-dzway-lur] drunk
hóngsède [hoong-sur-dur] red
hóngshuǐ [–shway] flood
hòu [hoh] thick
hòulái later; later on
hóulóng [hoh-loong] throat
hòumian [hoh-myen] behind
   zài hòumian [dzai] at the back
   zài-... hòumian behind-...
hòutiān [hoh-tyen] the day after tomorrow
hú lake
huā [hwah] flower
huà picture, painting
huāfèi [hwah-fay] spend

huài [hwai] bad
huàile [hwai-lur] broken
huáiyùn [hwai-yewn] pregnant
huáji [hwah-jee] funny
huàjù [hwah-jew] play (in theatre)
huáng [hwahng] yellow
huángdì emperor
huángfēng [–fung] wasp
huángjīn gold
huángsè [–sur] yellow
huānyíng dào-... [hwahn-ying dow] welcome to-...
huāpíng [hwah-ping] vase
huàr [hwar] painting, picture
huàxiàng [hwah-hsyang] portrait
huāyuán [hwah-yew-ahn] garden
huì [hway] meeting, conference
huílai come back
huīsède [hway-sur-dur] grey
huítóujiàn [hway-toh-jyen] see you later
huìyì [hway-yee] meeting, conference
hūnlǐ [hun-lee] wedding
huǒ [hwor] fire
huǒchái [hwor-chai] matches
huòchē [hwor-chur] van
huǒchē train
  zuò huǒchē [dzwor] by train
huǒchēzhàn [–jahn] railway station
huǒzāi [hwor-dzai] fire
huòzhe-... huòzhe-... [hwor-jur] either-... or-...
huòzhě or
hùshi [hoo-shur] nurse
hútòng [hoo-toong] lane; side street

hùzhào [hoo-jow] passport
húzi [hoo-dzur] beard

J

jì [jee] post, mail (verb)
jǐ few
jiā [jyah] home
  zài jiā [dzai] at home
jiàgé [jyah-gur] price
jiǎn [jyen] cut
jiàn measure word* used for things, affairs etc
Jiānádà [jyah-nah-dah] Canada; Canadian (adj)
jiānbǎng [jyen-bahng] shoulder
jiǎndān [jyen-dahn] simple, easy
jiāng [jyang] river
jiǎng speak
jiānglái [jyang-lai] future; in future
jiànkāng [jyen-kahng] healthy
jiànzhù [jyen-joo] building
jiǎnzi [jyen-dzur] scissors
jiǎo [jyow] foot (of person)
jiào call, greet
jiāochākǒu [jyow-chah-koh] junction
jiáodǐ sole (of foot)
jiǎo gēn [gun] heel (of foot)
jiāojuǎnr [jyow-jew-ahnr] film (for camera)
jiāoqū [jyow-chew] suburb
jiāoqūchē [–chur] bus (in suburbs)
jiàotáng [jyow-tahng] church
jiāotōng tú [jyow-toong] streetmap
jiāoyì huì [jyow-yee hway] exhibition, trade fair

jiáozhǐtou [jyow-jur-toh] toe

jiàqī [jyah-chee] holiday, vacation

jiàqián [jyah-chyen] cost (noun)

jiātíng family

jiǎyá [jyah-yah] dentures

jiāyóu zhàn [jyah-yoh jahn] petrol station, gas station

jiàzhí [jyah-jur] value

jiàzi [jyah-dzur] shelf

jíbìng illness, disease

jīchǎng bānchē [jee-chahng bahn-chur] airport bus

jiē(dào) [jyeh(-dow)] avenue; street

jiè [jyeh] borrow

jiěfū [jyeh-foo] brother-in-law (elder sister's husband)

jiéhūn [jyeh-hun] married
nǐ jiéhūnle ma? [jyeh-hun-lur mah] are you married?

jiějie [jyeh-jyeh] elder sister

jiémùdānr [jyeh-moo-dahnr] programme

jiérì [jyeh-rur] festival; holiday

jiēshi [jyeh-shur] strong

jièzhi [jyeh-jur] ring (on finger)

jīfèi diànhuà [jee-fay dyen-hwah] payphone

jǐge [jee-gur] several
jǐge? how much?, how many? (if answer is likely to be ten or fewer)

jíjiù [jee-jyoh] first aid

jíjiùxiāng [–hsyang] first-aid kit

jìn near

jǐngchá [jing-chah] police; policeman

jīngcháng [jing-chahng] often, frequent

jīngguò [jing-gwor] through; via

jīnglǐ manager

jǐngr view

jīngrén de [jing-run dur] astonishing

jìngzi [jing-dzur] mirror

jīnhuángsè [jin-hwahng-sur] blond

jìniànbēi [jee-nyen-bay] monument

jìniànpǐn [jee-nyen-pin] souvenir

jǐnjí(de) [–dur] urgent

jǐnjin just, only

jīnshǔ metal

jīntian [jin-tyen] today
jīntian wǎnshang [wahn-shahng] tonight

jìntóu [jin-toh] end (of street etc)

jīnwǎn [jin-wahn] tonight

jīnzi [jin-dzur] gold

jīqì [jee-chee] machine

jìshi-... yě [jee-shur-... yur] even if-...

jìsuànjī [jee-swahn-jee] computer

jiǔ [jyoh] nine; alcohol; alcoholic drink

jiù just; then; secondhand
jiù yìdiǎnr [yee-dyenr] just a little
jiù yìhuǐr [yee-hwayr] just a minute

jiǔbǎi nine hundred

jiǔbājiān [jyoh-bah-jyen] bar

jiùde [jyoh-dur] secondhand

jiùhùchē [jyoh-hoo-chur] ambulance

jiùjiu uncle (mother's brother)

jiǔshí [jyoh-shur] ninety
jiǔyuè [jyoh-yew-eh]
  September
juǎnqūde [jwahn-chew-dur] curly
jué búhuì [jew-eh boo-hway]
  never (referring to the future)
juéde [–dur] feel
juédìng decide; decision
juéduì bàng [–dway bahng]
  perfect
juéduìde! [–dur] absolutely!
júhuángsè [jyew-hwahng-sur]
  orange (colour)
jùlí [joo-lee] distance
jùyuàn [jyew-yew-ahn] theatre

K

kǎchē [kah-chur] lorry, truck
kāfēi diàn [kah-fay dyen] café
kāfēiguǎnr [–gwahnr] café
kāi open (adj)
kāichē [kai-chur] drive
kāide [kai-dur] open (adj)
kāile [kai-lur] open (adj)
kāishǐ [kai-shur] begin; start;
  beginning
  yì kāishǐ at the beginning
kāishuǐ [kai-shway] boiled water
kànbào [kahn-bow] read
  (newspaper)
kàngjūnsù [kahng-jyewn-soo]
  antibiotics
kànjian [kahn-jyen] see
kànshū [kahn-shoo] read (book)
kànyikàn [kahn-yee-kahn] have
  a look
kào [kow] near
kǎoshì [kow-shur] exam

kǎoxiāng [kow-hsyang] oven
kè [kur] lesson; gram(me)
kē measure word* used for
  trees etc
kěài lovely
kěnéng [kur-nung] maybe,
  perhaps; possible
kěpà [kur-pah] horrible
kèqi [kur-chee] polite
kèrén [kur-run] guest
kěshì [kur-shur] but
késou [kur-soh] cough
kètīng lounge
kěyi [kur-yee] be able
  kěyi qǐng [ching] yes please
  nín kěyi-... ma? [mah] could
  you-...?
kōng [koong] empty
kōngjiān [–jyen] room, space
kōngqì [–chee] air
kōngtiáo [–tyow] air-
  conditioning
kǒukě [koh-kur] thirsty
kǔ [koo] bitter
kū cry
kuài [kwai] quick, fast; sharp;
  soon; measure word* used
  for lumps or pieces
kuài chē [chur] express (train)
kuàidì express (mail)
kuài diǎnr! [dyenr] hurry up!
kuàilè [kwai-lur] happy
kuàir [kwai-r] piece
kuàizi [kwai-dzur] chopsticks
kuān de [kwahn dur] wide
kuāng [kwahng] basket
kuánghuānjié [–hwahn-jyeh]
  carnival
kùchǎ [koo-chah] underpants,

men's underwear

kūnchóng [kun-choong] insect

kùnle [kun-lur] sleepy

kùnnan [kun-nahn] difficult; difficulty

kùzi [koo-dzur] trousers, (US) pants

L

là [lah] hot, spicy

lā pull

lái come, arrive

láide: nǐ shì cóng nǎr láide? [shur tsoong nar lai-dur] where do you come from?

láihuí piào [lai-hway pyow] return/round-trip ticket

lājī [lah-jee] rubbish, trash

lājīxiāng [–hsyang] dustbin, trashcan

lán [lahn] blue

lǎn lazy

lánzi [lahn-dzur] basket

lǎo [low] old

lǎolao grandmother (maternal)

lǎoniánren [low-nyen-run] senior citizen

lǎoshī [low-shur] teacher

lǎoshǔ [low-shoo] rat; mouse

Lǎowō [low-wor] Laos

lǎoye [low-yeh] grandfather (maternal)

làzhú [lah-joo] candle

le [lur] sentence particle indicating something in the past which is still relevant to the present or a change of circumstances in the present

or future

-le [-lur] verb suffix indicating completion of action

lèi [lay] tired

léiyǔ [lay-yew] thunderstorm

lěng [lung] cold

li: zài-... li [dzai ... lee] inside-...

lí [lee] from; to; pear

-lǐ inside

liǎn [lyen] face

liǎng [lyang] two

liàng measure word* used for vehicles

liǎngcì [–tsur] twice

liǎngge dānrénchuáng [–gur dahn-run-chwahng] twin beds

liǎngge dōu [dow] both

liǎngge dōu bù [doh] neither (one) of them

liǎngge xīngqī [hsing-chee] fortnight

liángkuai [–kwai] cool

liángxié [–hsyeh] sandal

liánxi [lyen-hshee] contact

liányīqún [lyen-yee-chewn] dress

liányùn [lyen-yewn] connection

liǎobuqǐ [lyow-boo-chee] incredible, amazing

lièchē shíkè biǎo [lyeh-chur shur-kur byow] timetable, (US) schedule

lièzhì [lyeh-jur] poor

lǐfà [lee-fah] haircut

lǐfàdiàn [–dyen] hairdresser's; barber's

lǐfàshī [–shur] hairdresser's

líhūn [lee-hun] divorced

límǐ centimetre
límíng dawn
líng zero
lǐng take (someone somewhere)
lǐng tie, necktie
língqián [ling-chyen] change (noun: money)
lìngrén yúkuài [ling-run yew-kwai] pleasant
lǐngshìguǎn [ling-shur-gwahn] consulate
lìngwài another, different
líng yánglǎojīn de rén [–low-jin dur run] pensioner
lìng yígè [yee-gur] another, different; the other one
línyù [lin-yew] shower
  dài línyù with shower
lìrú for example
liù [lyoh] six
liùbǎi six hundred
liúgǎn [lyoh-gahn] flu
liúlì fluent
liùshí [lyoh-shur] sixty
liúxíng [lyoh-hsing] popular, fashionable
liúxíngxìng gǎnmào [gahn-mow] flu
liúxíng yīnyuè [yin-yew-eh] pop music
liùyuè [lyoh-yew-eh] June
lǐwù [lee-woo] present, gift
lìzi [lee-dzur] example; chestnut
lóng [loong] dragon
lóu [loh] floor, storey; building (with more than one storey)
lóushàng [loh-shahng] upstairs
lóutī [loh-tee] stairs

lóuxià [loh-hsyah] downstairs
lǚxíng [lyew-hsing] travel; tour; journey
lǚxíngshè [–shur] travel agent's
lǚxíngzhě [–jur] tourist
lǚxíng zhīpiào [jur-pyow] traveller's cheque
lǚyóuchē [lyew-yoh-chur] tourist bus, coach
lǚyóuzhě [lyew-joh-jur] tourist
lǚguǎn [lyew-gwahn] small hotel
lǜsède [lyew-sur-dur] green
lù road; way
lúntāi tyre
lúnzi [lun-dzur] wheel
lùtiān [loo-tyen] outdoors
lùxiàn [loo-hsyen] route
lùxiàngdài [loo-hsyang-dai] video tape
lúzào [loo-dzow] cooker

M

ma? [mah] question particle
mā mother
mǎ horse
mà scold
máfan [mah-fahn] trouble
mǎi buy
mài sell
mǎimài business deal
mǎn [mahn] full
màn slow; slowly
  hěn màn [hun] very slowly
  màn diǎnr! [dyenr] slow down!
mángmang [mahng–] busy
māo [mow] cat
máobèixīn [mow-bay-hsin] pullover

máojīn towel

màopáirhuò [mow-pai-r-hwor] fake

máotǎn [mow-tahn] blanket

máoyī sweater

màozi [mow-dzur] hat, cap

mǎshàng [mah-shahng] at once, immediately

mǎtóu [mah-toh] jetty

Máo zhǔxí [mow jyew-hshee] Chairman Mao

měi [may] each, every; beautiful

méi not; does not; no; have not

mèifū [may-foo] brother-in-law (younger sister's husband)

méi-...-guò [-gwor] has never; have never

měige [may-gur] every

měige dìfāng [dee-fahng] everywhere

měige rén [run] everyone

méi guānxi [gwahn-hshee] never mind, it doesn't matter

Měiguó [may-gwor] America; American (adj)

měijiàn shìqíng [may-jyen shur-ching] everything

měijiàn shìr [shur] everything

méi jìnr boring

měilì beautiful

mèimei younger sister

méiqì [may-chee] gas

měirén [may-run] everybody

méishìr le [may-shur lur] safe

měishùguǎn [may-shoo-gwahn] art gallery

měitiān [may-tyen] every day

méi wǎnshang [wahn-shahng] per night

méi wèntí! [wun-tee] no problem!

méixiǎngdào [may-hsyang-dow] amazing, surprising

měiyíge [may-yee-gur] each, every

měiyíge rén [run] everyone

méiyǒu [may-yoh] did not; has not, have not; without

méi-...-zhe [-zhur] was not-...-ing; is not-...-ing

-men suffix indicating the plural

mén [mun] door

Ménggǔ [mung-goo] Mongolia; Mongolian (adj)

mǐ metre; uncooked rice

Miǎndiàn [myen-dyen] Burma; Burmese (adj)

miǎn fèi [fay] free (no charge)

miánhuā [myen-hwah] cotton

miǎnshuì [myen-shway] duty-free goods

miǎo [myow] second (of time)

míngbai: wǒ míngba le [wor – lur] I see, I understand

míngpiàn [ming-pyen] card

míngtiān [ming-tyen] tomorrow

míngtiān zǎoshang [dzow-shahng] tomorrow morning

míngxìnpiàn [ming-hsin-pyen] postcard

míngzi [ming-dzur] name; first name

mòduān [mor-dwahn] end

mótuōchē [mor-twor-chur] motorbike

mǒudì [moh-dee] somewhere

mùdì cemetery

mùdìdì destination

mùjiān xiūxi [moo-jyen hsyoh-hshee] interval

mǔqīn [moo-chin] mother

mùtou [moo-toh] wood

N

ná [nah] carry; take

nà that; that one; the

nǎinai grandmother (paternal)

nǎiniú [nai-nyoh] cow

nǎli? [nah-lee] where?

nán [nahn] south; hard, difficult; man

nán cèsuǒ [tsur-swor] gents' toilet, men's room

nánfāng [nahn-fahng] in the south

Nánfēi [nahn-fay] South Africa; South African (adj)

nán fúwùyuán [foo-woo-yew-ahn] waiter; steward

nánguò [nahn-gwor] sad

nánhái boy

nánkàn [nahn-kahn] ugly

nán péngyou [pung-yoh] boyfriend

nánrén [nahn-run] man

nǎr? where?

zài nǎr? [dzai] where is it?

nǐ qù nǎr? [chew] where are you going?

nàr there

nà shí [nah shur] then, at that time

nà shì-... ma? [mah] is that-...?

nà shì shénme? [shun-mur] what's that?

názhe [nah-jur] keep

ne [nur] sentence particle which adds emphasis or conveys the idea 'and what about-...?'

nèi [nay] that; that one

nèi? [nay] which?

nèidì brother-in-law (wife's younger brother)

nèige [nay-gur] that; that one

nèige shíhou [shur-hoh] then, at that time

nèixiōng [nay-hsyoong] brother-in-law (wife's elder brother)

nèi yíge [yee-gur] that one

néng: nǐ néng-... ma? [nung-... mah] can you-...?

wǒ bù néng-... [wor] I can't-...

nǐ you (sing)

niàn [nyen] read (aloud)

nián year

niánjì [nyen-jee] age

nín duō dà niánjì le? [dwor dah nyen-jee lur] how old are you?

niánlíng: nín duō dà niánlíng? [nyen-ling] how old are you?

niánqīng [nyen-ching] young

niǎo [nyow] bird

niàobù [nyow-boo] nappy, diaper

Níbóěr [nee-bor-er] Nepal; Nepali (adj)

níde [nee-dur] your; yours (sing)

nǐ hǎo [nee how] hello; hi; how do you do?

nǐ hǎo ma? [mah] how are you?

nǐmen [nee-mun] you (pl)

nǐmende [–dur] your; yours (pl)

nín you (sing, pol)

nínde [nin-dur] your; yours (sing, pol)

niúzǎikù [nyoh-dzai-koo] jeans

nóng [noong] strong

nóngchǎng [–chahng] farm

nóngcūn [–tsun] countryside

nǚ'ér [nyew-er] daughter

nǚ cèsuǒ [tsur-swor] ladies' room, ladies' toilets

nǚ chènshān [nyew-chun-shahn] blouse

nǚ fúwùyuán [foo-woo-yew-ahn] waitress; maid; stewardess

nǚ háir [hai-r] girl

nǚpéngyou [nyew-pung-yoh] girlfriend

nǚshì [nyew-shur] Ms; lady

nǚzhāodài [nyew-jow-dai] waitress

nuǎnhuo [nwahn-hwor] warm; mild

nuǎnqì [nwahn-chee] heating; central heating; radiator

O

Ōuzhōu [oh-joh] Europe; European (adj)

P

pàichūsuǒ [pai-choo-swor] police station

pán [pahn] measure word* used for round objects

pàng [pahng] fat

páng side

pángbiān: zài-... pángbiān [dzai-... pahng-byen] beside the-..., next to-...

pánzi [pahn-dzur] plate

pǎo [pow] run

péngchē [pung-chur] van

pèngtóu dìdiǎn [pung-toh dee-dyen] meeting place

péngyou [pung-yoh] friend

pēnquán [pun-choo-en] fountain

piányi [pyen-yee] be inexpensive; inexpensive

piào [pyow] ticket; single ticket, one-way ticket

piàoliang [pyow-lyang] beautiful; pretty

pífu skin

pígé [pee-gur] leather

píng'ān [ping-ahn] safe

píngcháng [ping-chahng] usual, normal

pīngpāngqiú [ping-pahng-chyoh] table tennis

píngtǎn [ping-tahn] flat (adj)

píngzi [ping-dzur] bottle

pǔtōng [poo-toong] ordinary

Pǔtōnghuà [–hwah] Mandarin

Q

qī [chee] seven
qián [chyen] money
qiánbāo [–bow] wallet; purse
qiānbǐ pencil
qiánbianr: zài qiánbianr [dzai chyen-byenr] in front; at the front
qiáng [chyang] wall
qiángjiān [–jyen] rape
qiǎngle [–lur] robbed
qiánmiàn [chyen-myen] front
qiántiān [–tyen] the day before yesterday
qiántīng lobby
qiānwàn [–wahn] ten million
qiánxiōng [–hsyoong] breast; bust; chest
qián yì tiān [tyen] the day before
qiānzhèng [–jung] visa
qiānzì [–dzur] signature
qiáo [chyow] bridge
qiǎokèlì [–kur-lee] chocolate
qiāozhúgàng [–joo-gahng] rip-off
qībǎi [chee-bai] seven hundred
qìchē [chee-chur] car
  zuò qìchē [dzwor] by car
qìchē chūzū [choo-dzoo] car rental
qìchē zǒngzhàn [dzoong-jahn] bus station (for city buses)
qìchē xiūlíchǎng [hsyoh- lur-chahng] garage (for repairs)
qǐchuáng [chee-chwahng] get up (in the morning)

qiè [chyeh] cut
qǐfēi shíjiān [chee-fay shee-jyen] departure
qíguài(de) [chee-gwai(-dur)] weird, strange, odd
qí mǎ [chee mah] horse riding
qīng [ching] light (not heavy)
qǐng please; ask, request
qīngdàn [–dahn] mild
qǐng jìn come in
qīngshàonián [–show-nyen] teenager
qīngxīn [–hsin] fresh
qióng [chyoong] poor
qīshí [chee-shur] seventy
qítā [chee-tah] other
qìtǐng [chee-ting] motorboat
qiú [chyoh] ball
qiúmí sports fan
qiúpāi racket (tennis, squash)
qiūtian [chyoh-tyen] autumn, (US) fall; in the autumn/fall
qìxiè [chee-hsyeh] equipment
qìyóu [chee-yoh] petrol, (US) gas
qīyuè [chee-yew-eh] July
qīzi [chee-dzur] wife
qí zìxíngchē de rén [chee dzur-sing-chur dur run] cyclist
qù [chew] go; to
qǔ get, fetch
quánbù [choo-en-boo] all; all of it, the whole lot
quánguó [–gwor] national, nationwide
qùnián [chew-nyen] last year
qúnzi [chewn-dzur] skirt

qī:

R

ránhòu [rahn-hoh] then, after that

rè [rur] hot; heat

rèdù [rur-doo] temperature; fever

rèle [rur-lur] hot

rén [run] person

wǒ shì-... rén [wor shur] I come from-...

rènao [rur-now] busy, lively

rēng [rung] throw

rènhé [run-hur] any

rènhé rén anybody

rènhé shénme [shun-mur] anything

rénkǒu [run-koh] population

rénmín people

rénqún [run-chewn] crowd

rènshi [run-shur] know; recognize

rénxíng dào [run-hsing dow] pavement, sidewalk

rénxíng héngdào [hung-dow] pedestrian crossing

rèshuǐpíng [rur-shway-ping] Thermos® flask

Rìběn [ree-bun] Japan

rìjì [rur-jee] diary

róngyì [roong-yee] easy

ròu [roh] meat

ruǎn [rwahn] soft

ruǎnpán [rwahn-pahn] disk

ruǎnwò [–wor] soft sleeper, first class sleeper

ruǎnzuò [–dzwor] soft seat, first class seat

rúguǒ [roo-gwor] if

Ruìdiǎn [rway-dyen] Sweden

rùkǒu [roo-koh] entrance

ruò [rwor] weak

S

sāi cheek

sāizi [sai-dzur] plug (in sink)

sān [sahn] three

sānbǎi three hundred

sānděng [sahn-dung] third class

sǎngzi [sahng-dzur] Thursday

sānjiǎokù [sahn-jyow-koo] pants, panties

sānshí [sahn-shur] thirty

sānyuè [sahn-yew-eh] March

sēnlín [sun-lin] forest

shā [shah] sand; kill

shāfā [shah-fah] sofa

shǎguā [shah-gwah] idiot

shàiyīshéng [shai-yee-shung] clothes line

shān [shahn] mountain, hill

shāndòng [–doong] cave

shàng [shahng] up; above

zài-...-shàng [dzai] above-...

shàngdì God

shāngdiàn [–dyen] shop

shàngmian: zài-... shàngmian [dzai---myen] on-...

shàngtou: zài-... shàngtou [–toh] on top of-...

shāngǔ [shahn-goo] valley

shānguāngdēng [shahn-gwahng-dung] flash (for camera)

shàngwǔ a.m. (from 9 a.m. to noon)

shāngxīn [–hsin] sad

shàng xīngqī [hsing-chee] last week

shàngyī jacket

shàng yícì [yee-tsur] last time

shànzi [shahn-dzur] fan (hand-held)

shǎo [show] less

shāoshāng [show-shahng] burn (noun)

shǎoshù mínzú [show-shoo mind-zoo] nationality (for Chinese minorities)

shǎoyú [show-yew] under, less than

sháozi [show-dzur] spoon

shēchǐ [shur-chur] luxury

shéi? [shay] who?

shéide? [shay-dur] whose?

shēn [shun] deep

shēng [shung] be born; litre

shēng bìngle [shung bing-lur] ill

shèngdàn jié [–dahn jyeh] Christmas

shēngqì [–chee] angry

shēngrén [–run] stranger

shēngrì [–rur] birthday

shēngyi business

shēngyīn voice

shéngzi [–dzur] string; rope

shénjīngbìng [shun-jing-bing] crazy

shénkān [shun-kahn] shrine

shénme [shun-mur] anything; something

shénme? what?

shénme shíhòu? [shur-hoh] when?

shénme yàng de-...? [dur] what sort of-...?

nǐ shuō shénme? [shwor] sorry?, pardon (me)?

shénme yě méiyǒu [yur may-yoh] none

shēntǐ [shun-tee] body

shèshì [shur-shur] centigrade

shì [shur] to be; is; are; was; were; will be; it is; it was; yes, it is the case

shì-... ma? [mah] is it-...?

shí ten

shī wet

shíbā [shur-bah] eighteen

shìchǎng [shur-chahng] market

shìde [shur-dur] yes, it is the case

shí'èr [shur-er] twelve

shí'èr yuè [yew-eh] December

shìgù [shur-goo] accident

shíhou: zài-... de shíhou [dzai-... dur shur-hoh] during-...

shíjiān [shur-jyen] time

shíjiānbiǎo [–byow] timetable, (US) schedule

shìjiè [shur-jyeh] world

shíjiǔ [shur-jyoh] nineteen

shíliù [shur-lyoh] sixteen

shímáo [shur-mow] fashionable

shìnèi [shur-nay] indoors; indoor

shípǐn diàn [shur-pin dyen] food store

shíqī [shur-chee] seventeen; period (of time)

shìqūchē [shur-chew-chur] city bus

shìr [shur] thing, matter

shísān [shur-sahn] thirteen

shísì [shur-sur] fourteen

shíwàn [shur-wahn] hundred thousand

shíwù [shur-woo] food

shíwǔ fifteen

shíwù zhòngdú [joong-doo] food poisoning

shíyī [shur-yee] eleven

shíyīyuè [shur-yee-yew-eh] November

shíyuè [shur-yew-eh] October

shizhèngfǔ dàlóu [shur-jung-foo dah-loh] town hall

shì zhōngxīn [shur joong-sin] city centre

shízì lùkǒu [shur-dzur loo-koh] crossroads, intersection

shǒu [shoh] hand

shòu thin

shòu huānyíng [hwahn-ying] popular

shòuhuòtíng [shoh-hwor-ting] kiosk

shōujù [shoh-jew] receipt

shǒujuànr [shoh-jwahnr] handkerchief

shòupiàochù [shoh-pyow-choo] ticket office; box office

shòushāng [shoh-shahng] injured

shǒushi [shoh-shur] jewellery

shǒushù operation

shǒutào [shoh-tow] glove

shǒutíbāo [shoh-tee-bow] handbag, (US) purse

shǒutíxiāng [shoh-tee-hsyang] suitcase

shǒutí xíngli [shoh-tee hsing-lee] hand luggage

shǒuwànr [shoh-wahnr] wrist

shǒuxiān [shoh-hsyen] at first

shǒuyīnjī [shoh-yin-jee] radio

shǒuzhǐ [shoh-jur] toilet paper; finger

shǒuzhuó [shoh-jwor] bracelet

shū [shoo] book

shú ripe

shù tree

shuāng [shwahng] double

shuāngrén chuáng [–run chwahng] double bed

shuāngrén fángjiān [fahng-jyen] double room

shūdiàn [shoo-dyen] bookshop, bookstore

shūfu well; comfortable

shuǐ [shway] water

shuǐchí [–chur] sink; swimming pool

shuǐguǎnr [–gwahnr] pipe

shuǐguǒ [–gwor] fruit

shuìjiào [–jyow] sleep; asleep

shuǐlóng tóu [–loong toh] tap, faucet

shuìqún [–chewn] nightdress

shuìyī pyjamas

shùlín woods, forest

shuō [shwor] say

shuōhuà [–hwah] talk

shuōmíngshū leaflet; brochure

shūshu uncle (father's younger brother)

shùzì [shoo-dzur] number

sǐ [sur] die; dead

sì four; Buddhist temple

sìbǎi four hundred

sīchóu [sur-choh] silk

sì fēn zhī yī [fun jur] quarter

sījī [sur-jee] driver

sǐle [sur-lur] dead

sīrén(de) [sur-run(-dur)] private

sìshí [sur-shur] forty

sǐwáng [sur-wahng] death

sìyuàn [sur-yew-ahn] Buddhist monastery

sìyuè [sur-yew-eh] April

sòng [soong] deliver; send

sòng fàn fúwù [fahn foo-woo] room service

sòngxìn delivery (of mail)

suān [swahn] be sour; sour

suānténg [–tung] ache

Sūgélán [soo-gur-lahn] Scotland; Scottish

suíbiàn [sway-byen] informal

suídào [sway-dow] tunnel

suīrán [sway-rahn] although

sùliào [soo-lyow] plastic

sùliàodài plastic bag

sūnnǚr [sun-nyewr] granddaughter (son's daughter)

sūnzi [sun-dzur] grandson (son's son)

suǒ [swor] lock; locked; measure word* used for buildings

suǒyǒu de dōngxi [swor-yoh dur doong-hshee] everything

sùshài-r de [soo-shai-r dur] plain, not patterned

sùxiàng [soo-hsyang] statue

T

tā [tah] he; she; it; him; her

tǎ pagoda

tāde [tah-dur] his; her; hers; its

tài too (excessively)

tài duō [dwor] too much

Tàiguó [tai-gwor] Thailand

tàihǎole [tai-how-lur] fantastic; well done

tài shòu [tai shoh] skinny

tàiyáng sun

tàiyángjìng sunglasses

tāmen [tah-mun] they; them

tāmen quánbù [choo-en-boo] all of them

tāmende [tah-mun-dur] their; theirs

tān [tahn] greedy

tángdì [tahng-dee] cousin (son of father's brother)

tángjiě [–jyeh] cousin (daughter of father's brother)

tángkuàir [–kwai-r] sweets, candies

tángmèi [–may] cousin (daughter of father's brother)

tángniàobìng [–nyow-bing] diabetic

tángxiōng [–hsyoong] cousin (son of father's brother)

tǎnzi [tahn-dzur] blanket

táoqì [tow-chee] pottery

tàoshān [tow-shahn] jumper

tàozhuāng [tow-jwahng] suit

tèbié [tur-byeh] especially

téng [tung] pain, ache; painful
tiān [tyen] day; sky
tián sweet (taste)
tiándì field
tiānqi [tyen-chee] weather
tiáo [tyow] measure word★
  used for fish and long narrow
  objects
tiàowǔ [tyow-woo] dance
tiàozǎo [tyow-dzow] flea
tiělù [tyeh-loo] railway
tíng stop
tíngchē [–chur] park
tíngchēchǎng [–chahng] car
  park, parking lot; garage
tíngdiàn [–dyen] power cut
tíngzi [–dzur] pavilion
tíqián [tee-chyen] in advance
tìxūdāo [tee-hsyew-dow] razor
tǐyùguǎn [tee-yoo-gwahn] gym
tǒng [toong] bucket
tóngyì agree
tóu [toh] head
tōu steal
tóufa [toh-fah] hair
tóujīn headscarf
tòumíng jiāobù [jyow-boo]
  Sellotape®, Scotch tape®
tóuténg [toh-tung] headache
tóuyūn [toh-yewn] dizzy, faint
tú'àn [too-ahn] pattern
tuán [twahn] group
tuántǐ [twahn-tee] party, group
tuì [tway] cancel
tuǐ leg
tuī push
tuìkuǎn [tway-kwahn] refund
túpiàn [too-pyen] picture
tūrán [too-rahn] suddenly

W

-wài outside
wàigōng [wai-goong]
  grandfather (maternal)
wàiguó [wai-gwor] foreign
wàiguó rén [run] foreigner
wàimian [wai-myen] outside
wàipó [wai-por] grandmother
  (maternal)
wàisūn [wai-sun] grandson
  (daughter's son)
wàisūnnǚr [–nyewr]
  granddaughter (daughter's
  daughter)
wài sūnzi [sun-dzur] grandson
  (daughter's son)
wàitào [wai-tow] jacket
wàiyī jacket; coat
wǎn'ān [wahn-ahn] good night
wǎn [wahn] late (at night)
wàn ten thousand
wǎncān [wahn-tsahn] dinner
wǎndiǎn [wahn-dyen] delay
wǎnfàn [wahn-fahn] evening
  meal; supper
wàng [wahng] forget
wǎng towards; net (in sport)
wǎnhuì [wahn-hway] party
  (celebration)
wánjù [wahn-jyew] toy
wánquándi [wahn-choo-en-dee]
  completely
wánr [wahnr] play (verb)
wǎnshang [wahn-shahng]
  evening; in the evening
  jīntiān wǎnshang [jin-tyen] this
  evening

wánxiào [wahn-hsyow] joke

Wēi'ěrshì [way-er-shur] Welsh

wéi [way] hello

wèi because of; stomach; measure word* used politely to refer to ladies, gentlemen, guests etc

wèidao [way-dow] flavour

Wēiěrshì [way-er-shur] Wales

wèihūnfū fiancé

wèihūnqī [–chee] fiancée

wéijīn [way-jin] scarf

wèir [wayr] taste; smell

wèishēngjīn [way-shung-jin] sanitary napkin/towel

wèishēngzhǐ [way-shung-jur] toilet paper

wèishénme? [way-shun-mur] why?

  wèishénme bù? why not?

wēixiǎn [way-hsyen] dangerous

wèn [wun] ask (a question)

wénhuà dà gémìng [wun-hwah dah gur-ming] Cultural Revolution

wénjiàn [wun-jyen] document

wèntí [wun-tee] problem, question

wènxùnchù [wun-hsyewn-choo] information desk

wénzhàng [wun-jahng] mosquito net

wénzi [wun-dzur] mosquito

wǒ [wor] I; me

wǒde [wor-dur] my; mine

wǒmen [wor-mun] we; us

wǒmende [–dur] our; ours

wòpù [wor-poo] couchette; sleeper; berth

wòpù chēxiāng [chur-hsyang] sleeping car

wòshì [wor-shur] bedroom

wǔ [woo] five

wù mist; fog

wúbǎi [woo-fahn] five hundred

wǔfàn [woo-fahn] lunch

wùhuì [woo-hway] misunderstanding

wūjiǎor [woo-jyowr] in the corner of a room

wǔshí [woo-shur] fifty

wǔshù [woo-shoo] martial arts

wǔyuè [woo-yew-eh] May

X

xǐ [hshee] wash

xī west

xiā [hsyah] blind

xià down; below

  xià yícì [yee-tsur] next time

  xià yíge [yee-gur] next

  xià xīngqī [hsing-chee] next week

  zài-...-xià [dzai] under-...

xiàba [–bah] jaw, chin

xià chē [–chur] get out

xiàge [–gur] next

xiàmian: zài-... xiàmian [dzai–-myen] below-...

xiàn [hsyen] line; thread

xiān: nǐ xiān qǐng [ching] after you

xiàndài modern

xiǎng want; think

xiāngdāng [–dahng] quite, fairly

xiāngdāng duō [dwor] quite a lot

xiàngdǎo [–dow] guide

Xiānggǎng [–gahng] Hong Kong

xiàngjiāo [–jyow] rubber

xiàngjìn de [dur] similar

xiàngliàn [–lyen] necklace

xiàngpí rubber, eraser

xiàngqí [–chee] chess

xiāngshuǐr [–shwayr] perfume

xiāngxìn [–hsin] believe

xiāngyān [–yahn] cigarette

xiànqián [hsyen-chyen] cash

xiānsheng [hsyen-shung] Mr

xiānyàn [–yen] bright

xiànzài [–dzai] now

xiào [hsyow] laugh; smile

xiǎo little, small; tight

xiāofángduì [–fahng-dway] fire brigade

xiǎofèi [–fay] service charge; tip

xiǎo húzi [hoo-dzur] moustache

xiǎojiě [–jyeh] Miss

xiǎolù path

xiǎo qìchē [chee-chur] car

xiǎo sānjiǎokù [sahn-jyow-koo] pants, panties

xiǎoshān [–shahn] hill

xiǎosháor [–showr] spoon

xiǎoshí [–shur] hour

xiǎoshū brother-in-law (husband's younger brother)

xiāoxi [–hsee] information

xiǎoxī stream

xiǎoxīn! [–hsin] look out!

xiáozǔ [–dzyew] group

xiàshuǐdào [hsyah-shway-dow] drain

xiàtian [–tyen] summer; in the summer

xiàwǔ afternoon; in the afternoon; p.m.

jīntian xiàwǔ [jin-tyen] this afternoon

xià yíge [yee-gur] next

Xībānyá [hshee-bahn-yah] Spain; Spanish (adj)

xīběi [hshee-bay] northwest

xībiānr [–byenr] in the west

xīcān [–tsahn] Western-style food

xīcāntīng [–tsahn-ting] Western-style restaurant

xiě [hsyeh] blood; write

xié shoe

xiē a little bit

... xiē a bit more–...

xiédǐ [–dee] sole (of shoe)

xié hòugēn [hoh-gun] heel (of shoe)

xièxie [hsyeh-hsyeh] thank you

xièxie, wǒ bú yào [wor boo yow] no thanks

Xīfāng [hshee-fahng] West; in the West; Western

Xīfāng de [dur] Western (adj)

xīgài knee

xǐhǎo de yīfu [–how dur yee-foo] washing (clean)

xǐhuan [–hwahn] like

xìn [hsin] letter, message

xīn new

xī'nán [hshee-ahn] southwest

xìnfēng [hsin-fung] envelope

xíng [hsing] all right

xìng surname

xìnggǎn [–gahn] sexy

xìngkuī [–kway] fortunately

xíngle [–lur] that's OK

xǐngle awake

xíngli luggage, baggage

xīngqī [–chee] week

xīngqīèr [–chee-er] Tuesday

xīngqīliù [–lyoh] Saturday

xīngqīsān [–chee-sahn] Wednesday

xīngqītiān [–tyen] Sunday

xīngqīwǔ [–woo] Friday

xīngqīyī Monday

xìngqu [–chew] interest

xīngxing star

xìnhào [hsin-how] signal

xìnshǐ [hsin-shur] courier

xīnwén [hsin-wun] news (radio, TV etc)

xīnxiān [hsin-hsyen] fresh

xìnxiāng [hsin-hsyang] postbox, mailbox

Xīnxīlán [hsin-hshee-lahn] New Zealand

xìnyòng kǎ [hsin-yoong kah] credit card

xīnzàng [hsin-dzahng] heart

xiōng [hsyoong] chest

xiōngdì brother

xiōngkǒu [–koh] chest

xiōngzhào [–jow] bra

xiōngzhēn [–jun] brooch

xìshéng [hshee-shung] string

xīshì [hshee-shur] Western-style

xiūlǐ [hsyoh-lee] repair

xiūxiéjiàng [–hsyeh-jyang] shoe repairer

xiūxiépù shoe repairer

xiūxìshì [–hshee-shur] lounge

xiūxītīng foyer

xiùzhēn fàngyīnjī [–jun fahng-yin-jee] personal stereo

xiùzi [–dzur] sleeve

xīwàng [hshee-wahng] hope

xǐyīdiàn [–dyen] laundry (place)

xǐyījī washing machine

xīyǐnrén [–run] attractive

xīyǒu [–yoh] rare, uncommon

Xīzàng [–dzahng] Tibet

xǐzǎo [–dzow] bathe

xǐzǎojiān [–jyen] bathroom

xuǎn [hsyew-ahn] choose

xuányá [–yah] cliff

xǔduō [–dwor] a lot, lots, plenty of

xuě [hsyew-eh] snow

xuějiā [–jyah] cigar

xuéqī [–chur] term

xuésheng [–shung] student

xuéxí [–hshee] learn

xuéxiào [–hsyow] school

xuéyuàn [–yew-ahn] college

xuēzi [–dzur] boot (footwear)

xǔkě zhèng [hsyew-kur jung] permit (noun)

xūyào [hsyew-yow] need

Y

yá [yah] tooth

yágāo [yah-gow] toothpaste

yājīn [yah-jin] deposit

yákē dàifu [yah-kur] dentist

yákē yīshēng [yee-shung] dentist

yān [yen] smoke

nǐ chōu yān ma? [choh yen mah] do you smoke?

yāndǒu [yen-doh] pipe
yǎng itch
yángguāng [yang-gwahng] sunshine
yángmáo [yang-mow] wool
yángsǎn [yang-sahn] sunshade
yángtái balcony
yángwáwa [yang-wah-wah] doll
yànhuì [yen-hway] banquet
yǎnjing [yen-jing] eye
yǎnjìng glasses, eyeglasses
yǎnjìngdiàn [–dyen] optician
yǎnkē yīshēng [yen-kur yee-shung] optician
yánsè [yen-sur] colour
yǎo [yow] bite (by insect)
yāo waist; one
yào want; drug; Chinese medicine
  nǐ yào shénme? [shun-mur] what do you want?
yàobùrán [yow-boor-ahn] otherwise
yāodài [yow-dai] belt
yàodiàn [yow-dyen] pharmacy
yáodòng [yow-doong] cave (dwelling)
yàofāng [yow-fahng] prescription
yàogāo [yow-gow] ointment
yàomián [yow-myen] cotton wool, absorbent cotton
yāoqǐng [yow-ching] invitation; invite
yǎoshāng [yow-shahng] bite
yàoshi [yow-shur] key
yáshuā [yah-shwah] toothbrush
yáténg [yah-tung] toothache
yě [yur] also, too

yè night; page
yèli at night; p.m.
yéye [yur-yur] grandfather (paternal)
yèzǒnghuì [yur-dzoong-hway] nightclub
yī [yee] one
yìbǎi one hundred
yíbàn [yee-bahn] half
yìbāo [yee-bow] packet
yìbēi [yee-bay] cup
yīcéng [yee-tsung] ground floor, (US) first floor
yícì [yee-tsur] once
  xià yícì [hsyah] next time
yìdá [yee-dah] dozen
yídàkuàir [–kwai-r] a big bit
yīděng [yee-dung] first class
yìdiǎnr [yee-dyenr] a little bit
  ... yìdiǎnr a bit more-...
yìdiǎnrdiǎnr tiny
yídìng definitely
yīfu dress; clothes
yíge [yee-gur] one
  nǎ yíge? [nah yee-gur] which one?
yígèrén [yee-gur-run] alone
yígòng [yee-goong] altogether
yí guànr [gwahnr] can; jug
yǐhòu [yee-hoh] after; afterwards
yíhuìr [yee-hwayr] soon
yǐjīng already
yíkè [yee-kur] quarter past
yíkuàir [yee-kwai-r] piece
yīlǐng collar
yī lóu [loh] ground floor, (US) first floor
yílù shùnfēng! [yee-loo shun-

fung] have a good journey!

yímā [yee-mah] aunt (mother's sister)

yīmàojiān [yee-mow-jyen] cloakroom

yímǔ [yee-moo] aunt (mother's sister)

yín(zi) [yin(-dzur)] silver

Yìndu [yin-doo] India; Indian (adj)

yìng hard

yīngbàng [ying-bahng] pound sterling

yìngbì coin

yīng'ér [ying-er] baby

Yīngguó [ying-gwor] England; Britain; English; British

Yīngguóde [–dur] English; British

yìngwò [ying-wor] hard sleeper, second class sleeper

Yīngyǔ [ying-yew] English (language)

yìngzuò [ying-dzwor] hard seat, third class seat

yínháng [yin-hahng] bank

yínshuǐ lóngtóu [yin-shway loong-toh] fountain (for drinking)

yīnwèi [yin-way] because

yǐnyòngshuǐ [yin-yoong-shway] drinking water

yīnyuè [yin-yew-eh] music

yīnyuèhuì [–way] concert

yìqǐ [yee-chee] together

yìqián:-... yǐqián [yee-chyen] before-...

yìqiān one thousand

yírìyóu [yee-rur-yoh] day trip

yīsheng [yee-shung] doctor

yìshù [yee-shoo] art

yíwàn [yee-wahn] ten thousand

yǐxià: zài-... yǐxià [dzai-... yee-hsyah] below, less than

yìxiē [yee-hsyeh] a few

yí yì [yur yee] a hundred million

yīyuàn [yee-yew-ahn] hospital

yìzhí cháoqián [yee-jur chow-chyen] straight ahead

yǐzi [yee-dzur] chair

yòng [yoong] with; by means of; use; in

yōngjǐ [–jee] crowded

yǒu [yoh] have; there is; there are

yǒu-... ma? [mah] is there-...?; are there-...?

yòu right (not left)

yòubiānr [yoh-byenr] right

yòubìng [yoh-bing] ill, sick

yǒudúde [yoh-doo-dur] poisonous

yǒuguǐ diànchē [yoh-gway dyen-chur] tram

yǒuhǎo [yoh-how] friendly

yóujì [yoh-jee] post, mail (verb)

yóujiàn [yoh-jyen] post, mail

yóujú [yoh-jew] post office

yóulǎn [yoh-lahn] tour, visit

yǒu lǐmào [yoh lee-mow] polite

yǒu máobìng [yoh mow-bing] faulty

yǒumíng famous

yóunì [yoh-nee] greasy, oily (food)

yóupiào [yoh-pyow] stamp

yǒuqián [yoh-chyen] rich

yǒurén [yoh-run] somebody, someone; engaged, occupied

yŏushíhòu [yoh-shur-hoh] sometimes

Yóutàiren de [yoh-tai-run dur] Jewish

yóuxì [yoh-hshee] game

yŏuxiào [yoh-hsyow] valid

yòu yíge [yee-gur] another, one more

yŏu yìsi [yee-sur] interesting; funny, amusing

yóuyŏng [yoh-yoong] swim

yŏuyòng useful

yóuyŏngchí [–chur] swimming pool

yóuzhèng biānmă [yoh-jung byen-mah] postcode, zip code

yú [yew] fish

yù jade

yŭ rain

yuăn [yew-ahn] far; far away

yuănchù: zài yuănchù [dzai yew-ahn-choo] in the distance

yuánlái de [dur] usual

yuánzhūbĭ [–joo-bee] ballpoint pen

yúchŭn [yew-chun] stupid

yùdìng [yew-ding] reservation; reserve

yuè [yew-eh] month

yuèfù father-in-law

yuèfù yuèmŭ [yew-eh-moo] husband's parents-in-law

yuèliang [yew-eh-lyang] moon

Yuènán [yew-eh-nahn] Vietnam

yúkuài [yew-kwai] lovely

yúkuàide [yew-kwai-dur] enjoyable

yùndòng [yewn-doong] sport

yùndŏu [yewn-doh] iron

yùnqi [yewn-chee] luck

yŭsăn [yew-sahn] umbrella

yùshì [yew-shur] bathroom

yŭyán [yew-yahn] language

yŭyán kè [yew-yahn kur] language course

yŭyī [yew-yee] raincoat

yùyuē [yew-yew-eh] appointment

Z

záhuòdiàn [dzah-hwor-dyen] grocer's

zài [dzai] in; at; on; be in/at a place; again

zài năr? where is it?

zài-... de shíhou [dur shur-hoh] during-...

zài-... hòumian [hoh-myen] behind-...

zàijiàn [dzai-jyen] goodbye

zài nàr over there; up there

zájì acrobatics

zài-...-li inside-...

zài-...-pángbiān [pahng-byen] beside the-..., next to-...

zài-...-shàng [shahng] above-...

zài-...-shàngmian [shahng-myen] on-...

zài-...-xià [hsyah] under-...

zài-...-xiàmian [hsyah-myen] below-...

zài-...-yĭxià [yee-hsyah] below-..., less than-...

zài-...-zhījiān [jur-jyen] between-...

zài-...-zhōng [joong] among-...

zāng [dzahng] dirty, filthy

zànglǐ funeral

zǎo [dzow] good morning; early

yì zǎo early in the morning

zǎofàn [dzow-fahn] breakfast

zǎopén [dzow-pun] bathtub

zǎoshang [dzow-shahng] morning; in the morning; a.m. (up to 9 a.m.)

jīntiān zǎoshang [jin-tyen] this morning

zàoyīn [dzow-yin] noise

zázhì [dzah-jur] magazine

zéi [dzay] thief

zěnme? [dzun-mur] how?

zěnme huí shìr? [hway shur] what's happening?; what's up?, what's wrong?

zěnme le? [lur] what's happening?

zěnmele? what's wrong?, what's the matter?

zhǎi [jai] narrow

zhāng [jahng] measure word* used for tables, beds, tickets and sheets of paper

zhàngfu husband

zhānglǎng [–lahng] cockroach

zhàntái [jahn-tai] platform, (US) track

zhànxiàn [jahn-hsyen] engaged

zhànzhù [jahn-joo] stop

zhǎodào [jow-dow] find

zhàopiàn [jow-pyen] photo

zhāotiē [jow-tyeh] poster

zhàoxiàngjī [jow-hsyang-jee] camera

zhá tǔdòupiànr [jah too-doh-pyenr] crisps, (US) potato chips

zhè [jur] this; the

-zhe verb suffix indicating continuous action or two actions taking place at the same time

zhèi [jay] this; this one

zhèi? whose?

zhèicì [jay-tsur] this time

zhèige [jay-gur] this; this one

zhēn [jun] really

zhēnde [jun-dur] true; genuine, real; sure

zhèngcháng(de) [jung-chahng(-dur)] normal

zhèngfǔ [jung-foo] government

zhèngshì [jung-shur] formal

zhēnguì(de) [jung-way(-dur)] valuable

zhéngzhěng whole, full

zhēnjiǔ [jun-jyoh] acupuncture

zhēn láijìn exciting

zhěnsuǒ [jun-swor] clinic

zhèntou [jun-toh] pillow

zhènyǔ [jun-yew] shower

zhēnzhèng [jun-jung] genuine

zhèr [jer] here

zài zhèr [dzai] over here

zhī [jur] measure word* used for hands, birds, suitcases and boats

zhīdao [jur-dow] know

wǒ bù zhīdao [wor] I don't know

zhífēi [jur-fay] direct flight

zhījiān: zài-... zhījiān [dzai-... jur-jyen] between-...

zhíjiē [jur-jyeh] direct

zhǐjīn [jur-jin] tissue, Kleenex®

zhìliàng [jur-lyang] quality

zhínǚ [jin-yew] niece

zhǐshi [jur-shur] only

zhǐténgyào [jur-tung-yow] painkiller

zhíwù [jur-woo] plant

zhǐxuě gāobù [jur-hsyew-eh gow-boo] plaster, Bandaid®

zhǐyǒu [jur-yoh] only

zhìzào [jur-dzow] make (verb)

zhízi [jur-dzur] nephew

zhì [jur] cure (verb)

zhǐ just, only; paper

zhōng [joong] clock

-zhōng in the middle; between

zài-...-zhōng [dzai joong] among-...

zhòng heavy

zhǒng type; swollen

zhōngdiǎnzhàn [–dyen-jahn] rail terminus

Zhōngguó [joong-gwor] China; Chinese (adj)

Zhōngguó rén [run] Chinese (person)

Zhōngguó rénmín [run-min] the Chinese

Zhōnghuá Rénmín Gònghéguó [–hwah run-min goong-hur-gwor] People's Republic of China

zhōngjiān: zài zhōngjiān [dzai joong-jyen] in the middle

zhòngliàng [–lyang] weight

Zhōngshì [–shur] Chinese-style

Zhōngwén [–wun] Chinese (written language)

zhōngwǔ noon; at noon

zhōngxīn [–hsin] central; centre

zhòngyào [–yow] important

zhōngzhuǎn [–jwahn] connection

zhōumò [joh-mor] weekend

zhù [joo] live (verb)

nín zhù nǎr? what's your address?

zhuǎnxìn dìzhǐ [–hsin dee-jur] forwarding address

zhújiàn de [joo-jyen dur] gradually

zhǔnbèi hǎo le [jun-bay how lur] ready

zhù nǐ shùnlì! [joo nee shun-lee] good luck!

zhuōzi [jwor-dzur] table

zhǔyào de [joo-yow dur] main

zhǔyì [joo-yee] idea

zhúzi [joo-dzur] bamboo

zǐ [dzur] purple

zìdòng [dzur-doong] automatic

zìdòng qǔkuǎnjī [chew-kwahn-jee] cash dispenser, ATM

zìjǐ [dzur-jee] oneself

zìrán [dzur-rahn] natural

zìxíngchē [dzur-hsing-chur] bicycle

zìyóu [dzur-yoh] free

zìzhù [dzur-joo] self-service

zǒng [dzoong] always

zǒng fúwùtái reception desk

zǒnggòng [–goong] total

zǒngjī operator

zǒngjiào [–jyow] religion

zǒngsè [–sur] brown

zǒngshì [–shur] always

zǒu [dzoh] leave, depart, go

zǒuláng [dzoh-lahng] corridor

zǒuzou go for a walk

zū [dzoo] hire, rent

zuǐ [dzway] mouth
zuì drunk
 zuì-... ...-est, the most-...
zuǐba [-bah] mouth
zuì hǎo [how] best
zuìhòu [–hoh] eventually; last
zuì huài [hwai] worst
zuìjìn recently; last, latest
zuò [dzwor] by; do
 zuò fēijī [fay-jee] by air
 zuò huǒchē [hwor-chur] by rail
zuǒ left
zuǒbiānr [–byenr] left
zuò fānyì [fahn-yee] interpret
zuótiān [–tyen] yesterday
 zuótiān wǎnshang [wahn-shahng] last night
 zuótian zǎoshang [dzow-shahng] yesterday morning
zuòwei [–way] seat
zuòxià [–hsyah] sit down
zuǒyòu [–yoh] about
zúqiúsài football

Zu

Chinese

→

English
Signs and Notices

Contents

General Signs

危险 wēixiǎn danger

请勿乱踏草地 qǐng wù luàntà cǎodì keep off the grass

军事要地请勿靠近 jūnshì yàodì, qǐng wù kàojìn military zone, keep out

禁止入内 jìnzhǐ rù nèi no entry

外国人未经许可禁止超越 wàiguórén wèi jīng xúkě, jìnzhǐ chāoyuè no foreigners beyond this point without permission

请勿随地乱扔果皮纸屑 qǐng wù suídì luànrēng guǒpí zhǐxiè no litter

请勿大声喧哗 qǐng wù dàshēng xuānhuá no noise, please

禁止拍照 jìnzhǐ pāizhào no photographs

请勿吸烟 qǐng wù xī yān no smoking

请勿随地吐痰 qǐng wù suídì tǔtán no spitting

人行横道 rénxíng héngdào pedestrian crossing

肃静 sùjìng quiet

一慢二看三通过 yī màn, èr kàn, sān tōngguò slow down, look and then cross

闲人免进 xiánrén miǎn jìn staff only

楼下 lóuxià downstairs

楼上 lóushàng upstairs

Airport, Planes

机场 jīchǎng airport

机场班车 jīchǎng bānchē airport bus

来自 láizì arriving from

前往 qiánwǎng departing to

起飞时间 qǐfēi shíjiān departure time

终点站 zhōngdiǎnzhàn destination

预计到达时间 yùjì dàodá shíjiān estimated time of arrival

航班号 hángbānhào flight number

预计时间 yùjì shíjiān scheduled time

延误 yánwù delayed

经停站 jīngtíngzhàn via

国内航班进站 guónèi hángbān jìnzhàn domestic arrivals

国内航班出站 guónèi hángbān chūzhàn domestic departures

国际航班进站 guójì hángbān jìnzhàn international arrivals

国际航班出站 guójì hángbān chūzhàn international departures

登记牌 **dēngjìpái** boarding pass

日期 **rìqī** date

行李牌儿 **xínglipáir** baggage check

行李领取处 **xíngli língqǔchù** baggage claim

办理登机手续 **bànlǐ dēngjī shǒuxù** check-in

问讯处 **wènxùnchù** information desk

登机口 **dēngjīkǒu** gate

安全检查 **ānquán jiǎnchá** security control

中转旅客 **zhōngzhuǎn lǚkè** transfer passengers

中转 **zhōngzhuǎn** transfers

过境旅客 **guòjìng lǚkè** transit passengers

侯机室 **hòujīshì** departure lounge

免税商店 **miǎnshuì shāngdiàn** duty-free shop

系好安全带 **jìhǎo ānquándài** fasten seat belts

救生衣 **jiùshēngyī** life jacket

请勿吸烟 **qǐng wù xīyān** no smoking

座位号 **zuòwèihào** seat number

Banks, Money

帐户 **zhànghù** account

帐号 **zhànghào** account no.

银行 **yínháng** bank

中国银行 **Zhōngguó Yínháng** Bank of China

分行 **fēnháng** branch

营业时间 **yíngyè shíjiān** business hours

买价 **mǎijià** buying rate

交款处 **jiāokuǎnchù** cashier

信用卡 **xìnyòng kǎ** credit card

外币兑换 **wàibì duìhuàn** foreign exchange

中国人民银行 **Zhōngguó Rénmín Yínháng** People's Bank of China

卖价 **màijià** selling rate

今日牌价 **jīnrì páijià** today's exchange rate

旅行支票 **lǚxíng zhīpiào** traveller's cheque

元 **yuán** unit of currency

澳元 **Àoyuán** Australian dollar

加拿大元 **Jiānádà yuán** Canadian dollar

人民币 **Rénmínbì** Chinese currency

港币 **Gǎngbì** Hong Kong dollar

英镑 **Yīngbàng** pound sterling

美元 **Měiyuán** US dollar

Bus and Taxi Travel

长途汽车站 **chángtú qìchē zhàn** long-distance bus station

夜班车 yèbān chē all-night bus

公共汽车 gōnggòng qìchē bus

快车 kuàichē express bus

小公共汽车 xiǎo gōnggòng qìchē minibus

区间车 qūjiānchē part-route shuttle bus

无轨电车 wúguǐ diànchē trolley bus

游览车 yóulǎnchē tourist bus

售票处 shòupiàokǒu booking office

长途汽车时刻表 chángtú qìchē shíkèbiǎo long-distance bus timetable/schedule

城市交通图 chéngshì jiāotōngtú city transport map

始发站 shǐfāzhàn departure point

票价 piàojià fare

问讯处 wènxùnchù information office

月票 yuèpiào monthly ticket

一日游 yí rì yóu one-day tour

就近下车 jiùjìn xiàchē alight on request

先下后上 xiān xià hòu shàng allow passengers to alight before boarding

保持车内清洁 bǎochí chēnèi qīngjié keep the bus tidy

请勿与司机谈话 qǐng wù yǔ sījī tánhuà please do not speak to the driver

老弱病残孕专座 lǎoruò bìngcānyùn zhuānzuò seats for the elderly or disabled and for pregnant women

招手上车 zhāoshǒu shàngchē stop on request

小卖部 xiǎomàibù kiosk

小吃店 xiǎochīdiàn snack bar

候车室 hòuchēshì waiting room

出租汽车 chūzū qìchē taxis

Chinese Culture

寺 sì Buddhist temple

文化大革命 Wénhuà Dàgémìng Cultural Revolution (1966-1976)

天安门 Tiān'ānmén Gate of Heavenly Peace

长城 Chángchéng the Great Wall

五四运动 Wǔsì Yùndòng May 4th Movement (1919)

明 Míng Ming Dynasty (1368-1644)

十三陵 Shísānlíng Ming Tombs

年画 niánhuà New Year prints

塔 tǎ pagoda

故宫 Gùgōng Forbidden City

八达岭 Bādálǐng pass at Great

Wall
京剧 **Jīngjù** Peking opera
木偶戏 **mù'ǒuxì** puppet show
清 **Qīng** Qing Dynasty (1644-1911)
宋 **Sòng** Song Dynasty (960-1279)
颐和园 **Yíhéyuán** Summer Palace
唐 **Táng** Tang Dynasty (618-907)
宫 **gōng** Taoist temple
观 **guàn** Taoist temple
庙 **miào** temple
天坛 **Tiāntán** Temple of Heaven
兵马俑 **Bīngmǎyǒng** Terracotta Army
辛亥革命 **Xīnhài Gémìng** Xinhai Revolution (1911)

Countries, Nationalities

美国 **Měiguó** America; American
澳大利亚 **Àodàlìyà** Australia; Australian
缅甸 **Miǎndiàn** Burma; Burmese
加拿大 **Jiānádà** Canada; Canadian
中国 **Zhōngguó** China; Chinese
英国 **Yīngguó** England;

English; UK; British
法国 **Fǎguó** France; French
德国 **Déguó** Germany; German
香港 **Xiānggǎng** Hong Kong
印度尼西亚 **Yìndùníxīyà** Indonesia; Indonesian
爱尔兰 **Ài'ěrlán** Ireland; Irish
日本 **Rìběn** Japan; Japanese
朝鲜 **Cháoxiǎn** Korea; Korean
老挝 **Lǎowō** Laos; Laotian
马来西亚 **Mǎláixīyà** Malaysia; Malaysian
满 **Mǎn** minority people from North-East China
维吾尔 **Wéiwú'ěr** minority people from North-West China
傣 **Dǎi** minority people from South-West China
苗 **Miáo** minority people from South-West China
彝 **Yí** minority people from South-West China
僮 **Zhuàng** minority people from South-West China
蒙 **Měng** Mongol
蒙古 **Ménggǔ** Mongolia
回 **Huí** Muslim minority people
尼泊尔 **Níbó'ěr** Nepal; Nepali
中华人民共和国 **Zhōnghuá Rénmín Gònghéguó** People's Republic of China

菲律宾 **Fēilùbīn** Philippines; Filipino

俄国 **Éguó** Russia; Russian

苏格兰 **Sūgélán** Scotland; Scottish

新加坡 **Xīnjiāpō** Singapore; Singaporean

西藏 **Xīzàng** Tibet

藏 **Zàng** Tibetan

台湾 **Táiwān** Taiwan; Taiwanese

泰国 **Tàiguó** Thailand; Thai

威尔士 **Wēi'ěrshì** Wales; Welsh

Customs

中国海关 **Zhōngguó hǎiguān** Chinese Customs

海关 **hǎiguān** Customs

边防检查站 **biānfáng jiǎncházhàn** frontier checkpoint

免疫检查 **miǎnyì jiǎnchá** health inspection

护照检查 **hùzhào jiǎnchá** passport control

报关 **bàoguān** goods to declare

不用报关 **búyòng bàoguān** nothing to declare

绿色通道 **lǜsè tōngdào** green channel, nothing to declare

红色通道 **hóngsè tōngdào** red channel, goods to declare

入境签证 **rùjìng qiānzhèng** entry visa

出境签证 **chūjìng qiānzhèng** exit visa

护照 **hùzhào** passport

过境签证 **guòjìng qiānzhèng** transit visa

旅行证 **lǚxíngzhèng** travel permit

免税物品 **miǎnshuì wùpǐn** duty-free goods

Emergencies

救护车 **jiùhùchē** ambulance

太平门 **tàipíngmén** emergency exit

火警匪警 **huǒjǐng, féijǐng** emergency telephone number: fire, robbery

消防队 **xiāofángduì** fire brigade, fire department

急诊室 **jízhěnshì** first-aid room

派出所 **Pàichūsuǒ** local police station

警察 **jǐngchá** police

公安局 **gōng'ānjú** Public Security Bureau

Entertainment

售票处 **shòupiàochù** box office

入场券 **rùchǎngquàn** cinema

ticket

电影院 diànyǐngyuàn
cinema

迪斯科 dísīkē disco

夜场 yèchǎng evening
performance

全满 quánmǎn house full

休息 xiūxi interval

京剧 Jīngjù Peking Opera

节目单 jiémùdān
programme

排 ... pái row ...

号 ... hào seat number ...

票已售完 piào yǐ shòu wán
sold out

剧场 jùchǎng theatre

剧院 jùyuàn theatre

戏院 xìyuàn theatre

表演时间 biǎoyǎn shíjiān
times of performance

Forms

从何处来 cóng héchù lái
arriving from

出生年月 chūshēng niányuè
date of birth

籍贯 jíguàn father's place of
birth

到何处去 dào héchù qù
heading for

拟住天数 nǐ zhù tiānshù
length of stay

姓名 xìngmíng full name

国籍 guójí nationality

性别 xìngbié (nán/nǚ) sex
(male/female)

护照号码 hùzhào hàomǎ
passport number

永久地址 yóngjiǔ dìzhǐ
permanent address

旅客登记表 lǚkè dēngjìbiǎo
registration form

签名 qiānmíng signature

Geographical Terms

自治区 zìzhìqū autonomous
region

运河 yùnhé canal

市 shì city

国家 guójiā country

县 xiàn county

森林 sēnlín forest

岛 dǎo island

湖 hú lake

江 jiāng large river

地图 dìtú map

山 shān mountain, hill

山脉 shānmài mountains

海洋 hǎiyáng ocean

省 shěng province

河 hé river

海 hǎi sea

镇 zhèn town

山谷 shāngǔ valley

村 cūn village

树林 shùlín woods

Health

中医科 **zhōngyīkē** Chinese medicine department
中药房 **zhōngyàofáng** Chinese medicine dispensary
牙科 **yákē** dental department
急诊室 **jízhěnshì** emergency
外宾门诊部 **wàibīn ménzhěnbù** foreign outpatients
医院 **yīyuàn** hospital
住院处 **zhùyuànchù** hospital admissions office
内科 **nèikē** medical department
门诊部 **ménzhěnbù** outpatients
挂号 **guàhào** registration
西药房 **xīyàofáng** Western medicine dispensary

Hiring, Renting

出租自行车 **chūzū zìxíngchē** bikes to rent
租船 **zū chuán** boats to rent
出租 **chūzū** for hire, to rent

Hotels

中国国际旅行社 **Zhōngguó Guójì Lǚxíngshè** China International Travel Service
中国旅行社 **Zhōngguó Lǚxíngshè** China Travel Service
宾馆 **bīnguǎn** hotel
饭店 **fàndiàn** hotel
小卖部 **xiǎomàibù** kiosk
总服务台 **zǒng fúwùtái** reception
游艺室 **yóuyìshì** recreation room
电传室 **diànchuánshì** telex office

Lifts (Elevators)

关 **guān** close
下 **xià** down
电梯 **diàntī** lifts, elevators
开 **kāi** open
上 **shàng** up

Medicines

抗菌素 **kàngjùnsù** antibiotics
阿斯匹林 **āsīpǐlín** aspirin
咳鼻清 **kébìqīng** cough lozenges
棕色合剂 **zōngsè héjì** cough mixture
止咳糖浆 **zhǐké tángjiāng** cough syrup
止疼片儿 **zhǐténgpiànr** painkillers
青霉素 **qīngméisù** penicillin

含碘片 hándiǎnpiàn throat pastilles

剂量 jìliàng dosage

失效期 shīxiàoqī expiry date

初诊 chūzhěn first treatment

外用 wàiyòng for external use

一日三次 yírì sān cì three times a day

胃炎 wèiyán gastritis

饭前／后温开水送服 fàn qián/hòu wēnkāishuǐ sòngfú to be taken with warm water before/after food

每四／六小时服一次 měi sì/liù xiǎoshí fú yícì one dose every four/six hours

一日四次 yírì sìcì four times a day

内服 nèifú to be taken orally

每次一个 měi cì yì gé one measure at a time

每次一丸 měicì yì wán one pill at a time

每次一片儿 měicì yí piànr one tablet at a time

必要时服 bìyào shí fú when necessary

Notices on Doors

太平门 tàipíngmén emergency exit

入口 rùkǒu entrance

出口 chūkǒu exit

顾客止步 gùkè zhǐ bù no entry for customers

未经许可禁止入内 wèi jīng xúkě, jìnzhǐ rù nèi no entry without permission

拉 lā pull

推 tuī push

闲人免进 xiánrén miǎn jìn staff only

Phones

长途区号 chángtú qūhào area code

用卡电话亭 yòng kǎ diànhuà tíng cardphone

查号台 cháhàotái directory enquiries

分机 fēnjī extension

国际长途 guójì chángtú international call

长途电话 chángtú diànhuà long-distance call

电话卡 diànhuàkǎ phonecard

公用电话 gōngyòng diànhuà public telephone

总机 zǒngjī switchboard

电话簿 diànhuàbù telephone directory

一次一角(毛) yícì yìjiǎo (máo) ten fen per call

磁卡电话 cíkǎ diànhuà cardphone

Place Names

北京 **Běijīng** Beijing
成都 **Chéngdū** Chengdu
敦煌 **Dūnhuáng** Dunhuang
峨嵋山 **Éméishān** Emei Mountains
广州 **Guǎngzhōu** Canton
长城 **Chángchéng** the Great Wall
桂林 **Guìlín** Guilin
杭州 **Hángzhōu** Hangzhou
昆明 **Kūnmíng** Kunming
拉萨 **Lāsā** Lhasa
洛阳 **Luòyáng** Luoyang
南京 **Nánjīng** Nanjing
深圳 **Shēnzhèn** Shenzhen
天津 **Tiānjīn** Tientsin
西湖 **Xīhú** West Lake
西安 **Xī'ān** Xi'an
长江三峡 **Chángjiāng Sānxiá** Yangtze Gorges

Post Office

邮局 **yóujú** post office
开箱时间 **kāixiāng shíjiān** collection times
信封 **xìnfēng** envelope
邮筒 **yóutǒng** letterbox, mailbox
信函 **xìnhán** letters
杂志报刊 **zázhì bàokān** magazines and newspapers
包裹单 **bāoguǒdān** parcel form
包裹, 印刷品 **bāoguǒ, yìnshuāpǐn** parcels, printed matter
邮电局 **yóudiànjú** post and telecommunications office
信箱电报 **xìnxiāng** postbox
邮政编码 **yóuzhèng biānmǎ** postcode, zip code
邮票, 挂号 **yóupiào, guàhào** stamps, registered mail
电报纸 **diànbàozhǐ** telegram form
电报 **diànbào** telegram
电报大楼 **diànbào dàlóu** telegraph building

Public Buildings

浴池 **yùchí** baths
学院 **xuéyuàn** college
领事馆 **lǐngshìguǎn** consulate
大使馆 **dàshǐguǎn** embassy
工厂 **gōngchǎng** factory
游泳馆 **yóuyǒngguǎn** indoor swimming pool
图书馆 **túshūguǎn** library
博物馆 **bówùguǎn** museum
中学 **zhōngxué** secondary school
体育馆 **tǐyùguǎn** sports hall, indoor stadium
体育场 **tǐyùchǎng** stadium
大学 **dàxué** university

221

Restaurants, Cafés, Bars

酒吧 jiǔbā bar
咖啡店 kāfēidiàn café, coffee house
茶楼 chálóu café, teahouse
茶馆 cháguǎn café, teahouse
茶室 cháshì café, teahouse
收款台 shōukuǎntái cashier
冷饮店 lěngyǐndiàn cold drinks bar
中餐厅 Zhōng cāntīng Chinese dining room
清真饭店 qīngzhēn fàndiàn Muslim restaurant
面馆 miànguǎn noodle shop
菜馆 càiguǎn large restaurant
饭店 fàndiàn large restaurant
酒家 jiǔjiā large restaurant
酒楼 jiǔlóu large restaurant
餐厅 cāntīng restaurant; dining room
快餐 kuàicān snack bar
小吃店 xiǎochīdiàn snack bar
今日供应 jīnrì gòngyìng today's menu
素菜馆 sùcàiguǎn vegetarian restaurant
西餐厅 xī cāntīng Western dining room
西菜馆 xīcàiguǎn Western restaurant

Shopping

文物商店 wénwù shāngdiàn antique shop
工艺美术商店 gōngyì měishù shāngdiàn arts and crafts shop
自行车 zìxíngchē bicycles
收款台 shōukuǎntái cashier
烟酒糖茶 yān jiǔ táng chá cigarettes, wine, confectionery, tea
服装店 fúzhuāngdiàn clothes shop
男女服装 nánnǚ fúzhuāng clothing
化妆用品 huàzhuāng yòngpǐn cosmetics
百货商店 bǎihuò shāngdiàn department store
家用电器 jiāyòng diànqì domestic appliances
食品商店 shípǐn shāngdiàn food shop
食品糕点 shípǐn gāodiǎn food and confectionery
自由市场 zìyóu shìchǎng free market
友谊商店 yǒuyì shāngdiàn Friendship store
菜市场 càishìchǎng greengrocer
副食品商店 fùshípǐn shāngdiàn grocery store
五金交电 wǔjīn jiāodiàn

hardware and electrical goods

袜子鞋帽 wàzi xiémào
hosiery, shoes, hats

日用杂品 rìyòng zápǐn
household goods

橱房用品 chúfáng yòngpǐn
kitchenware

妇女用品 fùnǚ yòngpǐn
ladies' accessories

女装 nǚzhuāng ladies' wear

洗衣店 xǐyīdiàn laundry

皮革制品 pígé zhìpǐn leather
goods

市场 shìchǎng market

男装 nán zhuāng menswear

乐器行 yuèqì háng musical
instruments section

新华书店 xīnhuá shūdiàn
New China bookshop

夜市 yèshì night market

眼镜店 yǎnjìngdiàn optician

复印 fùyìn photocopying

照相器材 zhàoxiàng qìcái
photographic equipment

钱票当面点清过后该不
负责 qián piào dāngmiàn
diǎnqīng, guòhòu gāi bù fùzé
please check your change
before leaving as mistakes
cannot be rectified

雨伞雨具 yǔsǎn yǔjù
rainwear

大减价 dàjiǎnjià sale

古旧书店 gǔjiù shūdiàn
secondhand bookshop

购物中心 gòuwù zhōngxīn
shopping centre

体育用品 tǐyù yòngpǐn sports
goods

文具商店 wénjù shāngdiàn
stationery

文具用品 wénjù yòngpǐn
stationery

牙膏牙刷 yágāo yáshuā
toothpaste and toothbrushes

儿童玩具 értóng wánjù toys

针织用品 zhēnzhī yòngpǐn
underwear

Streets and Roads

大街 dàjiē avenue

胡同 hútòng lane

巷 xiàng lane

路 lù road

广场 guángchǎng square

街 jiē street

Toilets

有人 yǒurén engaged,
occupied

男厕所 náncèsuǒ gents'
toilet, men's room

男厕 náncè gents' toilet,
men's room

女厕所 nǚcèsuǒ ladies' toilet,
ladies' room

女厕 nǚcè ladies' toilet, ladies'

room

公厕 gōngcè public toilets, rest rooms

盥洗室 guànxǐshì toilet, rest room

无人 wúrén vacant, free

Train and Underground Travel

火车站 huǒchēzhàn station

火车 huǒchē train

列车到站时刻表 lièchē dàozhàn shíkèbiǎo arrival times

列车离站时刻表 lièchē lízhàn shíkèbiǎo departure times

开往 ... 方向 ... kāiwǎng ... fāngxiàng to ...

车次 chēcì train number

检票处 jiǎnpiàochù barrier

站台 zhàntái platform, (US) track

站台票 zhàntáipiào platform ticket

问讯处 wènxùnchù information desk

火车时刻表 huǒchē shíkèbiǎo timetable, (US) schedule

天 tiān day

特快 tèkuài express

直快 zhíkuài through train

快车 kuàichē fast train

客车 kèchē ordinary passenger train

站名 zhànmíng station name

开往 ... kāiwǎng ... to ...

旅游车 lǚyóuchē tourist train

车次 chēcì train number

星期 xīngqī week

行李寄存处 xíngli jìcúnchù left luggage, baggage checkroom

乘警 chéngjǐng railway police

售票处 shòupiàochù ticket office

候车室 hòuchēshì waiting room

餐车 cānchē dining car

硬席 yìngxí hard seat

硬席车 yìngxíchē hard seat carriage

硬卧 yìngwò hard sleeper

硬卧车 yìngwòchē hard sleeper carriage

软席 ruǎnxí soft seat

软席车 ruǎnxíchē soft seat carriage

软卧 ruǎnwò soft sleeper

软卧车 ruǎnwòchē soft sleeper carriage

紧急制动闸 jǐnjí zhìdòngzhá emergency brake

乘务员 chéngwùyuán train attendant

地铁 dìtiě underground, (US) subway

224

Menu Reader: Food

Contents

Essential Terms

碟子 **bowl** diézi [dyeh-dzur]

筷子 **chopsticks** kuàizi [kwai-dzur]

杯子 **cup** bēizi [bay-dzur]

甜品 **dessert** tiánpǐn [tyen-pin]

叉 **fork** (for eating) chā [chah]

炒面 **fried noodles** chǎomiàn [chow-myen]

炒饭 **fried rice** chǎofàn [chow-fahn]

玻璃杯 **glass** bōli bēi [bor-lee bay]

刀子 **knife** dāozi [dow-dzur]

菜单儿 **menu** càidānr [tsai-dahnr]

面条 **noodles** miàntiáo [myen-tyow]

盘子 **plate** pánzi [pahn-dzur]

米饭 **rice** mǐfàn [mee-fahn]

汤 **soup** tāng [tahng]

酱油 **soy sauce** jiàngyóu [jyahn-gyoh]

勺子 **spoon** sháozi [show-dzur]

桌子 **table** zhuōzi [jwor-dzur]

劳驾 **excuse me** láojià [low-jyah]

请帮我结帐好吗？ **could I have the bill, please?** qǐng bāng wǒ jiézhàng, hǎo ma? [ching bahng wor jyeh-jahng how mah]

Basic Foods

黄油 huángyóu [hwahng-yoh] butter

奶酪 nǎilào [nai-low] cheese

辣椒油 làjiāo yóu [lah-jyow yoh] chilli oil

辣椒酱 làjiāo jiàng [jyang] chilli paste

椰子油 yēzi yóu [yur-dzur yoh] coconut milk

奶油 nǎiyóu [nai-yoh] cream

豆腐干儿 dòufu gānr [doh-foo gahnr] dried bean curd

大蒜 dàsuàn [dah-swahn] garlic

黄米 huángmǐ [hwahng-mee] glutinous millet

豆瓣儿辣酱儿 dòubànr làjiàngr [doh-bahnr lah-jyengr] hot soya bean paste

玉米 yùmǐ [yoo-mee] maize

小米 xiáomǐ [hsyah-mee] millet

蚝油 háoyóu [how-yoh] oyster sauce

花生油 huāshēng yóu [hwah-shung yoh] peanut oil

咸菜 xiáncài [hsyen-tsai] pickles

松花蛋 sōnghuādàn [soong-hwah-dahn] preserved eggs

菜籽油 càizi yóu [tsai-dzur yoh] rape oil

大米 dàmǐ [dah-mee] rice

盐 yán [yahn] salt

芝麻油 zhīmā yóu [jur-mah yoh] sesame oil

高粱 gāoliáng [gow-lyang] sorghum (similar to corn)

豆油 dòuyóu [doh-yoh] soya bean oil

酱油 jiàngyóu [jyang-yoh] soy sauce

糖 táng [tahng] sugar

番茄酱 fānqié jiàng [fahn-chyeh jyang] tomato paste

素鸡 sùjī [soo-jee] 'vegetarian chicken' (made from soya beans)

小麦 xiǎomài [hsyow-mai] wheat

面粉 miànfěn [myen-fun] wheat flour

Basic Preparation and Cooking Methods

什锦 . . . shíjǐn . . . [shur-jin] assorted . . .

. . . 丸 . . . wán [wahn] . . . balls

. . . 圆 . . . yuán [yew-ahn] . . . balls

叉烧 . . . chāshāo . . . [chah-show] barbecued . . .

煮 . . . zhǔ . . . [joo] boiled . . .

烧 . . . shāo . . . [show] braised . . .

. . . 块儿 . . . kuàir [kwair] . . .

chunks, pieces

香酥 . . . **xiāngsū** . . . [hsyang-soo] crispy deep-fried . . .

咖喱 . . . **gāli** . . . [gah-lee] curried . . .

炸 . . . **zhá** . . . [jah] deep-fried . . .

. . . 丁 . . . **dīng** diced . . .

家常 . . . **jiācháng** . . . [jyah-chahng] home-style . . . (plain)

火锅 . . . **huǒguō** . . . [hwor-gwor] . . . in hot pot, i.e. served with a pot of boiling water in which the meat or fish is cooked, also creating a soup

烤 . . . **kǎo** . . . [kow] roasted, baked

. . . 片儿 . . . **piànr** [pyenr] . . . slices

蒸 . . . **zhēng** . . . [jung] steamed . . .

清蒸 . . . **qīngzhēng** . . . [ching-jung] steamed . . .

烩 . . . **huì** . . . [hway] stewed . . .

炒 . . . **chǎo** . . . [chow] stir-fried . . .

糖醋 . . . **tángcù** . . . [tahng-tsoo] sweet and sour . . .

三鲜 . . . **sānxiān** . . . [sahn-hsyen] 'three-fresh' . . . (with three ingredients which vary)

Bean Curd Dishes

麻婆豆腐 **mápó dòufu** [mah-por doh-foo] bean curd with minced beef in spicy sauce

三鲜豆腐 **sānxiān dòufu** [sahn-hsyen] 'three-fresh' bean curd (made with three ingredients)

沙锅豆腐 **shāguō dòufu** [shah-gwor] bean curd served with a pot of boiling water in which the bean curd is cooked, also creating a soup

麻辣豆腐 **málà dòufu** [mah-lah] bean curd with chilli and wild pepper

虾仁豆腐 **xiārén dòufu** [hsyah-run] bean curd with shrimps

家常豆腐 **jiācháng dòufu** [jyah-chahng] home-style bean curd

Beef Dishes

红烧牛肉 **hóngshāo niúròu** [hoong-show nyoh-roh] beef braised in brown sauce

麻酱牛肉 **májiàng niúròu** [mah-jyang] beef quick-fried in sesame paste

酱爆牛肉 **jiàngbào niúròu** [jyang-bow] beef quick-fried with black bean sauce

葱爆牛肉 **cōngbào niúròu** [tsoong-bow] beef quick-fried with spring onions

咖喱牛肉 **gāli niúròu** [gah-lee] curried beef

时菜牛肉片儿 **shícài niúròupiànr** [shur-tsai nyoh-roh-pyenr] shredded beef with seasonal vegetables

鱼香 牛肉 **yúxiāng niúròu** [yoo-hsyang nyoh-roh] stir-fried beef in hot spicy sauce

笋炒牛肉 **sǔnchǎo niúròu** [sun-chow] stir-fried beef with bamboo shoots

麻辣牛肉 **málà niúròu** [mah-lah] stir-fried beef with chilli and wild pepper

蚝 油 牛肉 **háoyóu niúròu** [how-yoh] stir-fried beef with oyster sauce

宫保牛肉 **gōngbǎo niúròu** [goong-bow] stir-fried beef with peanuts and chilli

茄汁牛肉 **qiézhī niúròu** [chyeh-jur] stir-fried sliced beef with tomato sauce

Bread, Dumplings etc

葱油饼 **cōngyóubǐng** [tsoong-yoh-bing] spring onion pancake

水饺 **shuǐjiǎo** [shway-jyow] Chinese ravioli

饺子 **jiǎozi** [jyow-dzur] dumplings

锅贴 **guōtiē** [gwor-tyeh] fried Chinese ravioli

馄饨 **húntun** small Chinese ravioli in soup

馒头 **mántou** [mahn-toh] steamed bread containing various fillings

蒸饺 **zhēngjiǎo** [jung-jyow] steamed Chinese ravioli

烧卖 **shāomài** [show-mai] steamed dumplings open at the top

包子 **bāozi** [bow-dzur] steamed dumplings with various fillings, usually minced pork

花卷儿 **huājuǎnr** [hwah-jwahnr] steamed rolls

三鲜水饺 **sānxiān shuǐjiǎo** [sahn-hsyen shoo-jyow] 'three-fresh' Chinese ravioli (pork, shrimps and chives)

面包 **miànbāo** [myen-bow] white bread

Cold Platters

什锦冷盘儿 **shíjǐn lěngpánr** [shur-jin lung-pahnr] assorted cold platter

海杂拌儿 **hǎi zábànr** [hai zah-bahnr] seafood cold platter

七彩冷拼盘儿 **qīcǎi lěng**

pīnpánr [chee-tsai lung pin-pahnr] 'seven colours' cold platter

Desserts

西瓜盅 xīguā zhōng [hshee-gwah joong] assorted fruit and water melon

什锦水果羹 shíjǐn shuǐguǒ gēng [shur-jin shway-gwor gung] fruit salad

莲子羹 liánzi gēng [lyen-dzur] lotus-seed in syrup

酸奶 suānnǎi [swahn-nai] yoghurt

Fish and Seafood

鲈鱼 lúyú [loo-yoo] bass

螃蟹 pángxiè [pahng-hsyeh] crab

鱼 yú [yoo] fish

鲳鱼 chāngyú pomfret

虾 xiā [hsyah] prawns

加级鱼 jiājí [jyah-jee] red snapper

鱿鱼 yóuyú [yoh-yoo] squid

红烧鲤鱼 hóngshāo lǐyú [hoong-show lee-yoo] carp braised in brown sauce

干烧桂鱼 gānshāo guìyú [gahn-show gway-yoo] Chinese perch braised with chilli and black bean sauce

咖喱鱿鱼 gālí yóuyú [gah-lee yoh-yoo] curried squid

茄汁石斑块儿 qiézhī shíbānkuàir [chyeh-jur shur-bahn-kwair] deep-fried grouper with tomato sauce

火锅鱼虾 huǒguō yúxiā [hwor-gwor yoo-hsyah] fish and prawns served with a pot of boiling water in which they are cooked, creating a soup

家常鱼块儿 jiācháng yúkuàir [jyah-chahng yoo-kwair] home-style fish

干烧黄鳝 gānshāo huángshàn [gahn-show hwahng-shahn] paddyfield eel braised with chilli and black bean sauce

时菜虾球 shícài xiāqiú [shoo-tsai hsyah-chew] prawn balls with seasonal vegetables

虾仁干贝 xiārén gānbèi [hsyah-run gahn-bay] scallops with shrimps

葱爆海参 cōngbào hǎishēn [tsoong-bow hai-shun] sea cucumber quick-fried with spring onions

蚝油鲍鱼 háoyóu bāoyú [how-yoh bow-yoo] stir-fried abalone with oyster sauce

滑溜鱼片儿 huáliū yúpiànr [hwah-lyoh yoo-pyenr] stir-fried fish slices with thick sauce

鱼香龙虾 yúxiāng lóngxiā

[yoo-hsyang loong-hsyah] stir-fried lobster in hot spicy sauce

冬笋炒海参 **dōngsǔn cháo hǎishēn** [doong-sun chow hai-shun] stir-fried sea cucumber with bamboo shoots

糖醋鱼块儿 **tángcù yúkuàir** [tahng-tsoo yoo-kwair] sweet and sour fish

Fruit

苹果 **píngguǒ** [ping-gwor] apple

杏 **xìng** [hsing] apricot

香蕉 **xiāngjiāo** [hsyang-jyow] banana

椰子 **yēzi** [yur-dzur] coconut

海棠果 **hǎitángguǒ** [hai-tahng-gwor] crab apple

枣 **zǎo** [dzow] date

葡萄 **pútao** [poo-tow] grape

广柑 **guǎnggān** [gwahng-gahn] Guangdong orange

哈密瓜 **hāmìguā** [hah-mee-gwah] honeydew melon

龙眼 **lóngyǎn** [loong-yahn] longan (similar to lychee)

荔枝 **lìzhī** [lee-jur] lychee

柑子 **gānzi** [gahn-dzur] orange

桔子 **júzi** [joo-dzur] orange

桃子 **táozi** [tow-dzur] peach

梨 **lí** [lee] pear

柿子 **shìzi** [shur-dzur] persimmon, sharon fruit

菠萝 **bōluó** [bor-lwor] pineapple

李子 **lǐzi** [lee-dzur] plum

石榴 **shíliu** [shur-lyoh] pomegranate

沙田柚 **shātiányòu** [shah-tyen-yoh] pomelo

橘子 **júzi** [joo-dzur] tangerine

蜜桔 **mìjú** [mee-joo] tangerine

西瓜 **xīguā** [hshee-gwah] water melon

Lamb and Mutton Dishes

咖喱羊肉 **gāli yángròu** [gah-lee yahn-roh] curried mutton

烤羊肉串儿 **kǎo yángròuchuànr** [kow yahng-roh-chwahnr] lamb kebabs

涮羊肉 **shuàn yángròu** [shwahn yang-roh] Mongolian lamb served with a pot of boiling water in which the meat is cooked, also creating a soup

红烧羊肉 **hóngshāo yángròu** [hoong-show] mutton braised in brown sauce

火锅羊肉 **huǒguō yángròu** [hwor-gwor] mutton served with a pot of boiling water in which the meat is cooked, also creating a soup

酱爆羊肉 jiàngbào yángròu [jyang-bow] mutton quick-fried with black bean sauce

葱爆羊肉 cōngbào yángròu [tsoong-bow] mutton quick-fried with spring onions

时菜羊肉片儿 shícài yángròupiànr [shur-tsai yang-roh-pyenr] shredded mutton with seasonal vegetables

麻辣羊肉 málà yángròu [mah-lah] stir-fried mutton with chilli and wild pepper

蚝油羊肉 háoyóu yángròu [how-yoh] stir-fried mutton with oyster sauce

Meats

牛肉 niúròu [nyoh-roh] beef

鸡 jī [jee] chicken

鸭 yā [yah] duck

羊肉 yángròu [yahng-roh] lamb; mutton

肉 ròu [roh] meat (usually pork)

猪肉 zhūròu [joo-roh] pork

Noodles

炒面 chǎomiàn [chow-myen] fried noodles

鸡丝炒面 jīsī chǎomiàn [jee-sur] fried noodles with shredded chicken

肉丝炒面 ròusī chǎomiàn [roh-sur] fried noodles with shredded pork

虾仁炒面 xiārén chǎomiàn [hsyah-run chow-myen] fried noodles with shrimps

炒米粉 cháomífěn [chow-mee-fun] fried rice noodles

面条 miàntiáo [myen-tyow] noodles

Pork Dishes

叉烧肉 chāshāo ròu [chah-show roh] barbecued pork

咖喱肉丸 gālí ròuwán [gah-lee roh-wahn] curried meatballs

狮子头 shīzi tóu [shur-dzur toh] a large meatball stewed with cabbage

火锅猪排 huǒguō zhūpái [hwor-gwor joo-pai] pork chop served with a pot of boiling water in which the meat is cooked, also creating a soup

酱爆三样 jiàngbào sānyàng [jyang-bow sahn-yang] pork, pig's liver and kidney quick-fried with black bean sauce

烤乳猪 káo rǔzhū [kow roo-joo] roast sucking pig

米粉蒸肉 mífěn zhēngròu [mee-fun jung-roh] steamed pork with rice

宫保肉丁 gōngbǎo ròudīng [goong-bow roh-ding] stir-fried

diced pork with peanuts and chilli

鱼香肉丝 yúxiāng ròusī [yoo-hsyang roh-sur] stir-fried shredded pork in hot sauce

冬笋肉丝 dōngsǔn ròusī [doong-sun] stir-fried shredded pork with bamboo shoots

榨菜炒肉丝 zhàcài chǎo ròusī [jah-tsai chow] stir-fried shredded pork with pickled mustard greens

笋炒肉片儿 sǔnchǎo ròupiànr [sun-chow roh-pyenr] stir-fried sliced pork with bamboo shoots

芙蓉肉片儿 fúróng ròupiànr [foo-roong] stir-fried sliced pork with egg white

青椒炒肉片儿 qīngjiāo chǎo ròupiànr [ching-jyow chow] stir-fried sliced pork with green pepper

时菜炒 肉片儿 shícài chǎo ròupiànr [shur-tsai] stir-fried sliced pork with seasonal vegetables

滑溜肉片儿 huáliū ròupiànr [hwah-lyoh] stir-fried sliced pork with thick sauce

回锅肉 huíguō ròu [hway-gwor roh] boiled then stir-fried pork

Poultry and Poultry Dishes

时 菜扒鸭 shícài páyā [shur-tsai pah-yah] braised duck with seasonal vegetables

佛跳墙 fó tiào qiáng [for tyow chyang] chicken with duck, pig's trotters and seafood stewed in rice wine (literally: Buddha leaps the wall)

茄汁鸡脯 qiézhī jīpú [chyeh-jur jee-poo] chicken breast with tomato sauce

咖喱鸡块儿 gālí jīkuàir [gah-lee jee-kwair] curried chicken pieces

酱爆鸡丁 jiàngbào jīdīng [jyang-bow jee-ding] diced chicken quick-fried with black bean sauce

冬笋鸡片儿 dōngsǔn jīpiànr [doong-sun jee-pyenr] chicken slices with bamboo shoots

冬菇鸡片儿 dōnggū jīpiànr [doong-goo] chicken slices with mushrooms

香酥鸡 xiāngsū jī [hsyang-soo jee] crispy deep-fried whole chicken

香酥鸭 xiāngsū yā [yah] crispy deep-fried whole duck

辣子鸡丁 làzi jīdīng [lah-dzur jee-ding] diced chicken with chilli

麻辣鸡丁 málà jīdīng [mah-lah] diced chicken with chilli and wild pepper

香菇鸭掌 xiānggū yāzhǎng [hsyang-goo yah-jahng] duck's foot with mushroom

茄汁煎软鸭 qiézhī jiān ruǎnyā [chyeh-jur jyen rwahn-yah] fried duck with tomato sauce

家常焖鸡 jiācháng mènjī [jyah-chahng mun-jee] home-style braised chicken

北京烤鸭 Běijīng kǎoyā [bay-jing kow-yah] Peking duck

酱爆鸭片儿菜心 jiàngbào yāpiànr càixīn [jyang-bow yah-pyenr tsai-hsin] sliced duck and green vegetables quick-fried with black bean sauce

葱爆烧鸭片儿 cōngbào shāoyāpiànr [tsoong-bow show-yah-pyenr] sliced duck quick-fried with spring onions

宫保鸡丁 gōngbǎo jīdīng [goong-bow jee-ding] stir-fried diced chicken with peanuts and chilli

怪味儿鸡 guàiwèirjī [gwai-wayr-jee] whole chicken with peanuts and pepper (literally: strange-tasting chicken)

汽锅蒸鸡 qìguō zhēngjī [chee-gwor jung-jee] whole chicken steamed in a pot

红烧全鸭 hóngshāo quányā [hoong-show choo-en-yah] whole duck braised in brown sauce

红烧全鸡 hóngshāo quánjī [choo-en-jee] whole chicken braised in brown sauce

Rice

炒饭 chǎofàn [chow-fahn] fried rice

蛋炒饭 dàn chǎofàn [dahn] fried rice with eggs

鸡丝炒饭 jīsī chǎofàn [jee-sur] fried rice with shredded chicken

肉丝炒饭 ròusī chǎofàn [roh-sur] fried rice with shredded pork

虾仁炒饭 xiārén chǎofàn [hsyah-run] fried rice with shrimps

米饭 mǐfàn [mee-fahn] rice

稀饭 xīfàn [hshee-fahn] rice porridge

叉烧包 chāshāobāo [chah-show-bow] steamed dumplings with pork filling

Seasonings, Spices

桂皮 **guìpí** [gway-pee] Chinese cinnamon

丁香 **dīngxiāng** [ding-hsyang] cloves

茴香 **huíxiāng** [hway-hsyang] fennel seed

五香面儿 **wǔxiāng miànr** [woo-hsyang myenr] 'five spice' powder

生姜 **shēngjiāng** [shung-jyang] ginger

辣椒 **làjiāo** [lah-jyow] chilli, chilli peppers

辣椒粉 **làjiāo fěn** [fun] chilli powder

胡椒 **hújiāo** [hoo-jyow] pepper

盐 **yán** [yahn] salt

醋 **cù** [tsoo] vinegar

Snacks

豆沙酥饼 **dòushā sūbǐng** [doh-shah soo-bing] baked flaky cake with sweet bean paste filling

火烧 **huǒshāo** [hwor-show] baked wheaten bun

糖火烧 **táng huǒshāo** [tahng] baked wheaten bun with sugar

油饼 **yóubǐng** [yoh-bing] deep-fried savoury pancake

油炸糕 **yóuzhágāo** [yoh-jah-gow] deep-fried sweet pancake

馅儿饼 **xiànrbǐng** [hsyenr-bing] savoury fritter

烧饼 **shāobǐng** [show-bing] sesame pancake

春卷儿 **chūnjuǎnr** [chun-jwahnr] spring rolls

豆沙包 **dòushābāo** [doh-shah-bow] steamed dumpling with sweet bean paste filling

油条 **yóutiáo** [yoh-tyow] unsweetened doughnut sticks

Soups

开水白菜 **kāishuǐ báicài** [kai-shway bai-tsai] Chinese cabbage in clear soup

酸辣汤 **suān là tāng** [swahn lah tahng] hot and sour soup

汤 **tāng** soup

竹笋鲜蘑汤 **zhúsǔn xiānmó tāng** [joo-sun hsyen-mor] soup with bamboo shoots and mushrooms

西红柿鸡蛋汤 **xīhóngshì jīdan tāng** [hshee-hoong-shur jee-dahn] soup with eggs and tomato

榨菜肉丝汤 **zhàcài ròusī tāng** [jah-tsai roh-sur] soup with shredded pork and pickled mustard greens

时菜肉片儿汤 **shícài ròupiànr tāng** 〖shur-tsai roh-pyenr〗 soup with sliced pork and seasonal vegetables

菠菜粉丝汤 **bōcài fěnsī tāng** 〖bor-tsai fun-sur〗 soup with spinach and vermicelli

三鲜汤 **sānxiān tāng** 〖sahn-hsyen〗 'three-fresh' soup (prawns, meat and a vegetable)

圆汤素烩 **yuántāng sùhuì** 〖ywahn-tahng soo-hway〗 vegetable chowder

Typical Combinations

红烧 . . . **hóngshāo** . . . 〖hoong-show〗 . . . braised in soy sauce

干烧 . . . **gānshāo** . . . 〖gahn-show〗 . . . braised with chilli and black bean sauce

麻酱 . . . **jiàngbào** . . . 〖jyang-bow〗 . . . quick-fried with black bean sauce

葱爆 . . . **cōngbào** . . . 〖tsoong-bow〗 . . . quick-fried with spring onions

鱼香 . . . **yúxiāng** . . . 〖yoo-hsyang〗 stir-fried . . . in hot spicy sauce (literally: fish fragrance; not always with fish)

笋炒 . . . **sǔnchǎo** . . . 〖sun-chow〗 stir-fried . . . with bamboo shoots

宫保 . . . **gōngbǎo** . . . 〖goong-bow〗 stir-fried . . . with peanuts and chilli

滑溜 . . . **huáliū** . . . 〖hwah-lyoh〗 stir-fried . . . with sauce

冬笋 . . . **dōngsǔn** . . . 〖doong-sun〗 . . . with bamboo shoots

辣子 . . . **làzi** . . . 〖lah-dzur〗 . . . with chilli

麻辣 . . . **málà** . . . 〖mah-lah〗 . . . with chilli and wild pepper

蟹肉 . . . **xièròu** . . . 〖hsyeh-roh〗 . . . with crab

火腿 . . . **huótuǐ** . . . 〖hwor-tway〗 . . . with ham

冬菇 . . . **dōnggū** . . . 〖doong-goo〗 . . . with mushrooms

香菇 . . . **xiānggū** . . . 〖hsyang-goo〗 . . . with mushrooms

蚝油 . . . **háoyóu** . . . 〖how-yoh〗 . . . with oyster sauce

榨菜 . . . **zhàcài** . . . 〖jah-tsai〗 . . . with pickled mustard greens

时菜 . . . **shícài** . . . 〖shur-tsai〗 . . . with seasonal vegetables

虾仁 . . . **xiārén** . . . 〖hsyah-run〗 . . . with shrimps

茄汁 . . . **qiézhī** . . . 〖chyeh-jur〗 . . . with tomato sauce

番茄 . . . **fānqié** . . . 〖fahn-chyeh〗 . . . with tomato sauce

Vegetables

茄子 qiézi [chyeh-dzur]
aubergine, eggplant

竹笋 zhúsǔn [joo-sun] bamboo
shoots

豆芽 dòuyá [doh-yah] bean
sprouts

卷心菜 juǎnxīncài [jwahn-hsin-
tsai] cabbage

胡萝卜 húluóbo [hoo-lwor-bor]
carrots

白菜 báicài [bai-tsai] Chinese
cabbage

青豆 qīngdòu [ching-doh]
green beans

蘑菇 mógu [mor-goo]
mushrooms

菠菜 bōcài [bor-tsai] spinach

红薯 hóngshǔ [hoong-shoo]
sweet potato

西红柿 xīhóngshì [hshee-
hoong-shur] tomato

蔬菜 shūcài [shoo-tsai]
vegetables

Vegetable Dishes

烧茄子 shāo qiézi [show
chyeh-dzur] stewed aubergine/
eggplant

烧胡萝卜 shāo húluóbo [hoo-
lwor-bor] stewed carrot

烧三鲜 shāo sānxiān [sahn-
hsyen] stewed 'three-fresh'

vegetables

炒玉兰片儿 chǎo yùlánpiànr
[chow yoo-lahn-pyenr] stir-fried
bamboo shoots

炒豆芽 chǎo dòuyá [doh-yah]
stir-fried bean sprouts

炒白菜 chǎo báicài [bai-tsai]
stir-fried Chinese cabbage

海米白菜 hǎimǐ báicài
[hai-mee] stir-fried Chinese
cabbage with dried shrimps

韭菜炒鸡蛋 jiǔcài chǎo
jīdàn [jyoh-tsai-chow jee-dyen]
stir-fried chives with eggs

黄瓜炒鸡蛋 huángguā chǎo
jīdàn [hwahng-gwah chow jee-
dahn] stir-fried cucumber
with eggs

鱼香茄子 yúxiāng qiézi [yoo-
hsyang chyeh-dzur] stir-fried
aubergine in hot spicy sauce

冬 笋扁豆 dōngsǔn biǎndòu
[doong-sun byen-doh] stir-fried
French beans with bamboo
shoots

烧二冬 shāo èr dōng [show er
doong] stir-fried mushrooms
and bamboo shoots with
vegetables

鲜蘑豌豆 xiānmó wāndòu
[hsyen-mor wahn-doh] stir-fried
peas with mushrooms

炒土豆丝 chǎo tǔdòusī
[chow too-doh-sur] stir-fried
shredded potato

炒萝卜丝 chǎo luóbosī 〖lwor-bor-sur〗 stir-fried shredded turnip

菠菜炒鸡蛋 bōcài chǎo jīdàn 〖bor-tsai — jee-dahn〗 stir-fried spinach with eggs

西红柿炒鸡蛋 xīhóngshì chǎo jīdàn 〖hshee-hoong-shur〗 stir-fried tomato with eggs

Menu Reader:
Drink

Contents

Essential Terms

啤酒 beer píjiǔ [pee-jyoh]

瓶子 bottle píngzi [ping-dzur]

咖啡 coffee kāfēi [kah-fay]

杯子 cup bēizi [bay-dzee]

玻璃杯 glass bōlibēi [bor-lee-bay]

牛奶 milk niúnǎi [nyoh-nai]

矿泉水儿 mineral water kuàngquánshuǐr [kwahng-choo-en-shwayr]

鲜橘汁 orange juice xiānjúzhī [hsyen-jyew-jur]

米酒 rice wine mǐjiǔ [mee-jyoh]

汽水儿 soft drink qìshuǐr [chee-shwayr]

糖 sugar táng [tahng]

茶 tea chá [chah]

水 water shuǐ [shway]

威士忌 whisky wēishìjì [way-shur-jee]

酒水在外 jiúshuǐ zài wài drinks not included

一杯茶／咖啡 a cup of tea/coffee, please yì bēi chá/kāfēi [bay]

请再来一杯啤酒 another beer, please qǐng zài lái yì bēi píjiǔ
[ching dzai lai yee bay pee-jyoh]

（来）一杯茅台酒 a glass of Maotai (lái) yì bēi Máotáijiǔ [yee
bay mow-tai-jyoh]

Beer

啤酒 píjiǔ [pee-jyoh] beer

冰镇啤酒 bīngzhèn píjiǔ [bing-jun] iced beer

青岛啤酒 Qīngdǎo píjiǔ [ching-dow] most famous type of Chinese beer

Coffee, Tea etc

红茶 hóngchá [hoong-chah] black tea

菊花茶 júhuāchá [joo-hwah-chah] chrysanthemum tea

咖啡 kāfēi [kah-fay] coffee

绿茶 lùchá [lyew-chah] green tea

茉莉花茶 mòli huāchá [mor-lee hwah-chah] jasmine tea

乌龙茶 wūlóngchá [woo-loong-chah] oolong tea, famous semi-fermented tea, half green, half black

花茶 huāchá [hwah-chah] scented tea

牛奶咖啡 niúnǎi kāfēi [nyoh-nai kah-fay] white coffee, coffee with milk

Soft Drinks

可口可乐 kěkou kělè [kur-koh kur-lur] Coke®

果子汁 guǒzizhī [gwor-dzur-jur]

fruit juice

冰水 bīngshuǐ [bing-shway] iced water

崂山可乐 Láoshān kělè [low-shahn kur-lur] Chinese variety of cola made from Laoshan water

柠檬汽水儿 níngméng qìshuǐr [ning-mung chee-shwayr] lemonade

牛奶 niúnǎi [nyoh-nai] milk

矿泉水儿 kuàngquánshuǐr [kwahng-chwahn-shwayr] mineral water

橘子汽水儿 júzi qìshuǐr [joo-dzur chee-shwayr] orangeade

橘子汁 júzizhī [joo-dzur-jee] orange juice

菠萝汁 bōluozhī [bor-lwor-jur] pineapple juice

酸梅汤 suānméitāng [swahn-may-tahng] sweet-sour plum juice

Wine, Spirits etc

白兰地 báilándì [bai-lahn-dee] brandy

香槟酒 xiāngbīnjiǔ [hsyang-bin-jyoh] champagne

白干儿 báigānr [bai-gahnr] clear spirit, distilled from sorghum grain

白酒 báijiǔ [bai-jyoh] clear

spirit, distilled from sorghum
grain

法国白兰地 **fǎguó báilándì**
[fah-gwor bai-lahn-dee] cognac

干红葡萄酒 **gān hóng
pútaojiǔ** [gahn hoong poo-tow-
jyow] dry red wine

干白葡萄酒 **gān bái pútaojiǔ**
dry white wine

金酒 **jīnjiǔ** [jin-jyoh] gin

果子酒 **guǒzijiǔ** [gwor-dzur-
jyoh] liqueur

茅台酒 **Máotáijiǔ** [mow-tai-
jyoh] Maotai spirit

红葡萄酒 **hóng pútaojiǔ**
[hoong poo-tow-jyoh] red wine

黄酒 **huángjiǔ** [hwahng-jyoh]
rice wine

老酒 **láojiǔ** [low-jyoh] rice wine

朗姆酒 **lángmújiǔ** [lahng-moo-
jyoh] rum

苏格兰威士忌 **Sūgélán
wēishìjì** [soo-gur-lahn] Scotch
whisky

汽水儿 **qìshuǐr** [chee-shwayr]
soda water

汽酒 **qìjiǔ** [chee-jyoh] sparkling
wine

味美思 **wèiměisī** [way-may-sur]
vermouth

俄得克酒 **édékèjiǔ** [ur-dur-kur-
jyoh] vodka

威士忌 **wēishìjì** [way-shur-jur]
whisky

白葡萄酒 **bái pútaojiǔ** [poo-
tow-jyoh] white wine

葡萄酒 [poo-tow-jyoh] **pútaojiǔ**
wine

How the
Language
Works

Pronunciation

Throughout this book Chinese words have been written in the standard romanized system known as pinyin (see below). Pinyin, which was introduced in China in the 1950s, can for the most part be used as a guide to pronunciation. However, some of the syllables are not pronounced in an immediately obvious way. For this reason, a simplified transliteration is also provided in almost all instances. This transliteration should be read as though it were English, bearing in mind the notes on pronunciation below:

Vowels

ah	long 'a' as in **a**rt	eh	'e' as in b**e**d
ai	'i' as in **I**, **eye**	oh	'o' as in g**o**, **oh**
ay	as in h**ay**	ow	as in c**ow**

Consonants

ch	as in **Ch**inese	ts	as in **ts**ar
dz	like the 'ds' in hea**ds**	y	as in **y**es
g	hard 'g' as in **g**et		

Pinyin

Chinese words are made up of one or more syllables, each of which is represented in the written language by a character. These syllables can be divided into initials (consonants) and finals (vowels or vowels followed by either n or ng). In spoken Chinese, the consonant finals are often not fully sounded. A full list of initials and finals, along with the closest equivalent sound in English appears below. There are, however, some sounds that are unlike anything in English. In this pronunciation guide, words containing these sounds are given in Chinese characters as well; ask a Chinese person to pronounce them for you.

Initials

f, l, m, n, s, w and y	are all similar to English
b, d, g	similar to English, but a shorter sound
p, t, k	a more emphatic pronunciation as in **p**op, **t**ap and **c**ap (more strongly pronounced than b, d and g above)
h	slightly harsher than an **h** in English, closer to the **ch** sound in lo**ch** or Ba**ch**
j, q, x	pronounced with the lips positioned as if you were smiling:
j	'j' as in **j**eer
q	'ch' as in **ch**eer
x	'sh' as in **sh**eer, but say it with your lips in a smile and the tip of your tongue pointing up. This sound is shown in the book with **hs**
c	'ts' as in **ts**ar 菜
z	'ds' as hea**ds** 自
ch, sh, zh, r	the last group of initials is the most difficult for a non-Chinese to perfect; they are all pronounced with the tip of the tongue curled back till it touches the palate:
ch	as ch in bir**ch** 茶
sh	as sh in **sh**ower 少
zh	as ge in bud**ge** 中
r	as r in **r**ung 人

Finals

a	as in **a**rt
ai	as in **ai**sle
an	as in r**an**, but with a longer 'a' as in **a**rt
ang	as in h**ang**, but with a longer 'a' as in **a**rt
ao	'ow' as in c**ow**

e	like the 'e' in th**e** or the 'u' in f**u**r
ei	as in w**ei**ght
en	as in shak**en**
eng	like 'en' followed by a softly spoken 'g'
er	similar to **err**, pronounced with the tongue curled back so that it touches the palate
i	usually pronounced as in marga**ri**ne; however, after the initials c, ch, r, s, sh, z and zh it is pronounced like the 'i' in sh**i**rt or f**i**rst
ia	'ya' as in **ya**rn
ian	similar to **yen**
iang	**yang** ('i' plus 'ang', but with shorter 'a' sound)
iao	'yow' as in **yow**l
ie	'ye' as in **ye**ti
in	as in d**in**
ing	as in br**ing**
iong	**yoong** ('i' plus 'ong')
iu	'yo' as in **yo-yo**
o	as in l**o**re
ou	like **oh**
ong	**oong** ('ung' as in l**u**ng, with the vowel given a longer, more rounded sound)
u	as in r**u**le; or like French **u**ne or German **ü**ber
ua	**wah** ('wa' plus 'a' as in **a**rt)
uai	similar to **why**
uan	**wahn** in most cases ('w' plus 'an'); after 'y', the second pronunciation of 'u' plus 'an'
uang	**wahng** ('w' plus 'ang')
ue	the second pronunciation of 'u' plus 'e' as in b**e**t
ui	'wai' as in **wai**t
un	as in f**un**gi
uo	similar to **war**
ü	like French **u**ne or German **ü**ber
üe	'ü' followed by 'e' as in b**e**t

Northern Chinese

In Northern Chinese, the suffix **r** is often placed at the end of a syllable, producing a sound reminiscent of the burr of southwest England. This is represented in pinyin by the addition of an **r** to the syllable so that **men** (door), for example, becomes **menr**, with the 'n' barely pronounced. Such pronunciation is most apparent in Beijing.

Tones

The Chinese language only uses about four hundred different sounds. The number of sounds available is increased by the use of tones: the particular pitch at which a word is pronounced determines its meaning. The same combination of letters pronounced with a different tone will produce different words. There are four tones: first tone (ˉ), second tone (ˊ), third tone (ˇ) and fourth tone (ˋ).

Not all syllables are pronounced with tones; where there is no tone, the syllable is written without a tone mark. Often when you have a word consisting of two syllables, the second syllable, for example, **xuésheng** (student), is written without a tone.

In Chinese, the tone is as important a part of the word as the consonant and vowel sounds. Context usually makes the meaning clear, but it is still important whenever possible to use the correct tone in order to reduce the chance of misunderstanding. The character **ma** [mah] has five meanings, differentiated by the tones:

mā	妈	mother
má	麻	hemp
mǎ	马	horse
mà	骂	abuse, scold
ma	吗	(added to the end of a sentence to turn it into a question)

To help you get a clearer idea of how the tones sound, Chinese character equivalents are given for the words in this section. Ask a Chinese speaker to read the words for you so that you can hear the tonal differences.

First tone (‾). High, level tone, with unchanging volume, held briefly:

gū [goo]	孤	solitary
guān [gwahn]	观	look at
kāi	开	open (verb)
yān [yahn]	烟	cigarette

Second tone (´). Starting about mid-range, rising quickly and becoming louder; a shorter sound than the first tone, similar to a question showing surprise such as 'eh?':

héng [hung]	衡	balance (verb)
rén [run]	人	person
shí [shur]	十	ten
yán [yahn]	言	speech

Third tone (ˇ). Starts low and falls before rising again to slightly above the starting point; starts quietly then increases in volume; slightly longer than first tone:

běn [bun]	本	book
fǎ [fah]	法	law
qǐ [chee]	起	rise (verb)
yǎn [yahn]	掩	cover (verb)

Fourth tone (`). Starts high, falling abruptly in pitch and volume; shorter than the second tone:

bèn [bun]	笨	stupid
dà [dah]	大	big
pà [pah]	怕	fear (verb)
yàn [yahn]	雁	wild goose

The tones can be illustrated in diagram form like this:

In speech, a third tone which precedes another third tone becomes a second tone.

Abbreviations

adj	adjective
pl	plural
pol	polite
sing	singular

General

The Chinese language has a number of characteristics which are very different from European languages, the most important of these being that there are no inflections for case, number or gender and that verbs do not decline. References to past, present or future are identified by context and the addition of various time words such as **míngtian** [ming-tyen] (tomorrow), **jīntian** [jin-tyen] (today), or **qùnián** [chew-nyen] (last year). In both the written and spoken language, statements are kept short and the repetition of what has already been expressed is avoided. Pronouns, both personal and impersonal, are often omitted.

Nouns

Singular and plural forms of nouns are nearly always the same. For example, **shū** can mean either 'book' or 'books' depending on the context:

wǒ mǎile yìběn shū
wor mai-lur yee-bun shoo
I bought one book

wǒ mǎile liǎngběn shū
wor mai-lur lyang-bun shoo
I bought two books

The few exceptions tend to be nouns used in addressing groups of people, in which case the suffix **-men** is added to the end of the noun:

péngyoumen
pung-yoh-mun
friends

háizimen
hai-dzur-mun
children

However, **-men** is not used for the plural when numbers are involved as the plural is obvious from the context:

sìge péngyou
sur-gur pung-yoh
four friends

Articles

There is no equivalent in Chinese for either the definite article 'the' or the indefinite articles 'a' and 'an'. The exact meaning will be clear from the context or word order. Therefore, **zázhì** (magazine) can mean 'a magazine' or 'the magazine' depending on the context.

If you want to be more precise, you can use **nèi** (that) or **zhèi** (this) with the appropriate measure word (see page 262).

The number **yī** (one), along with the appropriate measure word (see page 262) can also be used to translate 'a/an'. But often in such sentences **yi** is either unstressed or omitted altogether, leaving just the measure word:

> **wǒ xiǎng mǎi yìběn zázhì**
> wor hsyang mai yee-bun dzah-jur
> I am going to buy a magazine

or:

> **wǒ xiǎng mǎi běn zázhì**
> I am going to buy a magazine

Adjectives

Adjectives are placed before the noun and usually the word **de** is added between the adjective and the noun:

piányi de shū	**hěn suān de sùcài**
pyen-yee dur shoo	hun swahn dur soo-tsai
cheap book(s)	very sour vegetable dish(es)

The **de** is frequently omitted if the adjective is monosyllabic:

gǔ huà	**hǎo bànfǎ**
goo hwah	how bahn-fah
ancient paintings	a good method

Some nouns can be used adjectivally:

lìshǐ	lìshǐ xiǎoshuō
lee-shur	lee-shur hsyow-shwor
history	historical novel(s)

shùxué	shùxué jiàokēshū
shoo-hsyew-eh	shoo-hsyew-eh jyow-kur-shoo
mathematics	maths textbook

Adjectival Verbs

Some verbs also function as adjectives and are known as adjectival verbs. In sentences using an adjectival verb, the word order is:

noun subject + **hěn** + adjectival verb

The word **hěn** has little meaning, unless it is stressed, when it means 'very'.

sùcài hěn suān	shū dōu hěn piányi
soo-tsai hun swahn	shoo doh hun pyen-yee
the vegetable dish is very sour	the books are all cheap

Suàn means 'to be sour' and **piányi** 'to be cheap'.

For greater emphasis, add **tài** to mean 'very', 'really' or 'extremely':

tài hǎole
tai how-lur
that's really great

Comparatives

To form the comparative (more ..., ...-er) in sentences when only one thing is referred to, most often in response to a question, an adjectival verb is used by itself. In the following two examples, the adjectival verbs **hǎokàn** (attractive) and **guì** (expensive) are used:

zhèige hǎokàn
jay-gur how-kahn
this (one) is more attractive

nèige guì
nay-gur gway
that (one) is more expensive

The above phrases can also be translated as 'this one is attractive' and 'that one is expensive', but the exact meaning will be clear from the context. The following are added after the adjective or adjectival verb to indicate the degree of comparison:

... diǎnr	[dyenr]	more ...
... xiē	[hsyeh]	a bit more ...
... yìdiǎnr	[yee-dyenr]	a bit more ...
... de duō	[dur dwor]	much more ...
... duōle	[dwor-lur]	far more ...
... gèng	[gung]	even more ...

zhèige guì (yi)diǎnr/xiē
jay-gur gway (yee-)dyenr/hsyeh
this (one) is (a bit) more expensive

zhèige guì de duō
jay-gur gway dur dwor
this (one) is much more expensive

zhèige guì duōle
jay-gur gway dwor-lur
this (one) is far more expensive

zhèige gèng guì
jay-gur gung gway
this (one) is even more expensive

To compare two nouns, the word order is:

subject + **bǐ** + object of comparison + adjectival verb

Fǎguó bǐ Zhōngguó xiǎo
fah-gwor bee joong-gwor hsyow
France is smaller than China

qùnián bǐ jīnnián rè
chew-nyen bee jin-nyen rur
last year was hotter than this year

zhèige bǐ nèige gèng měilì
jay-gur bee nay-gur gung may-lur
this one is even more beautiful than that one

Superlatives

To form the superlative (most ..., ...-est), place **zuì** before the adjective or adjectival verb:

zuì guì de zixíngchē
dzway gway dur dzur-hsing-chur
the most expensive bicycle

zhèige fàndiàn zuì dà
jay-gur fahn-dyen dzway dah
this hotel is the largest

Adverbs

Adverbs usually have the same form as adjectives, but are sometimes repeated for emphasis (**mànmàn** below):

tā mànmàn de kànle nǐde xìn
tah mahn-mahn dur kahn-lur nee-dur hsin
he/she read your letter slowly

Adverbs can also be formed by placing **de** after an adjective:

nǐ dàshēng de gēn tā shuō ba
nee dah-shung dur gun tah shwor bah
speak loudly to him/her

When **de** appears after a verb, the subsequent adjective takes on an adverbial function:

tāmen qǐde hén wǎn
tah-mun chee-dur hun wahn
they got up late

tā zúqiu tīde hén hǎo
tah dzoo-chyew tee-dur hun how
he plays football well

Pronouns

Personal Pronouns

wǒ	[wor]	I; me
nǐ	[nee]	you (sing)
nín	[nin]	you (sing, pol)
tā	[tah]	he; him; she; her; it
wǒmen	[wor-mun]	we; us
nǐmen	[nee-mun]	you (pl)
tāmen	[tah-mun]	they; them

There are no different forms for subject and object in Chinese:

wǒ rènshi tā
wor run-shur tah
I know him/her

tā rènshi wǒ
tah runshur wor
he/she knows me

zhèi shì géi nǐ de
jay shur gay nee dur
this is for you

Tā can also mean 'it', though this is not a common usage. Generally, there is no need to refer to 'it' in a sentence as the context usually makes it clear:

shū hěn wúqù – wǒ bù xǐhuan
shoo hun woo-choo – wor boo hshee-hwahn
the book is boring – I don't like it

wǒ xǐhuan nèiběn shū – hén yǒu yìsi
wor hshee-hwahn nay-bun shoo – hun yoh yee-sur
I like that book – it's very interesting

Like tā, tāmen referring to inanimate things is rarely used.

Demonstrative Pronouns

zhè [jur] this

zhè búshì tāde
jur boo-shur tah-dur
this is not his

nà [nah] that

nà tèbié hǎo
nah tur-byeh how
that's awfully good

In order to translate 'this one' or 'that one' as the object of a sentence, a measure word (see page 262) must be added:

wǒ xǐhuan zhèige/nèige
wor hshee-hwahn jay-gur/nay-gur
I like this (one)/that (one)

Possessives

In order to form possessive adjectives and pronouns, add the suffix **-de** to the personal pronouns on page 260:

wǒde	[wor-dur]	my; mine
nǐde	[nee-dur]	your; yours (sing)
nínde	[nin-dur]	your; yours (sing, pol)
tāde	[tah-dur]	his; her; hers; its
wǒmende	[wor-mun-dur]	our; ours
nǐmende	[nee-mun-dur]	your; yours (pl)
tāmende	[tah-mun-dur]	their; theirs

wǒde zhuōzi	**tāde péngyou**
wor-dur jwor-dzur	tah-dur pung-yoh
my table	his/her friend

tāmende péngyou	**zhè shì nǐde**
tah-mun-dur pung-yoh	jur shur nee-dur
their friend	this is yours

De equates to 'of' or apostrophe 's' in English. **De** phrases always precede the noun to be described:

Shànghǎi de fēngjǐng	**qiūtiān de tiānqi**
shahng-hai dur fung-jing	chyew-tyen dur tyen-chee
the scenery of Shanghai	autumn weather

wǒ qīzi de yīxiāng
wor chee-dzur dur yee-hsyang
my wife's suitcase

If a relationship or possession is obvious from the context, it is common to omit **de**:

wǒ àiren	**tā jiā**	**wǒ péngyou**
wor ai-run	tah jyah	wor pung-yoh
my wife	his/her home	my friend

wǒ mǎile chēpiào le
wor mai-lur chur-pyow lur
I've bought my train ticket

Dependent Clauses and 'de'

Dependent clauses precede the noun to be modified and **de** is inserted between the clause and the noun:

tā jì de xìn	**wǒ kàn de shū**
tah jee dur hsin	wor kahn dur shoo
the letter which he sent	the book(s) (which/that) I read

zuótian kàn de nèibù diànyǐng
dzwor-tyen kahn dur nay-boo dyen-ying
that film I saw yesterday

Measure Words

Demonstrative Adjectives and Measure Words

Nouns or groups of nouns in Chinese have specific measure words which are used when counting or quantifying the noun or nouns, i.e. which are used in conjunction with demonstratives and numerals. The demonstrative adjective is usually formed with the demonstrative **nèi** (that) or **zhèi** (this) followed by a measure word. Measure words, of which there are around fifty in common usage, are added to the end of the demonstrative (or numeral) and precede the noun. Some measure words can be readily translated into English while others cannot, for example:

gōngjīn	**mǐ**	**píng**
goong-jin	mee	ping
kilogram	metre	bottle

sāngōngjīn lí	**sānmǐ miánbù**
sahng-goong-jin lee	sahn-mee myen-boo
three kilos of pears	three metres of cotton

nèipíng píjiǔ
nay-ping pee-yoh
that bottle of beer

The most common measure words are:

bǎ	[bah]	chairs, knives, teapots, tools or implements with handles, stems, bunches of flowers
bēi	[bay]	cups, glasses
běn	[bun]	books, magazines
fēng	[fun]	letters
ge	[gur]	general measure word
jiàn	[jyen]	things, affairs, shirts etc
kē	[kur]	trees
kuài	[kwai]	lumps, pieces
liàng	[lyang]	vehicles
pán	[pahn]	round objects
suǒ	[swor]	buildings
tiáo	[tyow]	fish and various long narrow things
wèi	[way]	polite measure word used for gentlemen, ladies, guests etc
zhāng	[jahng]	tables, beds, tickets, sheets of paper
zhī	[jur]	hands, birds, suitcases, boats

zhèiběn shū	**nèijiàn lǐwù**
jay-bun shoo	nay-jyen lee-woo
this book	that present

nèikē shù	**zhèiliàng zìxíngchē**
nay-kur shoo	jay-lyang dzur-hsing-chur
that tree	this bicycle

nèisuǒ yīyuàn	**sāntiáo chuán**
nay-swor yee-ywahn	sahn-tyow chwahn
that hospital	three boats
nèiwèi láibīn	**sānzhāng piào**
nay-way lai-bin	sahn-jahng pyow
that guest	three tickets

The most common of all measure words is **ge**:

zhèige shāngdiàn	**nèige zhěntou**
ay-gur shang-dyen	nay-gur jun-toh
this shop	that pillow

When the correct measure word is not known, the best solution is to use **ge**.

In a dialogue, when it is clear from the context what is being referred to, then the noun may be omitted and only the demonstrative and measure word are used:

wǒ xǐhuan nèige	**zhèibēi chá hěn hǎohē**
wor hshee-hwahn nay-gur	jay-bay chah hun how-hur
I like that (one)	this is a lovely cup of tea

zhèiwèi shì ...
jay-way shur
this is ... (introducing people)

Numbers and Measure Words

As is the case with demonstrative adjectives, you must use a measure word with numbers when they are linked with nouns:

sìkē shù	**sānshíwǔběn shū**	**sìshíge rén**
sur-kur shoo	sahn-shur-woo-bun shoo	sur-shur-gur run
four trees	thirty-five books	forty people

See page 282 for the use of **liǎng** (two) with measure words. Similarly, when ordinal numbers are linked with a noun, it is necessary to include a measure word:

dìsānsuǒ fángzi
dee-sahn-swor fahng-dzur
the third house

dìsìtiáo lù
dee-sur-tyow loo
the fourth road

Demonstratives and Numbers

If a demonstrative and a number are used together in a sentence, the word order is:

demonstrative + number + measure word + noun

nèi sānběn shū
nay sahn-bun shoo
those three books

zhèi bāwèi láibīn
jay bah-way lai-bin
these eight guests

nèi liùge
nay lyoh-gur
those six

Verbs

There is no change in Chinese verbs for first, second or third person subjects, both singular and plural:

wǒ zǒu
wor dzoh
I walk, I am walking

tā zǒu
tah dzoh
he/she walks, he/she is walking

tāmen zǒu
tah-mun dzoh
they walk, they are walking

Chinese verbs also have no tenses:

wǒ míngtian zǒu
wor ming-tyen dzoh
I will go for a walk tomorrow

wǒ zuótian zǒu de shíhou, tiānqi hěn hǎo
wor dzwor-tyen dzoh dur shur-hoh tyen-chee hun how
when I was walking yesterday, the weather was lovely

The future and past are indicated in the above sentences by the time words **míngtian** (tomorrow) and **zuótian** (yesterday), while the form of the verb **zǒu** does not change.

The meaning of verbs is also influenced by a number of suffixes and sentence particles (see pages 268 and 270).

A verb used by itself usually implies either a habitual action:

> **Zhōngguórén chī mǐfàn**
> joong-gwor-run chur mee-fahn
> Chinese people eat rice

or an imminent action:

> **nǐ qù nǎr?**
> nee chew nar
> where are you going?

To Be

The verb 'to be', when followed by a noun, is **shì**, which corresponds to all the forms of the verb 'to be' in English ('am', 'are', 'is', 'were' etc):

> **tā shì wǒde péngyou**
> tah shur wor-dur pung-yoh
> she is my friend

> **zhè shì shénme?**
> jur shur shun-mur
> what is this?

> **tāmen shì xuésheng**
> tah-mun shur hway-shung
> they are students

The verb **shì** is not required when adjectival verbs are used (see page 257).

The preposition **zài** (in, at) is used as a verb to convey the meaning of 'to be in or at' a particular place (see page 274).

Negatives

To form a negative sentence, use the word **bù** (not); when **bù** precedes a word with a fourth tone, the tone changes to a second tone (**bú**):

wǒ búyào nèiběn shū
wor boo-yow nay-bun shoo
I do not want that book

tā bú qù
tah boo chew
he's not going

nà wǒ bù zhīdao
nah wor boo jur-dow
I didn't know that

Bù is also the negative used with adjectives/adjectival verbs:

bùmǎn
boo-mahn
dissatisfied, discontented

fángzi bú dà
fahng-dzur boo dah
the building isn't big

With the verb **yǒu** (to have), **méi** is used as a negative rather than **bù**:

tā yǒu kòng
tah yoh koong
he/she has time

wǒ méiyǒu kòng
wor may-yoh koong
I don't have time

Méi can also be used on its own to mean 'have not':

wǒ méishir
wor may-shur
I have nothing to do

Yǒu also means 'there is/are':

shāngdiànli méiyǒu niúnǎi
shahng-dyen-lee may-yoh nyoh-nai
there's no milk in the shop

méiyǒu bànfǎ
may-yoh bahn-fah
there's nothing to be done, there's nothing you can do about it

yǒu rén

yoh run

there is someone there; engaged, occupied (on a toilet door)

Verb Suffixes

Suffixes are added to Chinese verbs to modify their meaning.

The addition of the suffix -le indicates a changed situation; often this means that the action of the verb has been completed:

wǒ mǎile sānge píngguǒ
wor mai-lur sahn-gur ping-gwor
I bought three apples

tā yǐjing líkāile
tah yee-jing lee-kai-lur
he/she has left already

wǒ zài nàr zhùle jiǔnián
wor dzai nar joo-lur jyoh-nyen
I lived there for nine years

hēwánle chá wǒ jiù kàn diànshì
hur-wahn-lur chah wor jyoh kahn dyen-shur
when I have finished my tea, I am going to watch television

As the fourth example shows, the completed action need not necessarily be in the past.

In order to express the negative form of a completed action, either **méi** or **méi yǒu** is placed before the verb and **-le** is omitted:

wǒ méi(yǒu) kàn diànshì
wor may(-yoh) kahn dyen-shur
I didn't watch television

tā méi(yǒu) líkāi
tah may(-yoh) lee-kai
he hasn't left

Continuous or prolonged action is expressed by the suffix -zhe:

tā chōuzhe yān
tah choh-jur yahn
he/she is smoking a cigarette

tā zài shāfāshang zuòzhe
tah dzai shah-fah-shahng dzwor-jur
he/she is sitting on the sofa

The suffix **-zhe** can also be used to convey the idea of doing more than one thing at the same time:

tā hēzhe chá kàn shū
tah hur-jur chah kahn shoo
he read a book while drinking tea

When the **-zhe** suffix is used, **méi** is placed before the verb to form the negative:

tā méi chuānzhe zhōngshānzhuāng
tah may chwahn-jur joong-shahn-jwahng
he/she isn't wearing a Mao suit

Note that **-zhe** has no connection with tense. Depending on the context, the above sentences could be translated as: 'he/she was smoking a cigarette', 'he/she wasn't wearing a Mao suit'.

Another way of indicating continuous action is to place the word **zài** in front of the verb:

tā zài chōuyān
tah dzai choh-yahn
he is smoking

nǐ zài kàn shénme?
nee dzai kahn shun-mur
what are you reading?

The suffix **-guo** is used to indicate a past experience:

wǒ qùguo Zhōngguó
wor chew-gwor joong-gwor
I have been to China

wǒ kànguo nèiběn shū
wor kahng-gwor nay-bun shoo
I have read that book

When the suffix **-guo** is used, **méi** is placed before the verb to form the negative:

wǒ méi qùguo Shànghǎi
wor may chew-gwor shahng-hai
I have never been to
  Shanghai

tā méi hēguo Yìndù chá
tah may hur-gwor yin-doo chah
he's/she's never drunk
  Indian tea

Sentence Particles

The particle **le** at the end of a sentence either indicates that something happened in the past which is still relevant to the present or implies a change of circumstances in the present or future:

tā mǎi bàozhǐ qù le
tah mai bow-jur chew lur
he/she has gone to buy a paper

wǒ zài Lúndūn zhùle liùnián le
wor dzai lun-dun joo-lur lyoh-nyen lur
I have been living in London for six years

gūafēng le
gwah-fung lur
it's windy (now)

wǒ xiànzai bú è le
wor hsyahn-dzai boo ur lur
I'm not hungry any more

píngguǒ dōu huài le
ping-gwor doh hway lur
the apples have all gone bad

wǒmen zǒu le
wor-mun dzoh lur
we are leaving (now)

The particle **ne** adds emphasis to what is said:

tā hái méi líkāi ne
tah hai may lee-kai nur
he still hasn't gone

zuò chángtú qìchē kě bù fāngbiàn ne
dzwor chahng-too chee-chur kur boo fahng-byen nur
(but) it's so inconvenient to go by bus

nǐ zuò shénme ne?
nee dzwor shun-mur nur
well, what are you going to do?

On its own, often in response to an earlier question, **ne** can be used to express the idea 'and what about ...?':

zhèishuāng xié tài guì – nèishuāng ne?
jay-shwahng hsyeh tai gway – nay-shwahng nur
this pair of shoes is too expensive – what about that pair?

The particle **ba** indicates a suggestion:

zǒu ba!
dzoh bah
let's go!

nǐ kǎolǜ yíxià ba
nee kow-lyew yee-syah bah
think about it, consider it

It can also mean 'I suggest' or 'I suppose':

nǐ shì lǎo Zhāng ba?
nee shur low jahng bah
I suppose you must be old Zhang?

nǐmen dōu hěn lèi ba?
nee-mun doh hun lay bah
you are all very tired, aren't you?

Questions

There are a number of ways of forming questions in Chinese. One way is to add the particle **ma** to the end of a sentence to turn it into a question without changing the word order:

tā shì Rìběrén ma?
tah shur ree-bur-run mah
is he/she Japanese?

nǐ mǎi zhèifèn bàozhǐ ma?
nee mai jay-fun bow-jur mah
are you buying this newspaper?

nǐ è ma?
nee ur mah
are you hungry?

nǐ qùguo Běijīng ma?
nee choo-gwor bay-jing mah
have you ever been to Beijing?

nǐ yǒu háizi ma?
nee yoh hai-dzur mah
do you have any children?

Alternatively, the verb is repeated along with the negative **bù** or **méi**:

tāmen shì búshì Yīngguórén?
tah-mun shur boo-shur ying-gwor-run
are they British?

jīntian rè bú rè?
jin-tyen rur boo rur
is it hot today?

nǐ è bú è?
nee ur boo ur
are you hungry?

tā chīguo Zhōngcān méiyǒu?
tah chur-gwor joong-tsahn may-yoh
has he/she ever eaten
    Chinese food?

ní yǒu méiyou háizi?
nee yoh may-yoh hai-dzur
do you have any children?

Shéi (who?) and **shénme** (what?) are the main interrogative pronouns. Interrogative pronouns are placed in the same position in the sentence as the noun in the answer that is implied:

tā shì shéi?
tah shur shay
who is he?

tā shì wǒ péngyou
tah shur wor pung-yoh
he's my friend

shéi fù qián?
shay foo chyen
who is going to pay?

tā fùqián
tah foo-chyen
he is going to pay

ní mǎi shénme?
nee mai shun-mur
what are you going to buy?

wó mǎi yìjié diànchí
wor mai yee-jyeh dyen-chur
I'm going to buy a battery

The other common interrogatives are:

nǎr/nǎli?	[nar/nah-lee]	where?
duōshǎo?	[dwor-show]	how many?, how much?
nèi?	[nay]	which?
shéide?	[shay-dur]	whose?
zěnme?	[dzun-mur]	how?
wèishénme?	[way-shun-mur]	why?

shāngdiàn zài nǎr?
shahng-dyen dzai nar
where is the shop?

duōshǎo qián?
dwor-show chyen
how much is that?

nǎige fàndiàn zuì guì?
nay-gur fahn-dyen dzway gway
which hotel is most expensive?

nǐ xǐhuan něige?
nee hshee-hwahn nay-gur
which one would you like?

zhè shì shéide?
jur shur shay-dur
whose is this?

nǐ shì zěnme láide?
nee shur dzun-mur lai-dur
how did you get here?

tāmen wèishénme bú shàng huǒchē?
tah-mun way-shun-mur goo shahng hwor-chur
why aren't they getting on the train?

Háishi (or) is used in questions posing alternatives:

nǐ xiǎng mǎi zhèige háishi nèige?
nee hsyahng mai jay-gur hai-shur nay-gur
do you wish to buy this one or that one?

Prepositions

Some common prepositions are:

cóng	[tsoong]	from
dào	[dow]	to
duì	[dway]	towards, with regard to
gěi	[gay]	for
gēn	[gun]	with
lí	[lee]	from/to (in expressions of distance)
wèile	[way-lur]	because of
yòng	[yoong]	with, by means of,
zài	[dzai]	in, at (see page 274)

wǒmen míngtian dào Shànghǎi qù
wor-mun ming-tyen dow shahng-hai chew
we're going to Shanghai tomorrow

cóng sāndiǎnbàn dào sìdiǎn
tsoong sahn-dyen-bahn dow sur-dyen
from three thirty to four o'clock

Yīngguó lí Fǎguó bù yuǎn
ying-gwor lee fah-gwor boo ywahn
Britain is not far from France

wǒmen shì zuò chuán láide
wor-mun shur dzwor chwahn lai-dur
we came by boat

wǒ géi ní mǎile yìxiē píngguǒ
wor gay nee mai-lur yee-hsyeh ping-gwor
I've bought some apples for you

qǐng gēn wǒ lái
ching gun wor lai
please come with me

tā wèi tā háizi hěn zháojí
tah way tah hai-dzur hun jow-jee
she was very worried about her child

Zài (in, at) is also used as a verb meaning 'to be in/at':

tā zài nǎr?	**tāmen zài Shànghǎi**
tah dzai nar	tah-mun dzai shahng-hai
where is he/she?	they are in Shanghai
zhuōzi zài wàibiānr	**wǒ zài Shànghǎi méiyǒu qīnqī**
jwor-dzur zai wai-byenr	wor dzai shahng-hai may-yoh ching-chee
the table is outside	I don't have any relatives in Shanghai

Place Word Suffixes

Various suffixes are added to nouns to indicate location and are nearly always used in conjunction with the preposition **zài**. The most important are:

lǐ	[lee]	inside, in
shàng	[shahng]	above, on
wài	[wai]	outside
xià	[hsyah]	below
zhōng	[joong]	in the middle, between

nǐde bàozhǐ zài dàizili
nee-dur bow-jur dzai dai-dzur-lee
your newspaper is in your bag

chéngwài yǒu fēijīchǎng
chung-wai yoh fur-jee-chahng
there's an airport outside the town

nǐde zhàoxiàngjī zài chuángshàng
nee-dur jow-hsyahng-jee dzai chwahng-shahng
your camera is on the bed

nǐde yīxiāng zài chuángxià
nee-dur yee-hsyahng dzai chwahng-hsyah
your suitcase is under the bed

zài shānlǐ
dzai shahn-lee
in the mountains

Yes and No

Chinese has no standard words for 'yes' and 'no', but you can often use **shì(de)** (yes, it is the case), **duìle** (yes, that's right) and **bú shì** (no, it is not the case).

The most common way of saying 'yes' is to repeat the verb of the question; to say 'no', repeat the verb of the question together with **bù** or **méi** as required:

nǐ yǒu kòng ma?	yǒu	méi yǒu
nee yoh koong mah	yoh	may yoh
do you have any free time?	yes	no

tā shì xuésheng ma?		shì	bú shì
tah shur hsyeh-shung mah		shur	boo shur
is he a student?		yes	no

nǐ qùguo Chángchéng méi yǒu?
nee chew-gwor chahng-chung may yoh
have you been to see the Great Wall?

qùguo	méi yǒu/méi qùguo
chew-gwor	may yoh/may chew-gwor
yes	no

Imperatives

To make an imperative in Chinese, pronounce the verb in an emphatic way:

zhànzhù!	gǔnchūqu!
jahn-joo	gun-choo-chew
stop!	get out!

Imperatives are rarely used because they sound too abrupt. The verb is more likely to be preceded by **qǐng** (please) or followed by **ba** (see page 271) to make the command sound more polite:

qǐng zuò ba
ching dzwor bah
please sit down

Negative imperatives are formed using either **bié** or **bú yào** (don't):

bié zǒule	bú yào zài shuō
byeh dzoh-lur	boo yow dzai shwor
don't go	say no more

Dates

Dates in Chinese are written in the following order:

> year + month + number

To write the year, place the relevant numbers in front of **nián** (year); this is followed by the month and then the number of the day plus **hào**:

九月一号
jiǔyuè yīhào
jyoh-yew-eh yee-how
the first of September

十二月二号
shíèryuè èrhào
shur-er-yew-eh er-how
the second of December

五月三十号
wǔyuè sānshíhào
woo-yew-eh sahn-shur-how
the thirtieth of May

二零零六年五月三十一号
èrlínglíngliù nián wǔyuè sānshíyīhào
ur-ling-ling-lyoh nyen woo-yew-eh
  sahn-shur-yee-how
the thirty-first of May, 2006

一九四二年
yījiǔ sìèr nián
yee-jyoh sur-er nyen
1942

Days

Sunday xīngqītiān 〖hsing-chee-tyen〗 星期天
Monday xīngqīyī 〖hsing-chee-yee〗 星期一
Tuesday xīngqīèr 〖hsing-chee-er〗 星期二
Wednesday xīngqīsān 〖hsing-chee-sahn〗 星期三
Thursday xīngqīsì 〖hsing-chee-sur〗 星期四
Friday xīngqīwǔ 〖hsing-chee-woo〗 星期五
Saturday xīngqīliù 〖hsing-chee-lyoh〗 星期六

Months

January yīyuè 【yee-yew-eh】 一月
February èryuè 【er-yew-eh】 二月
March sānyuè 【sahn-yew-eh】 三月
April sìyuè 【sur-yew-eh】 四月
May wǔyuè 【woo-yew-eh】 五月
June liùyuè 【lyoh-yew-eh】 六月
July qīyuè 【chee-yew-eh】 七月
August bāyuè 【bah-yew-eh】 八月
September jiǔyuè 【jyoh-yew-eh】 九月
October shíyuè 【shur-yew-eh】 十月
November shíyīyuè 【shur-yee-yew-eh】 十一月
December shíèryuè 【shur-er-yew-eh】 十二月

Time

■

When telling the time, the word **diān** is added to the number to indicate the hours. **Zhōng** (clock) is optional and is placed at the end of most time expressions. The word **fēn** (minutes) is added to the number of minutes.

what time is it? jǐdiǎn le? 【jee-dyen lur】 几点了？
o'clock diǎn zhōng 【dyen joong】 点钟
one o'clock yìdiǎn (zhōng) 【yee-dyen】 一点（钟）
two o'clock liǎngdiǎn (zhōng) 【lyang-dyen】 两点（钟）
at one o'clock yìdiǎn (zhōng) 【yee-dyen】 一点（钟）
it's one o'clock yìdiǎn (zhōng) 一点（钟）
it's two o'clock liǎngdiǎn (zhōng) 【lyang-dyen】 两点（钟）
it's ten o'clock shídiǎn (zhōng) 【shur-dyen】 十点（钟）
five past one yìdiǎn wǔfēn 【yee-dyen woo-fun】 一点五分
ten past two liǎngdiǎn shífēn 【lyang-dyen shur-fun】 两点十分
quarter past one yìdiǎn yíkè 【yee-dyen yee-kur】 一点一刻
quarter past two liǎngdiǎn yíkè 【lyang-dyen yee-kur】 两点一刻
half past two liǎngdiǎn bàn 【bahn】 两点半
half past ten shídiǎn bàn 【shur-dyen】 十点半

twenty to one yìdiǎn chà èrshí [yee-dyen chah er-shur] 一点差二十
twenty to ten shídiǎn chà èrshí [shur-dyen] 十点差二十
quarter to one yìdiǎn chà yíkè [yee-dyen chah yee-kur] 一点差一刻
quarter to two liǎngdiǎn chà yíkè [lyang-dyen] 两点差一刻
a.m. (early morning up to about 9) zǎoshang [dzow-shahng] 早上
(from about 9 till noon) shàngwǔ 上午
p.m. (afternoon) xiàwǔ [hsyah-woo] 下午
(evening) wǎnshang [wahn-shahng] 晚上
(night) yèli [yur-lee] 夜里
2 a.m. língchén liǎngdiǎn [ling-chun lyang-dyen] 凌晨两点
2 p.m. (14.00) xiàwǔ liǎngdiǎn [hsyah-woo] 下午两点
6 a.m. zǎoshang liùdiǎn [dzow-shahng lyoh-dyen] 早上六点
6 p.m. (18.00) wǎnshang liùdiǎn [wahn-shahng] 晚上六点
10 a.m. shàngwǔ shídiǎn [shahng-woo shur-dyen] 上午十点
10 p.m. wǎnshang shídiǎn [wahn-shahng] 晚上十点
noon zhōngwǔ [joong-woo] 中午
midnight bànyè [bahn-yur] 半夜
hour xiǎoshí [hsyow-shur] 小时
minute fēn [fun] 分
two minutes liǎng fēnzhōng [lyang fun-joong] 两分钟
second miǎo [myow] 秒
quarter of an hour yí kèzhōng [kur-joong] 一刻钟
half an hour bàn xiǎoshí [bahn hsyow-shur] 半小时
three quarters of an hour sān kèzhōng [sahn kur-joong] 三刻钟
nearly three o'clock kuài sān diǎn le [kwai sahn dyen lur] 快三点了

Numbers

See **Measure Words** on page 262.

0	líng	零
1	yī [yee]	一
2	èr, liǎng [lyang]	二
3	sān [sahn]	三
4	sì [sur]	四
5	wǔ	五

6	liù [lyoh]	六
7	qī [chee]	七
8	bā [bah]	八
9	jiǔ [jyoh]	九
10	shí [shur]	十
11	shíyī [shur-yee]	十一
12	shí'èr [shur-er]	十二
13	shísān [shur-sahn]	十三
14	shísì [shur-sur]	十四
15	shíwǔ [shur-woo]	十五
16	shíliù [shur-lyoh]	十六
17	shíqī [shur-chee]	十七
18	shíbā [shur-bah]	十八
19	shíjiǔ [shur-jyoh]	十九
20	èrshí [er-shur]	二十
21	èrshíyí [er-shur-yee]	二十一
22	èrshí'èr [er-shur-er]	二十二
30	sānshí [sahn-shur]	三十
31	sānshíyī [sahn-shur-yee]	三十一
32	sānshí'èr [sahn-shur-er]	三十二
40	sìshí [sur-shur]	四十
50	wǔshí [woo-shur]	五十
60	liùshí [lyoh-shur]	六十
70	qīshí [chee-shur]	七十
80	bāshí [bah-shur]	八十
90	jiǔshí [jyoh-shur]	九十
100	yìbǎi	一百
101	yìbǎi líng yī	一百零一
102	yìbǎi líng èr	一百零二
110	yìbǎi yìshí [yee-shur]	一百一十
111	yìbǎi yīshíyī [shur-yee]	一百一十一
200	èrbǎi	二百
201	èrbǎi líng yī	二百零一
202	èrbǎi líng èr	二百零二
210	èrbǎi yìshí [yee-shur]	二百一十

300	sānbǎi [sahn-bai]	三百
1,000	yìqiān [yee-chyen]	一千
2,000	liǎngqiān [lyang-chyen]	两千
3,000	sān qiān [sahn chyen]	三千
4,000	sìqiān [sur-chyen]	四千
5,000	wǔqiān [woo-chyen]	五千
10,000	yíwàn [yee-wahn]	一万
50,000	wǔwàn	五万
100,000	shíwàn [shur-wahn]	十万
1,000,000	bǎiwàn	百万
10,000,000	qiānwàn [chyen-wahn]	千万
100,000,000	yí yì	一亿

When counting 'one, two, three' and so on, **yī** (one) is written and said with the first tone. In other situations, the fourth tone is used:

yī, èr, sān	**yìtiáo yú**	**yìkē shū**
yee er sahn	yee-tyow yoo	yee-kur shoo
one, two, three	a fish	a tree

The exception to the above is if **yì** is followed by a fourth tone, in which case it changes to second tone:

yíjiàn dōngxi
yee-jyen doong-hshee
an object

In number sequences **yāo** is used for 'one' instead of **yī**, as in the two examples below:

sān-èr-wǔ-yāo-bā	**yāoyāojiǔ**
sahn-er-woo-yow-bah	yow-yow-jyoh
32518	number one hundred and nineteen
(phone number)	(room number)

There are two words for two in Chinese: **èr** and **liǎng**. **Èr** is used in counting or for phone, room or bus numbers:

yī, èr, sān ...	èr hào	èr lù chē
yee er sahn	er how	er loo chur
one, two three ...	number two	number two bus
	(room, house etc)	

Èr also occurs in compound numbers:

sānshí'èr [sahn-shur-er] thirty-two

Liǎng is similar to 'a couple' in English and is used with measure words (see page 262):

liǎngwèi péngyou	liǎngsuǒ fángzi
lyang-way pung-yoh	lyang-swor fahng-dzur
two friends	two buildings

The numbers 11-19 are made up of shí (ten) followed by the numbers yī (one) to jiǔ (nine):

shíyī   eleven
shí'èr   twelve
shísān   thirteen

Multiples of ten are formed by adding the numbers two to nine to shí (ten):

èrshí   twenty
sānshí   thirty
sìshí   forty

The numbers 21 to 29, 31-39 etc are formed by adding one to nine to the above numbers èrshí, sānshí and so on:

èrshíyī   twenty-one
sìshíqī   forty-seven
bāshíwǔ   eighty-five

A similar pattern is used with bǎi (hundred), qiān (thousand) and wàn (ten thousand):

sìbǎi	sìbǎi jiǔshí
sur-bai	sur-bai jyoh-shur
four hundred	four hundred and ninety

bābǎi sìshí liù
bah-bai sur-shur lyoh
eight hundred and forty-six

jiǔqiān sìbǎi qīshí
jyoh-chyen sur-bai chee-shur
nine thousand four hundred
and seventy

qīwàn sìqiān bābǎi
chee-wahn sur-chyen bah-bai
seventy-four thousand eight
hundred

For numbers in the thousands and millions, **shí**, **bǎi**, **qiān** and **wàn** are added to **wàn**:

shíwàn
shur-wahn
a hundred thousand

bǎiwàn
bai-wahn
a million

qiānwàn
chyah-wahn
ten million

yí yì
a hundred million

Líng (zero) is used when there are zeros in the middle of a number sequence:

yìbǎi líng sān
yee-bai ling sahn
one hundred and three

yìqiān líng sān
yee-chyen ling sahn
one thousand and three

yìqiān líng bāshí
yee-chyen ling bah-shur
one thousand and eighty

Ordinals

1st	dì yī	第一	6th	dì liù [lyoh]	第六
2nd	dì èr	第二	7th	dì qī [chee]	第七
3rd	dì sān [sahn]	第三	8th	dì bā	第八
4th	dì sì [sur]	第四	9th	dì jiǔ [jyoh]	第九
5th	dì wǔ	第五	10th	dì shí [shur]	第十

Conversion Tables

1 centimetre = 0.39 inches	1 inch = 2.54 cm
1 metre = 39.37 inches = 1.09 yards	1 foot = 30.48 cm
1 kilometre = 0.62 miles = 5/8 mile	1 yard = 0.91 m
	1 mile = 1.61 km

km	1	2	3	4	5	10	20	30	40	50	100
miles	0.6	1.2	1.9	2.5	3.1	6.2	12.4	18.6	24.8	31.0	62.1

miles	1	2	3	4	5	10	20	30	40	50	100
km	1.6	3.2	4.8	6.4	8.0	16.1	32.2	48.3	64.4	80.5	161

1 gram = 0.035 ounces	1 kilo = 1000 g = 2.2 pounds

g	100	250	500
oz	3.5	8.75	17.5

1 oz = 28.35 g
1 lb = 0.45 kg

kg	0.5	1	2	3	4	5	6	7	8	9	10
lb	1.1	2.2	4.4	6.6	8.8	11.0	13.2	15.4	17.6	19.8	22.0

kg	20	30	40	50	60	70	80	90	100
lb	44	66	88	110	132	154	176	198	220

lb	0.5	1	2	3	4	5	6	7	8	9	10	20
kg	0.2	0.5	0.9	1.4	1.8	2.3	2.7	3.2	3.6	4.1	4.5	9.0

1 litre = 1.75 UK pints / 2.13 US pints

1 UK pint = 0.57 l	1 UK gallon = 4.55 l
1 US pint = 0.47 l	1 US gallon = 3.79 l

centigrade / Celsius $\quad$ °C = (°F - 32) x 5/9

°C	-5	0	5	10	15	18	20	25	30	36.8	38
°F	23	32	41	50	59	64	68	77	86	98.4	100.4

Fahrenheit $\quad$ °F = (°C x 9/5) + 32

°F	23	32	40	50	60	65	70	80	85	98.4	101
°C	-5	0	4	10	16	18	21	27	29	36.8	38.3